Finding Refuge

Finding Refuge

A Year in His Story

For Judge Oliver Green,

Always thankful for faithful men in influential roles. Thanking God for you,

Jodie Montgomery

Psalm 2:12

JODIE MONTGOMERY
ILLUSTRATIONS BY LOURDES SANABRIA

XULON ELITE

Xulon Press Elite
2301 Lucien Way #415
Maitland, FL 32751
407.339.4217
www.xulonpress.com

Printed in the United States of America.

ISBN 13: 978-1-54565-000-4

Table of Contents

For Scott Montgomery, my hero

Introduction

I struggled for years as an anorexic Christian—I hadn't learned how to properly nourish my faith. I trusted Christ as my Savior as a teenager while visiting my aunt and uncle's church but had not discovered the value of discipleship. Thankfully, when I was working for an engineering consulting firm as a chemical engineer, a colleague of mine who professed to be an atheist had a wife who wanted to do a Bible study. When she invited me to her study, I thought the least I could do was encourage her. I thank God for that woman; thank you Jennifer.

Bible study revealed what I was missing as a baby Christian: truth, God's Revelation of Himself, a Light unto my path. I knew how to be saved, but I didn't know my Savior. I wanted to do God's will, but you cannot know someone's desires without spending time listening to them, discovering their heart. I relate this to my marriage relationship. When I married Scott Lewis Montgomery, I knew many details about him but until we really talked, sometimes for hours, I couldn't really know his heart. He had to personally reveal his heart to me. Knowing his heart is important because our value systems either unite us or divide us. There is joy in doing life together when we are unified in our beliefs which motivate us and give us purpose. Life with God begins at salvation and blossoms as I discover what would best represent His character. It brings peace to my soul and happiness to my step when I beautifully represent the One I love as I'm jealous for His dignity. His name is my name too and so lifting up His name dignifies me.

God has a purpose for His children. The believer is called to walk by faith. This is also referred to in the Bible as walking in the Light, and walking in the Spirit. I learned that faith isn't blind, it has a foundation to it. The Christian faith is based in God's character revealed in His Word and grounded by historical, archaeological, and cultural data points throughout His Word. "Faith comes from hearing, and hearing from the Word of Christ" (Romans 10:17) and "Establish Your word to Your servant, as that which produces reverence for You" (Psalm 119:38[1]). You cannot be sanctified apart from His Word.

Bible study steadied my walk of faith. It saved my marriage. It redirected my path to worship, to family, to friends. It delighted my heart. It strengthened my convictions. It sent me to seminary. It lifted my head. It opened my eyes to life and my heart to love.

Now after years of study, a renewed love for my husband, a huge career change, three children raised in His truth, a ministry to thousands of women, and a lot of chocolate, I am purposing to share some devotional time with you. When I started studying the Bible, I got caught up in specific portions that were wonderful truths to learn in the moment, but I missed His story in its entirety; the way God progressed His plan through history. Learning to read the Bible as one story has helped me to interpret the smaller meals more accurately and it has helped me to feast on His sovereign ways throughout history—His Story.

Seminary professor Dr. Charles Baylis and his wife Sharon have spent countless hours discussing God's Word with me and my husband Scott. I'm grateful for their time. I've referred frequently to Dr. Baylis' website, The Biblical Story,[2] while writing this book. Many of our discussions are written out in these devotionals. Dr. Baylis directed me to see Psalm 2 as an overview of the Bible, and I go back to this Psalm repeatedly. In Psalm 2, I hear a dear and powerful Father revealing to His precious child how to escape the impending war of the worlds as He advises His child to take refuge in the Son. I was so taken with this guidance that I wrote and taught a study on the Psalms one summer centered on seeking His refuge. The Good Father's provision of refuge is throughout the Biblical story. The reader grasps God's provision by simply adopting a

---

[1]   Unless otherwise noted, all Scripture references are from the New American Standard Bible.

[2]   http://thebiblicalstory.org

humble fear of Holy God and the realization that the Son is our only hope for Life.

Through the years I've written several Bible studies and blogs to exhort believers to be steadfast in their faith. I decided to write this book as I see the need for a devotional that encourages the reader to see the Bible as a story worth reading regularly and straight through (no skipping around and getting off track or confused in the story). God's entire story within a year . . . or less. The book is set up for forty-four weeks of reading and eight weeks for rest or catching up. The rest/catchup weeks provide space for you, if you wish, to journal on what has stood out to you in your reading. Each day's reading is divided into a "Read It All" track that, once completed for all the weeks, will yield a full portion of His Story. There is also a "Read a Bit" track for those with time constraints who may be snacking on the run. I advise the full portion.

Some weeks have days with a lot of text to take in, so pace yourself to enjoy it. Psalms and Jeremiah stand out to me as lengthy reads in a week, but I don't want to drag them out and the plan is very doable. I prefer reading on my lounger near the bird feeders. I enjoy nature and sudden appearances of hummingbirds, woodpeckers or a Carolina chickadee feeding as I feast. Some may prefer to use an audible Bible for the reading portions. Reading Jeremiah in a week is more doable for me if I listen to the text as I make dinner or drive in the car. There are many apps that you can download and have handy as you purpose to digest His Word.

I've added summaries to repeatedly remind readers where they are in the story. Repetition is the mother of all learning. I've also included a devotional for each day so you know you have a companion on your journey who is also feasting with you for steady spiritual health. My encouragement is to keep persistently working your way through the Bible text. Somewhere in the midst of reading the prophets, I realize that I am so ready for Christ to physically appear in the story. I'm anticipating His incarnation just as the prophets described and it is a great joy to read God with us when I finally get to the gospels.

I have discovered in study that we are edified by:

- seeing His Revelation so clearly that we can summarize our reading for ourselves and others,
- focusing on the integrity of our Savior and His representatives,
- discovering the dignity He bestows on His beloved,

- reviewing how His children are united in His truth, and
- prioritizing our walk with Him.

Therefore, the weekly sections of the devotional address thoughts on His Revelation in Summary, Integrity, Dignity, Unity, and Priority. Integrity and dignity are very similar characteristics. Integrity is exemplified by a person who has a worthy value system. Dignity is portrayed by a high level of respect based on one's integrity. Integrity focuses on the inner man and dignity on relational worth. The devotionals on integrity and dignity will overlap a bit as dignity is dependent on integrity and God's love for His children is the source of their dignity while His Spirit within the believer is how He bestows integrity. Unity is more directly focused on Biblical truths that unite His children, His church. Priority has to do with worshipping God through living out the Gospel in our lives.

In weeks where more than one Bible book is included in the reading plan, the Revelation in Summary will be the focus in the devotional unless the books are divided into parts, 1 & 2 Peter for example. In those cases, the summary is not repeated as it was covered for the first book in the series. I like the topics for the devotional sections, but there is so much more to say and so many topics that could be developed that I'm concerned you will find the order a bit random. That is how it is on our journeys, not everything so perfectly laid out, so even the randomness has an application, an authenticity to it. I've attempted to provide a bit of a GPS for you by summarizing the definitions for the devotional headings on a page at the end of this introduction so you may refer back to the definitions as needed in your journey. Take note, this isn't a commentary even though I make lots of comments on the text. I hope you will feel like you have a companion on your journey through His Story. A companion that enjoys discussing the reading with you and celebrating His gift of truth through the ages. Know that I struggle with taking on too big a mouthful at times, so feel free to determine right good portions for yourself.

Studying God's Word is to fall in love with the Author. I have led women's ministry and served in the church for several decades now, and I realize that His name can only be glorified by a people fed well on His truth. The spiritual health of His children is an eternal matter. Our local bodies long to do great compassionate helps in His name, but we have so many members who are suffering from spiritual malnutrition that they cannot serve others when they do not know how to reach His bountiful provision for themselves. God exhorts us to be secure in Him, fully realizing that because of His imputed righteousness, we are His beloved, beyond reproach, holy and blameless ambassadors of reconciliation to the world. *"Therefore as you have received Christ Jesus the Lord, so walk in Him, having been firmly rooted and now being built up in Him and established in your faith, just as you were instructed, and overflowing with gratitude"* (Colossians 2:6-7).

Lourdes Sanabria has added her Scripture art for the eight sections that make up the fifty-two weeks comprising this devotional. These sections are *Old Testament Pentateuch, Old Testament History, Old Testament Wisdom Writings, Old Testament Major & Minor Prophets, New Testament Gospels, New Testament Acts, New Testament Letters,* and *New Testament Revelation.* Thank you for adding such beauty, Lourdes!

I want to thank my children for loving me even as I repeatedly use our relationships for illustrations. I love you dearly Samuel, Sarah, and Susan. Scott made my heart beat, and you made it full. I also mention the wonderful son-in-laws, Gannon and Cody. Thank you, Mom (Janet B. Townsend), for your strength and overwhelming support. Thank you to my most influential Bible teachers; there are many of you that have served in area studies, as my pastors and small group leaders through the years. I thank God for Linda DeVore's quick edit and wisdom.

It is my hope that this devotional will be shared with the next generation as a guide to His faithful, steadfast love. So often we forget to prioritize time with those who love us most, and devotionals are just that, devoted time with truth I value, truth from the One I love. God is holy and He will settle all His accounts justly. Heed His Word and take refuge in His Son. *"The Father loves the Son and has given all things into His hand. He who believes in the Son has eternal life; but he who does not obey the Son will not see life, but the wrath of God abides on him"* (John 3:35-36). I do not apologize for the directness of the text. I lovingly call us all to awareness of His holiness and to Life in His provided Refuge.

Psalm 2

Why are the nations in an uproar
And the peoples devising a vain thing?
The kings of the earth take their stand
And the rulers take counsel together
Against the Lord and against His Anointed, saying,
"Let us tear their fetters apart
And cast away their cords from us!"
He who sits in the heavens laughs,
The Lord scoffs at them.
Then He will speak to them in His anger
And terrify them in His fury, saying,
"But as for Me, I have installed My King
Upon Zion, My holy mountain."
"I will surely tell of the decree of the Lord:
He said to Me, 'You are My Son, today I have begotten You.
Ask of Me, and I will surely give the nations as Your inheritance,
And the very ends of the earth as Your possession.
You shall break them with a rod of iron,
You shall shatter them like earthenware.'"
Now therefore, O kings, show discernment;
Take warning, O judges of the earth.
Worship the Lord with reverence
And rejoice with trembling.
Do homage to the Son,
that He not become angry,
and you perish in the way,
For His wrath may soon be kindled.
How blessed are all who take refuge in Him!

Definitions for Devotional Thoughts

Revelation in Summary – Recaptures the main themes of the Bible book being read for the week.

Integrity – The quality of being honest, upright; indicative of wholeness, being undivided. Summed up in the character of God. In these devotionals, the integrity sections focus on the inner man as set apart by God Almighty, bestowed with integrity through His Holy Spirit filling the believer.

Dignity – The state of being worthy of respect or honor. God bestows dignity on His children by adopting them. Dignity indicates relational worth; depends on integrity. The devotionals on dignity remind the believer that God's love for His children is the source of their dignity.

Unity – Focuses on Biblical truths that unite His children, His church.

Priority – These devotionals on priority address how the believer adds intention in worshiping God through living out the Gospel daily, moment by moment.

And I
will put
enmity
between you
and the woman,
and between
your seed
and her seed
Genesis 3:15

OLD TESTAMENT
PENTATEUCH

In the Protestant Christian Bible, 39 books make up the Old Testament writings and 27 books comprise the New Testament. These books are revealed to be God's Words given through His Spirit guiding human authors. Jesus and the apostles referred to the Old Testament writings as the teachings, prophets, and writings, or the Law and the Prophets. The believer is directed to hear and apply the Law and the Prophets for Life in Christ.

The Pentateuch is the first five books of the Old Testament. Ancient Jewish literature is the basis for the Protestant Christian Bible, and the first five books in the ancient writings are also The Pentateuch but are known as The Torah. These first five books (Genesis, Exodus, Leviticus, Numbers, and Deuteronomy) provide the main characters, setting, plot, tension, and hope in the story of God's creation. From early in the story, God provides His Revelation on how He will redeem His people from the consequences of their sin. The Pentateuch introduces us to Holy God, His delight in showing mercy, and the depth of His love exhibited in His covenant care. The Pentateuch readies us for Life in the promised Seed of the woman.

GENESIS

Week 1, Day 1
Read It All: Genesis 1-12
Read a Bit: Genesis 1-3; 11

The Revelation in Summary

Interesting Detail: Job is believed to have been written during the same period as Genesis. Job is one of the most ancient of Biblical texts.

Genesis 1:1 — *In the beginning God created the heavens and the earth.*

Genesis is the book of beginnings: the beginning of creation, the beginning of mankind, the beginning of family, the beginning of sin, the beginning of sorrow, the beginning of hope, the beginning of nations, the beginning of rivalries, the beginning of a redemptive plan. Genesis 1-2 introduce the wondrous Creator of all, God, but we do not linger at creation. The tension in the big story is quickly disclosed as Genesis 3 records the Fall of mankind by Adam and Eve, the representatives of all. God's love of His creation is demonstrated through His provision of deliverance to fallen humanity. In the midst of the consequences of the Fall (hardship and death), God promises He will ultimately deliver mankind from its sinful state and domination by the serpent Satan through the Seed of the woman (Genesis 3:15). From this point in the story, the reader should be expectantly looking, even longing, for the Seed that will redeem. Mankind has hope in contrast to the finality of death.

The first twelve chapters of Genesis cover thousands of years and how evil and death rule. God reveals how the individual may represent Him, bear His image to all, and show His character through a national representative, Israel. Genesis13-50 provides the historical details of Abraham's family as Abraham's Seed-line develops into God's national representative over a few hundred years. God established a nation through the Seed of Abraham to bless many nations, providing a land of refuge and hope under the One True God. God reveals that full life is in representing our Creator.

Genesis presents God as Creator, Companion, and Redeemer and residing everywhere. One of the biggest steps of faith for anyone is to believe that the Creator of the universe also cares about you specifically.

Genesis reveals the Creator as lovingly, personally interested in His creation, particularly mankind, as a good Father who loves his child. God created mankind in His image so that each person has the capacity to bear His image, as a representative of the Covenant Blesser, to a world that needs specific revelation about God in order to have Life. (Not all choose to bear His image well, of course.) God also reveals Himself through His national representative, Israel, as God's character is complex, and some aspects of His interaction with humanity require a corporate representative. Scripture also provides that marriage, the family, and the church are endowed by God with the sacred task of representing His love in a distinct way so that those who witness His people in relationships may witness His love and find Life.

Genesis introduces the reader to a Covenant-keeping God that is purposing to set the stage so that those who value the Revelation of God will live by faith that God will provide a way for the sinner to have Life everlasting. Genesis reveals that God cares about His creation. God loves you.

Week 1, Day 2

Read It All: Genesis 12-20
Read a Bit: Genesis 12; 15; 19

Integrity

Genesis 19:6 — *But Lot went out to them at the doorway, and shut the door behind him, and said, "Please, my brothers, do not act wickedly."*

It would be so simple if mankind was good. Why God created us with the ability to choose right or wrong is constantly questioned and mourned. We appreciate not being puppets for the Lord, for He could definitely control every detail of our lives, but our ability and propensity to choose poorly is at the center of all pain. In our own relationships, love is reflected when another chooses us: time with us, enjoying us, walking with us. God too values love over force or pre-programming His creation to be good.

Genesis reveals God's integrity and long-suffering nature in contrast to that of humankind. God continues to reveal Himself and what it means to have His life while people continue to prefer their reasoning over the Revelation of God. Mankind loves themselves. In Genesis we discover: brother killing brother (Cain), a wicked destructive race ridiculing one faithful man (Noah), the people who long to make a name for themselves (Babel) instead of praising God, a lying patriarch risking the Seed-line to gain security for self (Abraham), a city sexually obsessed (Sodom), and a highly dysfunctional family (the Seed-line of Abraham). Holy God and mankind seem to have nothing in common. Yet God promises and covenants with mankind's representatives that He will purify a people and secure them in a great kingdom to come. God is long-suffering.

The Bible teaches that no one can have a right relationship with God without holiness (Hebrews 12:14). Thankfully, the resolution to our problem of our lack of holiness is dependent on the integrity of a good God and not on ourselves or on one of the pagan false gods that love playing tricks on us. The One True God reveals Himself through the creation around us, through the consciousness within us, and through the Word before us. God's program is to mercifully bless many. Our hope is in continuing to seek the Seed of the woman for deliverance.

Week 1, Day 3

Read It All: Genesis 21-25
Read a Bit: Genesis 21; 22:1-19; 25:29-34

Unity

Genesis 22:18 — *The Angel of the Lord to Abraham, "In your Seed all the nations of the earth shall be blessed, because you have obeyed My voice."*

Abraham's obedience at Mount Moriah resulted in God's declaration to bless all the nations of the earth with a righteousness that exists in identifying with the Seed of Abraham, the promised Messiah. Believers are united in the promises of God to Abraham by belief in the Seed.

God reveals through Abraham that offerings are necessary for mankind to be right with Holy God. The offering must be something meaningful, precious to the giver, as it symbolizes the loss of all that is good through sin. Abraham was willing to sacrifice his own son at Mount Moriah. This projects a future sacrifice of God's own Son on Mount Calvary. Abraham believed that even death wouldn't separate him from his dearly beloved son. This prefigures hope in the resurrection, Christ being the resurrected Seed, having fully settled mankind's debt before God. Mercifully, God did not require Abraham to kill his son and took it upon Himself to provide the ram for the offering. God points out the ram to Abraham amidst the thicket (I envision a crown of thorns). God is steadfastly revealing His plan of redemption to all through the life of Abraham. It is imperative at this point in the story that the genealogy of the Christ, the validation of the promised Seed, be preserved through the years as a record of God's faithful covenant relationship to mankind through Abraham. The details are important. They give the seeker a basis for faith. They reveal the hope of having an inheritance in God's kingdom plan. Hold on! Don't sell your birthright like Esau did.

Week 1, Day 4

Read It All: Genesis 26-36
Read a Bit: Genesis 27; 33; 35:23-29

Dignity

Genesis 28:3 — Isaac to Jacob: *"May God Almighty bless you and make you fruitful and multiply you, that you may become a company of peoples. May He also give you the blessing of Abraham, to you and to your descendants with you, that you may possess the land of your sojournings, which God gave to Abraham."*

Dignity: the state or quality of being worthy of honor or respect. I have witnessed dignity defined. My friend Julie Oliver was physically diminishing as she battled cancer. She was bed-ridden in her home. Dignity is a husband of many years, holding his wife's hand, praying, reading Scripture, and singing as his wife battles a mean disease. Dignity is a beautiful daughter with her head resting near as she waits with her mom for promised life. Dignity is sons who are present and providing updates that are honoring and considerate to family and friends. Dignity is praying, protecting, and patient in the midst of great sorrow. Dignity is loving friends experiencing life and death with you. It is pretty black and white photos of family and friends at a bedside. Dignity is loving hands tenderly caring for a temporary body. It is tears of mourning, appreciation, laughter, memories, and angst. Dignity is being recognized as created in the image of God and as a precious life from God. Dignity honors and respects the value of each life.

To God be the glory for the life of our loved ones. I am so thankful for our value in Him. "God created man in His own image, . . . male and female He created them" (Genesis 1:27).

We live in this tension of being capable of many things as even though we are highly dependent upon our Maker, we are given His dignity as we are created in His image. The tension is to walk according to His revealed word or to value our own reasoning about what is good and best. We can seem pretty successful and we can escape some temporary trials with our human reasoning. We struggle with humble reliance on anyone, as we are equipped with many great resources including the capacity to think and feel for ourselves. There seems to be much we can do within ourselves and our own little realms.

Isaac's prayer for his son is that he will live in the blessing of his Maker. Through God our lives have meaning. Through God we form a community, that can collectively bless many others and, in doing so, restore dignity to humanity. Through God we have a future, a promised victory over our great enemy death, and a land in His kingdom to come.

Isaac has a bigger picture of what is most important for his son than his son has for himself. Isaac longs for Jacob to be restored to the dignity given him by God prior to all his failures and self-centered doings. Isaac sees a way for Jacob to overcome his greatest fears. Mankind longs for God's dignity to be revealed, as the blessed person is the one who realizes that true dignity comes from identification with the people of God, with the Seed of the Woman.

Week 1, Day 5

Read It All: Genesis 37-50
Read a Bit: Genesis 37; 49; 50:22-29

Priority

Genesis 50:24 — *Joseph said to his brothers, "I am about to die, but God will surely take care of you and bring you up from this land to the land which He promised on oath to Abraham, to Isaac and to Jacob."*

Genesis teaches us about many beginnings, but it also heavily schools us on death as the unwavering consequence of sin. Death is not a reflection of the Creator, but of man. God counters death.

The story unfolding in Genesis centers on a hope in God as Redeemer. The reader can evaluate the hope or hopelessness of all the deaths listed in Genesis based on whether the dead believed in the promises of God . . . or not.

Genesis ends with a death, that of Joseph. In his last moments, Joseph assured those surrounding his deathbed that God would surely take care of them as promised. Joseph died in Egypt and longed for his people to take his bones with them to the promised land, as he knew they would go there just as God said. Joseph focuses on his hope in redemption.

I haven't been to Egypt like Joseph, but I have stood in his land of promise, Israel. I've walked a graveyard in Nazareth, and I thought a lot about death as it confronted me in tomb after tomb. I learned that if the tall, wrought-iron gates to the cemetery were open, then it was permissible to walk the cemetery. My husband and I did just that one early morning in Nazareth. As a result of the geology of Israel, graves are above ground, stone containers one upon another. I felt like I was walking through a dense, white maze as the tombs were piled well above my head. I became a little uncomfortable following the path and going farther from the gate, as I couldn't see what was around the next corner, and I wasn't sure I would be able to go back to the gate correctly. If another person turned up, I would have been startled.

The tombs there are often marked with an engraved picture of the deceased. Some crypts have the inhabitant's information etched in three languages. Visitors place flowers, memorabilia, and pictures near their loved one's remains. If it weren't for these mementos, I would not believe that many came to the cemetery. It was mainly empty of life. That walk through the mausoleum reminded me that our days are numbered and few.

I came back to the cemetery on another morning with another member of the mission group I had traveled with. When we arrived at the gates, a man (presumably the caretaker) motioned for us to follow him. As we did, he started putting his finger to his head, signifying a shooting. I would have turned and fled except that his expression held sorrow, not hate. He led us to a vault that was further back in the cemetery than I preferred to go, but it seemed a dishonor not to see what he had to share. The tomb was of a young man whose face was etched on the stone, a young man who had been killed in some crossfire. The caretaker continued to mourn the loss of life due to a lack of peace in the land. Only the Maker of the heavenlies can provide victory over such sorrow. In Genesis, we meet the Maker Who purposes to do just that, make a way of deliverance instead of death.

"The last enemy that will be abolished is death".
1 Corinthians 15:26

EXODUS

Let's review before launching into Exodus:

Genesis revealed the beginning of life, the establishment of family, the sinfulness of humanity, the means of overcoming suffering and death, and a national representative of God (Israel). Most importantly, God promised a Redeemer to defeat the enemy serpent Satan. The Redeemer's lineage will trace back to the Seed of the woman through the line of Abraham. Creation is under the control of Satan, but God is establishing a nation through Jacob (aka Israel) to preserve the Seed-line and bear the ultimate ruler of mankind. The tension in the story is whether those representing God will trust in His Word over their own reasoning. Enter Moses.

Week 2, Day 1

Read It All: Exodus 1-14
Read a Bit: Exodus 1-3; 6:1-13; 14

The Revelation in Summary

Exodus 14:31 — *When Israel saw the great power which the Lord had used against the Egyptians, the people feared the Lord, and they believed in the Lord and in His servant Moses.*

Exodus contains the historical account of God supernaturally identifying Israel as His covenant people in contrast to the mighty nation Egypt and its false gods. God equips Israel to represent Him by revealing His delivering power as He raises up the prophet Moses to lead them from captivity, covenants with them at Mount Sinai, and provides instructions on how to dwell with Him.

Exodus is a remarkable account of redemption from slavery by a merciful God. The heart of Moses is contrasted with the heart of Pharaoh such that the reader witnesses the greatest potential and greatest tragedy of life: choosing to be a Covenant representative of God versus a hardened enemy of God. The heart is a main character in this historical account.

Exodus reveals the heart of God portrayed in His commandments. To know another is to know what they consider good and bad, right and wrong. On Mount Sinai, God provides Moses, and ultimately all mankind, with His character, His value system, and His moral code. This is the pinnacle of equipping a people. The giving of the Law enables the people to know their God and represent His heart to all nations. Today, readers learn from Israel's exodus of the greater exodus when God's Son, the Greater Prophet than Moses, the Lord Jesus Christ, will return to make a way for all enslaved to sin to have life. This final deliverance will result in rest for the people of God, a rest that reflects joy and celebration in His presence as the enemies of God are removed from the land.

Week 2, Day 2

Read It All: Exodus 15-18
Read a Bit: Exodus 15:1-20; 16:22-35; 18:24-27

Integrity

Exodus 3:14 — *God said to Moses, "I AM WHO I AM"; and He said, "Thus you shall say to the sons of Israel, 'I AM has sent me to you.'"*

People of integrity speak what is true, particularly about themselves. In John 8:58, Jesus said to the people, "Truly, truly, I say to you, before Abraham was born, I am." Jesus made a very clear claim of deity to the people. If His statement was not true, then the people would respond by demanding His death. They picked up stones to throw at Him, but Jesus hid Himself and went out of the temple. The response of the crowd reveals how controversial, how direct Jesus is when He claims to be "I am." "I am" is the name God revealed to Moses when He appeared to Moses in the burning bush. The hearer of "I am" in Jesus' day knew that Christ was claiming full deity in his statement.

In Exodus, the Great I Am was equipping Moses to represent I Am through delivering the oppressed Israelites from Egypt. This deliverance reveals to the world in every age that God is a Covenant-keeping God, the faithful One. When Jesus proclaims that He is I Am, Jesus clearly identifies Himself as God. Jesus asserts that He existed before Abraham, which is before Israel's founding father, and directly links Himself to the Old Testament teachings. I Am is the pinnacle of unity with God and gives Him membership in the Godhead.

Under the Old Testament law, the people were to stone anyone who falsely professed they were God. The response of the people in grabbing stones is a direct application of the law if Jesus is making a false claim, but the law also served to help the people see their Deliverer, the fulfillment of the law, when He "tabernacled" with them. In this case, with Christ in their midst, the people miss the fulfillment of the law by refusing to believe Christ is Lord. Again, humanity is surprised by the Creator of the universe valuing a residence in their midst. The shock of God with us, possible in the Old Testament tabernacle, the New Testament Incarnate God, and His Spirit indwelling the believer, creates an obstacle to embracing His presence. The people were not seeing the signs that would direct them to the Greater Moses, the Ultimate Deliverer, the Lord Jesus Christ. They were missing Life.

John wrote about Christ's life specifically to emphasize the signs that verified Christ as Messiah so that the reader would see and believe (John 20:31). You and I need a Deliverer. You and I can never fulfill the law in ourselves. God is holy. God is also good. He, the Great I Am, has sent His Son to deliver you and me. May we have ears to hear the great prophet Moses, the apostle John, and the very Spirit of God so that we see our Deliverer has come.

Week 2, Day 3

Read It all: Exodus 19-24
Read a Bit: Exodus 19-20; 23:10-19

Dignity

Exodus 20:1-2 — *Then God spoke all these words, saying, "I am the Lord your God, who brought you out of the land of Egypt, out of the house of slavery."*

There is such a lack of respect for the Law today that I fear people have forgotten that laws aren't put into effect to frustrate and humiliate but rather to protect, to instill justice. We fear getting caught more than being hurt or hurting others by breaking the law. I avoided the Old Testament books on the Law for years, thinking that they were a cumbersome, boring read and that for the most part I knew what was wrong and right. Then, in seminary, I discovered that to understand the Bible, you needed to understand the character of God and the character of God is righteousness as revealed in the Law. I learned that so many of the New Testament teachings about the Lord Jesus Christ were directly out of passages in the Law. I jumped into Deuteronomy with renewed passion and found not a boring, predictable, controlling God but a loving, merciful Father who desired to help His people and make every way possible for them to be protected and valued. God's Law showed He specifically hunted out the needy, the alien, the widow, the Fatherless and made a place for them. My Father abandoned me in high school so I took great comfort in seeing God's provision in the Law for the fatherless. God's Law revealed that He purposed for His people to be instruments of mercy in the land, a blessing to those cursed in a world of unbelief. God's Law indicated a high view of man and the perfection of the Creator. God's Law does protect His people but even more it reveals how to more fully represent the Lord Himself. The Law guides us into the abundant Life of the believer.

I pray you enjoy your time in His character, the Law of God.

Week 2, Day 4

Read It all: Exodus 25-31
Read a Bit: Exodus 25:1-9; 31

Unity

Exodus 25:1-2, 8 — *Then the Lord spoke to Moses, saying, "Tell the sons of Israel to raise a contribution for Me; from every man whose heart moves him you shall raise My contribution. . . . Let them construct a sanctuary for Me, that I may dwell among them."*

A doctrine (teaching) that unites us all is the doctrine of original sin. This is the state of man since the fall of Adam and Eve in the garden. We rebel against the Revelation of God and choose to live for ourselves. We resist His love and loving others as we primarily love ourselves. Every person is enslaved to sin apart from the redeeming power of God. Sin separates us from our Maker and thus from Life.

God pictures this enslavement to sin in Exodus through the enslavement of the nation Israel in Egypt. The Israelites are woefully entrapped by a people who believe in mean, angry gods that the people perfectly reflect. God acknowledges hearing the cries of the enslaved people and caring deeply for their state of destruction. He has been waiting for their cries, waiting a planned amount of time that in prophetic fulfillment will rebuild their weakened faith in Him.

We learn through the deliverance of Israel that God is specific in His care. He longs to tabernacle (reside) with His people, and His character is as merciful as it is holy and just. These attributes are intricately interwoven. There is no love apart from justice.

The longing for freedom is still the cry of the human heart. We groan in this body of sin, knowing there is something much better. Our ability to love is constantly challenged by our propensity to pridefully elevate ourselves. We are an enslaved people unified in our longing for the Great Emancipator and the new heart only He provides.

Week 2, Day 5

Read It all: Exodus 32-40
Read a Bit: Exodus 32-34:28; 40:34-38

Priority

Exodus 33:17 — *The Lord said to Moses, "I will also do this thing of which you have spoken; for you have found favor in My sight and I have known you by name."*

Exodus 34:34-38 – *Then the cloud covered the tent of meeting, and the glory of the Lord filled the tabernacle. Moses was not able to enter the tent of meeting because the cloud had settled on it, and the glory of the Lord filled the tabernacle. Throughout all their journeys whenever the cloud was taken up from over the tabernacle, the sons of Israel would set out; but if the cloud was not taken up, then they did not set out until the day when it was taken up. For throughout all their journeys, the cloud of the Lord was on the tabernacle by day, and there was fire in it by night, in the sight of all the house of Israel.*

If you could capture a Bible moment in time, this might be one you would wish to witness. God with us. God in His tabernacle and clearly guiding His people into His promises. They were not making a move without Him. Surely this is the ultimate peace.

God has always been evident in His creation, but this time in the wilderness, filling the man-made tabernacle was divinely unique. God authenticated His message to the nations through Moses and Israel by physically dwelling with them. God was visibly present.

I live in Florida. I crave His presence too, and so somedays I head outdoors to enjoy the grandness of the Creator. I make enjoying His presence a priority. The beach is a great location to reflect on the majesty of God.

> *"For since the creation of the world His invisible attributes, His eternal power and divine nature, have been clearly seen, being understood through what has been made, so that they are without excuse."* Romans 1:20

When I go to the beach I am comforted by my insignificance. The ocean is massive and I am small (regardless of how I felt bathing suit shopping). God's creative genius and overwhelming power are before all, and the skies display His glory. It is good to see that so much of what consumes me is temporary and little.

I still enjoy building sand castles or some sand art. We write the occasion for the beach trip in the sand and take our pictures with our artwork to date our visit. Sometimes we create a large sand mural and then rush down later in the day to see if any of it remains. We are designers with no control over the future of our creations. We are reminded of the Great Designer and the security we have in Him.

I think I live better at the beach. The heat helps me to value the lighter fare, salads and fresh fruit. I delight in long morning walks and searching the shore for unique shells, birds, and sea creatures. I am intentional about enjoying the sunsets. I love sharing these moments with family and friends and am quicker to run a few steps, to play harder. I see life.

When storms come in at the beach, I see how cleansing they can be. The sand-covered walkways are rinsed. The ocean takes away the stuff left randomly along the shore. The dead palm branches are shaken away. I appreciate the storms and the subsequent calm. The contrast helps me understand the precious gift of each moment.

Time at the beach refreshes my sense of awe and wonder. Sometimes the most biblical thing I can do is to rest and remember He is, to tabernacle with God. *"Return to your rest, O my soul, for the Lord has dealt bountifully with you"* Psalm 116:7

LEVITICUS

Week 3, Day 1

Read It All: Leviticus 1-7
Read a Bit: Leviticus 5:14-19; 6:24-30; 7:37-38

The Revelation in Summary

To encourage you: Many struggle in reading Leviticus. The key is looking for how God makes a way for sinful man to dwell with Holy God.

Leviticus 7:37-38 — *This is the law of the burnt offering, the grain offering and the sin offering and the guilt offering and the ordination offering and the sacrifice of peace offerings, which the Lord commanded Moses at Mount Sinai in the day that He commanded the sons of Israel to present their offerings to the Lord in the wilderness of Sinai.*

Exodus revealed that even though God would deliver His people and keep covenant with them, they would continue to struggle in loving God. It seems impossible for mankind to tabernacle with holiness. How could this relationship endure when Holy God, in all His essence, destroys all sin in His path? There is an aspect to total goodness that is dangerous. It reveals sin wherever it goes, and many of us do not appreciate opportunities to repent.

God reveals in Leviticus the way of reconciling sinful mankind to righteous God. The sin, personal and corporate, of Israel separates them from God, so God sets up a system to ritually purify Israel and all associated with Israel. God's cleansing provisions are part of His redemptive plan. The provisions direct the people to their need of a Savior who will completely atone for their sin. The details provided in Leviticus depict how ritual and moral purity should be highly regarded by the people, as purity is essential for relationship with Holy God. The required offerings in Leviticus direct the people to their need of a perfect representative before God. The many cultural, symbolic requirements in Leviticus for the people and the priesthood teach that God's purity should be considered in every aspect of our lives.

Death is a key character in Leviticus. Death stands in contrast to the life that is God. The Israelites learned that to be on this earth is to be associated with some aspect of death and that results in impurity. It isn't always our own sin that causes us to be impure before God. Sometimes we are impure as we are impacted by the death around us. The commandments in Leviticus address this aspect of cultural impurity due to the world in which we reside.

Leviticus cautions the reader about making anything related to God common. God is life, and our deadly impurities should not be ignored as we seek the presence of God. His people should take time to purify themselves before approaching Him in worship and prayer. He clearly reveals that the consequence of unholiness, sin, is death. People should not be flippant about death. It is the ultimate separation from a living, Holy God if we die apart from the Lord Jesus Christ.

Leviticus reveals the uniqueness of God and the importance of His people being different from all that would belittle the revelation of God. Richard Melick Jr. says, "When we think of God's holiness, the most common thought is how different He is from us. He's above human frailty, impurity, and sin."[3] The symbols for God's holiness in Leviticus are valuable in directing the world to their Savior. Our response to God's purity requirements reveals whether our hearts are truly His.

Week 3, Day 2

Read It All: Leviticus 8-15
Read a Bit: Leviticus 10

Integrity

Leviticus 8:10 — *Moses then took the anointing oil and anointed the tabernacle and all that was in it, and consecrated them.*

Consecration means "association with the sacred." Moses, as God's representative, authoritatively declares the elements of worship for the Israelites as sacred unto the Lord as directed by the Lord from the tabernacle. God is continuing to equip His people Israel to display His holiness to all. God's holy integrity is a hard thing to communicate to the world. Unless God reveals His nature to the people, there will be

---

[3]   Richard Melick Jr., *Called to Be Holy* (Nashville, TN: Lifeway Press, 2014), 14.

great confusion about who this I Am truly is. God is providing many symbols and pictures of His redemptive plan so humanity can receive His redemptive life.

Integrity implies consistency, a continual, nonstop righteousness. Though the people, even God's representative nation, continue to be wayward, God is steadfast in His righteousness and provision of mercy to all who would seek refuge in Him. The details of Leviticus direct everyone on God's provisional path of purity. To enter the presence of God, to be with God, man must also be fully righteous. Many say this is impossible, and it would be impossible if God did not provide the steps for purification. Leviticus demands that readers stop in their own approach and adopt God's way of righteousness.

Aaron's sons Nadab and Abihu decided to ignore Moses' directions and worship God as they desired, but they were consumed by fire and died before the Lord. The just nature of God includes being consistent in dispensing judgment on those who dishonor His authority and directions. At this point in time, it was essential that the details given Moses were followed by the leadership. It is in these details that all nations would be directed to the Seed of the woman, the Savior. Representing God is a high calling that includes obedience to His revelation of Himself.

Week 3, Day 3

Read It All: Leviticus 16-17
Read a Bit: Leviticus 16:29-34

Dignity

Leviticus 16:29-30 — *This shall be a permanent statute for you: in the seventh month, on the tenth day of the month, you shall humble your souls and not do any work, whether the native, or the alien who sojourns among you; for it is on this day that atonement shall be made for you to cleanse you; you will be clean from all your sins before the Lord.*

Unbelievable! A day each year set aside for humility and corporate acknowledgement of the nation's need for God's cleansing, an annual celebration of His provision of restored purity and forgiveness. This is humanity's greatest need, reconciliation with God and with our neighbors.

I envy Israel's Day of Atonement. Not because it was a day off of work, but because it was a day of restoration with God and with all the people. I know that a simple "I'm sorry" is key to living well and loving one another, but I struggle to see my own sin or to know when "bringing it up" will just make it more dramatic and awkward. The idea of everyone doing this in community is restorative for all, a good example of honoring God and valuing one another.

We struggle with apologies. We'd rather forgive without even having to explain the offense. This is avoidance, not forgiveness. Forgiveness cannot be accomplished without an identification and admission of sin. The Day of Atonement called all the people to recognize the destructive nature of sin, their need for confession and repentance, and the joy of restoration.

Saying "I'm sorry" is a matter of dignity and humility. In our humility, we exalt the Savior and in our apology, we uplift the person hurt. The dignity of the one hurt is restored, as these little words validate their pain and their worth. Confronting the guilty party aids their restoration as the confrontation indicates we believe they are capable of repentance, of doing what is right. In Christ, all believers have a Day of Atonement when they realize that He is the blood sacrifice prefigured in Leviticus. To God be the glory for His atoning life.

Week 3, Day 4

Read It All: Leviticus 18-22
Read a Bit: Leviticus 19

Unity

Leviticus 19:2 — *Speak to all the congregation of the sons of Israel and say to them, "You shall be holy, for I the Lord your God am holy."*

In describing God's holiness, Richard Melick Jr. writes, "Perhaps the most fundamental principle of the universe is God's holiness. His holiness explains how He can reign in righteousness, unaffected by the evil that influences His creation. When the power of God is manifest, it's often associated with His holiness. God's intervention in the affairs of life is always redemptive or corrective, with moral implications properly associated with holiness.

34

Because He is holy, He always wills what's right. Therefore, the relationship between God and people is based on holiness."[4]

The details in this section of Leviticus can be shocking. Is mankind capable of such horrific acts? Apparently the answer is yes, and God knows us well. We are unified in our depravity. Leviticus includes laws regarding immoral relationships, idolatry, bestiality, shaming one another, cheating, ignoring your neighbor's hunger, wrong with a harlot, human sacrifice, and more!

You would think that the laws regarding human sacrifice and trafficking would be unnecessary in our modern culture, our higher learning, but there are more humans trafficked and aborted today than possibly ever as a result of larger populations and our adeptness at trapping and killing. Abortion is legal. We do not value the unborn. Trafficking is big business as we traffic for child labor, which enables excesses for adults and sexual pleasure, again to "benefit" "adults." We disgust ourselves and marvel that our Creator doesn't wipe us off the face of His earth.

Instead, His Word continually calls us to reassess what it means to be holy. Unholy people need the teaching of Leviticus. We need to be reminded of the seriousness of sin. The ritualistic and symbolic cleansings described in Leviticus reveal that it is necessary to offer a perfect life to atone for sin. As we participate in God's Word and in His means of forgiveness, we express responsibility for our sins and attempt to bring our best to God. His Word is shared so that we might hear and repent. Holy God establishes our path to His refuge.

Week 3, Day 5

Read It All: Leviticus 23-27
Read a Bit: Leviticus 26

Priority

Leviticus 26:13 — *I am the Lord your God, who brought you out of the land of Egypt so that you would not be their slaves, and I broke the bars of your yoke and made you walk erect.*

---

4   Melick.

Once in a while, there is a song that seems to play on the radio just when I need it most. This was the case with the song "Touch the Sky" by Hillsong United. I would pull over when it would play and rest in the truth celebrated in the lyrics. There is a phrase in the song that really appealed to me; it is in the chorus:

> My heart beating, my soul breathing
> I found my life when I laid it down
> Upward falling, spirit soaring
> I touch the sky when my knees hit the ground

The phrase that strikes me is "upward falling." I like the contradiction in it and the fact that it isn't really contradictory when you consider the context of the song and, more importantly, the significance of contrition in a child's relationship with their Father. Every good parent embraces and celebrates the child who comprehends their wickedness and turns to their parent for help doing right. As we admit our wrong, our loved ones pick us up. "Upward falling" reminds me of contrition and its restorative work.

Contrition, the state of feeling remorseful and penitent, is a priority in the life of the believer. Contrition comes from an old French and late Latin word which means "ground down."

I'm reminded of some Bible promises related to the contrite:

"The sacrifices of God are a broken spirit; a broken and a contrite heart, O God, You will not despise." Psalm 51:17

"For thus says the high and exalted One Who lives forever, whose name is Holy, 'I dwell on a high and holy place, and also with the contrite and lowly of spirit in order to revive the spirit of the lowly and to revive the heart of the contrite.'" Isaiah 57:15

"For My hand made all these things, Thus all these things came into being," declares the Lord. "But to this one I will look, to him who is humble and contrite of spirit, and who trembles at My word." Isaiah 66:2

I've learned, in my walk of faith, that God does honor the contrite, for it takes contrition to realize how critical our need is for a Savior, for the Lord Jesus Christ. I cannot approach my holy heavenly Father without a grinding down of my self-righteousness. It is when I recognize my need of His provision of righteousness in His Son that my "falling" takes me upward as I take refuge in the Son and experience restored life. If only I would learn how to more readily fight the urge to "hide," ignore, or rationalize my sin, I could rest in my Father's care without a hindered relationship. God's Spirit fills the contrite believer, and He dwells with them just as He dwells in the heavenly realm. These are lofty thoughts, and I would question their truth were it not for His revelation of Himself and my discovery of His merciful grace. So I go back to singing and enjoying His willingness to lift me up as I humbly bow before the One Who loves in a manner far beyond what I can comprehend.

NUMBERS

Week 4, Day 1

Read It All: Numbers 1-10
Read a Bit: Numbers 1; 6:22-27; 9

The Revelation in Summary

Numbers 2:1-2 — *Now the Lord spoke to Moses and to Aaron, saying, "The sons of Israel shall camp, each by his own standard, with the banners of their fathers' households; they shall camp around the tent of meeting at a distance."*

Who can pay attention through reading lists of the numbers of groups of people? Numbers can be a tiring read unless you realize that the listing is a testimony of the faithfulness of God. Though Israel has not been faithful, God continues to execute His plan to bring a Redeemer through the Israelite nation. The Book of Numbers is named after the two numberings of the Israelites during their 38 years of wilderness wanderings. God honors His covenant while preserving a remnant of believing Israelites to fulfill His Word.

God had promised Abraham the land of Canaan as confirmation of God's covenant with Abraham's descendants. Moses is blessed with the task of leading the descendants of Abraham to the Promised Land. Numbers records the journey of Israel from Mount Sinai to the plains of Moab on the border of Canaan. This journey was lengthy due to the unbelief of the people and the judgment from God that this generation would wander the dessert because of their murmuring and rebellion. Though these wanderings were a judgment from God, they also depict His detailed care of them as He met their needs in the wilderness.

I feel for Moses. I cannot imagine leading a multitude through the desert. I got frustrated leading my three children into McDonald's while skirting the drive through line. When Moses hits the rock with his staff, I cringe. I remember kicking a hole in my wall when I was trying to herd my three out of the house to go to the zoo with friends. I was in air conditioning, not the desert. Shockingly, my three didn't rebel against me, but ran to see what I did to the wall. The sensitive one did end up crying but clung to me amidst the tears. I felt awful. The youngest pointed out the spot on the wall to our house guests for many weeks. Moses and I have had our moments.

Week 4, Day 2

Read It All: Numbers 11-20
Read a Bit: Numbers 11; 13-14; 20:23-29

Integrity

Numbers 14:22-23 — *Surely all the men who have seen My glory and My signs which I performed in Egypt and in the wilderness, yet have put Me to the test these ten times and have not listened to My voice, shall by no means see the land which I swore to their fathers, nor shall any of those who spurned Me see it.*

It seems dark.

Devastated homes breeding devastated lives. A bride remembering being a child repeatedly raped by Mom's boyfriends and now resisting a Good Father she cannot comprehend. A failing marriage, panicked parents that cannot say anything nice and blaming everyone, still not teachable, seems hopeless. Children witnessing it all. An abusive husband manipulating the mother of his children, using them as ammunition in his continued war to control. Gossip ruining friendships. The bottle that shatters homes, deceiving many into thinking it is filled with joy. Anxiety over petty things. Leadership with secrets. There seems to be no way to revive character. Unbelief in power. Unopened Bibles and low attendance in study. Shock when someone bows to pray. Slavery today while the Emancipator is ignored. Children with no consistent place to lay their heads and no consistent person to show them value.

It seems overwhelmingly dark.

God is good, but there is evil, and He allows humankind to rebel against God-ordained responsibilities . . . repeatedly. God is good, and the evil is us. We need the Redeemer every moment of our lives.

> "*Let love be without hypocrisy. Abhor what is evil; cling to what is good.*" Romans 12:9

> "*Never pay back evil for evil to anyone. Respect what is right in the sight of all men.*" Romans 12:17

"Do not be overcome by evil, but overcome evil with good".
Romans 12:21

Persevere to do right; we are not home yet. Your acts of right make a tremendous difference in this wrong world. He is the Lifter of our heads and He does so through His Body of believers. Be an instrument of His Light, as darkness is readily consumed by even small flickers as they try to take flame.

> *"Blessed is a man who perseveres under trial; for once he has been approved, he will receive the crown of life which the Lord has promised to those who love Him. Let no one say when he is tempted, "I am being tempted by God"; for God cannot be tempted by evil, and He Himself does not tempt anyone"* James 1:12-13.

Week 4, Day 3

Read It All: Numbers 21-26
Read a Bit: Numbers 21:1-9; 24

Dignity

Numbers 21:9 — *And Moses made a bronze serpent and set it on the standard; and it came about, that if a serpent bit any man, when he looked to the bronze serpent, he lived.*

> *"As Moses lifted up the serpent in the wilderness, even so must the Son of Man be lifted up; so that whoever believes will in Him have eternal life"* John 3:14-15.

God provided so many illustrations of the life of Christ in the Old Testament that are fulfilled in the Gospels. The bronze serpent in the wilderness is one of the most powerful illustrations.

Historically, God had just delivered Israel from a mighty Canaanite King that had taken some of the Israelites captive. It was an incredible victory. As the people continued their journey to the Promised Land, they became impatient and complained about God and Moses. God had repeatedly warned the people against complaining about the leader He had anointed for the nation. The Israelites loathed God's provision of leadership and food in the wilderness.

In response, the Lord sent fiery serpents among the people and many died. The people confessed their sin and begged Moses to intercede for them. The Lord directed Moses to make a replica of the serpent and set it on a standard so that everyone who was bitten could look at the standard and live.

The apostle John refers back to this time in Numbers to relate God's deliverance of the people in the past with His provision of another standard raised for all to see. Christ on the cross is healing for all who look to His death for the forgiveness of their sins. The cross was taught through Moses hundreds of years before crucifixion existed. God continues to mercifully give life to complainers today. He is the Psalm 3 Lifter of our heads.

Week 4, Day 4

Read It All: Numbers 27-32
Read a Bit: Numbers 27:1-14; 31

Unity

Numbers 27:6-7 — *Then the Lord spoke to Moses, saying, "The daughters of Zelophehad are right in their statements. You shall surely give them a hereditary possession among their father's brothers, and you shall transfer the inheritance of their father to them."*

Prior to becoming a Christian, I believed that Christianity held women back. I believed that a faith based on a society called "patriarchal" would diminish females. I believed the Bible taught a disparity in valuing people based on gender. I was ignorant of God's character. I was wrong.

Teachers may warp the Gospel and add horrific philosophies to the Gospel message due to human reasoning and bias, but the Gospel restores dignity to all. The Gospel is the great equalizer. When you visit the land of Christ's incarnation, you see the prominence of women in the biblical story. You see the countercultural teaching of God regarding women. Numbers 27:6-7 and the inheritance for the daughters of Zelophehad was revolutionizing text. God values women.

In the New Testament, God proclaims the comforting presence of women in the tortured life of His Son. Consider that the Deliverer is anticipated through the Seed of a woman (Eve), an interesting phrase unless a virgin birth is involved. Deborah, Ruth, a quiet servant girl to Naaman's wife, the Queen of Sheba, Esther and the Proverbial Woman all demonstrate strong devotion to the ways of God at crisis moments in the Holy Land. The birth of Christ is accompanied by the account of the incredible faith of a young woman named Mary. Christ's first public sign of His relationship to God is brought about by the urging of a woman. Many of the New Testament parables involve women, and these women are heroes in the parables in contrast to the self-righteous male leaders. The word "ministry" is associated with women in the New Testament, particularly women who minister to Christ through physical nourishment, moments of generous worship, or steadfast support at the foot of the cross. Women are noted for their incredible recognition of Christ's deity while many others reject Him and His teaching. The Samaritan woman sets the example for readily sharing Christ with the neighbors. The Syrophoenician woman sets the example for quick-witted humility in begging help for her daughter and comparing herself to the dogs that value crumbs. The risen Jesus reveals Himself first to the women who honor Him by returning to the tomb. The early church is established through the aid of many women acknowledged in epistle after epistle. Women are frequently listed as sharing in the struggle for the cause of the Gospel. The church itself is pictured as the precious Bride of Christ. Thank You, Lord, for so thoroughly validating women. You are our integrity.

> *"For all of you who were baptized into Christ have clothed yourselves with Christ. There is neither Jew nor Greek, there is neither slave nor free man, there is neither male nor female; for you are all one in Christ Jesus. And if you belong to Christ, then you are Abraham's descendants, heirs according to promise"* (Galatians 3:27-29).

Week 4, Day 5

Read It All: Numbers 33-36
Read a Bit: Numbers 33:50-56; 36

Priority

Numbers 32:18 — *We will not return to our homes until every one of the sons of Israel has possessed his inheritance.*

The word "inheritance" occurs repeatedly in Numbers. God is implementing His plan to secure an inheritance for His children. He cares about each person's future and their capacity to pass life on to the next generation.

In studying the Pentateuch, we not only have great reminders of the reality of God, but evidence of His loving care. The writings are also good warnings about my weaknesses, especially my propensity to be unbelieving like the people in Numbers. I'm reminded of my dependence on my Maker for life and rest. I'm reminded to beware of times when I am presumptuous in thinking I am strong.

> *"Therefore let him who thinks he stands take heed that he does not fall"* 1 Corinthians 10:12.

Amazingly, in the midst of studying about the weakness of man, I see the love of God. G. K. Chesterton, a great twentieth century writer, said, "All men matter. You matter. I matter. It's the hardest thing in theology to believe."[5] I'm seeing this truth as a theme in the pages of the Pentateuch. In particular, the Book of Numbers reveals a faithful God who continually teaches, directs, and disciplines a people because they matter to Him. This is an extraordinary concept to modern man, as we are known for abandoning people when they are not "nice" to us. It is hard for us to really comprehend that God is faithful. I readily give up, go with the crowd, and seek my own selfish interests. I do this out of unbelief that God is good and that His ways are best. I need to learn from the example set by Israel in Numbers. Unbelief leads to disobedience and death. I am learning the character of God in the midst of His peoples' unbelief and disobedience. God is patient. My disobedience doesn't result in God abandoning me; rather it distances me from the rest I could have in Him and the enjoyment of Him. People matter to God, and it is good to serve Him.

---

[5]   G. K. Chesterton, *The Scandal of Father Brown* (Cornwall, UK: The Stratus House, 2001), 34.

The Book of Hebrews gives commentary on Israel's unbelief and applies the lessons to believers through the ages. I'm taking a moment to consider the warnings in this text and to turn from unbelief. How about you?

"Therefore, just as the Holy Spirit says, 'Today if you hear His voice, do not harden your hearts as when they provoked Me, as in the day of trial in the wilderness, where your fathers tried Me by testing Me, and saw My works for forty years.' Therefore I was angry with this generation, and said, 'They always go astray in their heart, and they did not know My ways'; As I swore in My wrath, 'They shall not enter My rest' Take care, brethren, that there not be in any one of you an evil, unbelieving heart that falls away from the living God. . ., but encourage one another day after day, as long as it is still called "Today," so that none of you will be hardened by the deceitfulness of sin. For we have become partakers of Christ, if we hold fast the beginning of our assurance firm until the end, while it is said, 'Today if you hear His voice, do not harden your hearts, as when they provoked Me.' For who provoked Him when they had heard? Indeed, did not all those who came out of Egypt led by Moses? And with whom was He angry for forty years? Was it not with those who sinned, whose bodies fell in the wilderness? And to whom did He swear that they would not enter His rest, but to those who were disobedient? So we see that they were not able to enter because of unbelief" Hebrews 3:7-19.

DEUTERONOMY

Week 5, Day 1

Read it All: Deuteronomy 1-4
Read a Bit: Deuteronomy 1-4 (It's not long!)

The Revelation in Summary

Deuteronomy 1:43 — *So I spoke to you. . ., but you would not listen. Instead you rebelled against the command of the Lord, and acted presumptuously and went up into the hill country.*

Deuteronomy is the final book in the Torah or Pentateuch. It begins with Moses explaining God's revelation to the next generation as they stand at the border of the Promised Land. Moses gives a history lesson on Israel to remind the people that life is to be lived for God, their faithful Deliverer during the wilderness wandering years. The impact of unbelief and disobedience on their lives is emphasized as Moses purposes to prepare the next generation to obey God by reminding them of all God has done.

Deuteronomy gets its name from a word meaning the second law. Moses is conveying the character of the Lord to the people by reiterating the Law of God. The book centers on Moses' two speeches to the people and on his death. Moses does not enter the Promised Land at this time; his disobedience resulted in his own death prior to experiencing the promises of God on this earth.

Moses is thankful for God's patience with Israel and understands that God could have rightly wiped out the people from the face of the earth but that He graciously preserved a remnant to declare His name to the nations. Moses is passionate about making sure that his listeners live purposeful lives for God, blessed by God, and are careful to preserve a godly heritage to their children. Moses says, "Only give heed to yourself and keep your soul diligently, so that you do not forget the things which your eyes have seen and they do not depart from your heart all the days of your life; but make them known to your sons and your grandsons" (Deuteronomy 4:9).

Moses reviews the stipulations of the Law in great detail so that Israel will learn how to be blessed by God for obedience rather than cursed by

God for disobedience. The people make an oath to God to obey His Word rather than to live by their own faulty standards and reasoning. Moses knows that the people will continue to disobey, but he hopes that they will remember when they are suffering because of disobedience that the Lord will continue to hear their cries for deliverance and respond to them. The faithfulness of God is the basis for Moses calling the people to choose life not death.

Week 5, Day 2

Read It All: Deuteronomy 5-11
Read a Bit: Deuteronomy 5; 6:1-9; 7:17-19; 8:1-10; 10:12-22

Integrity

Deuteronomy 6:4-9 — *Hear, O Israel! The Lord is our God, the Lord is one! You shall love the Lord your God with all your heart and with all your soul and with all your might. These words, which I am commanding you today, shall be on your heart. You shall teach them diligently to your sons and shall talk of them when you sit in your house and when you walk by the way and when you lie down and when you rise up. You shall bind them as a sign on your hand and they shall be as frontals on your forehead. You shall write them on the doorposts of your house and on your gates.*

Moses summarizes what the Lord requires of Israel in Deuteronomy 6:4. The passage reveals that God is the only God, worthy of their worship. God's people are to love Him with all their heart, soul, and might. Moses knows that this has been impossible for all previous generations, but he believes God will do this through the people by giving them new hearts. This hope anticipates the coming of the Seed of the woman who will perfectly represent God and fulfill humanity's need for holiness by sending His Spirit as each person's new nature.

If Israel obeys these words of God through Moses, they will become a place of refuge for all the nations. This would fulfill the Abrahamic Covenant of a people set apart to bless others in God's name. The nations Israel was to conquer as they move into the Promised Land were known for their horrific practices, idol worship, and devaluation of life. God's people would be a community that helped the hurting, the widow, the orphan, and the foreigner. God's people would purify the land as they established a nation under His authority.

Caring for others takes effort and planning. More churches are getting intentional about supporting the families within the church that foster children. This is making a difference in the number of families that continue to foster following their first experience. Seeing pictures and hearing the stories of the families in training to foster and to support foster families reminds the entire Body that children are in need of homes and families in our area and that His church can help. In some cases, fostering leads to adoption which should resonate with His children as we have been adopted into God's family. God revealed Himself in the Law, He is a God that cares deeply about the weak and hurting.

Week 5, Day 3

Read It All: Deuteronomy 12-26
Read a Bit: Deuteronomy 12:1-7; 13:1-5; 15:1-6; 18:9-22; 26:16-19

Dignity

Deuteronomy 18:15 — *The Lord your God will raise up for you a prophet like me from among you, from your countrymen, you shall listen to him.*

The prophet that God will raise up, the Greater Prophet than Moses, is the Lord Jesus Christ. The promise of this prophet is in the midst of a section on spiritism and false prophets. Those who would teach contrary to God's Word are the greatest threat to the people of God as they lead the people away from the truth of God and away from their equipping to give the message of redemption to the world. Too often, our hunger for the spiritual and someone to worship leads us to idolize appearances of spirituality. This mars our dignity. We base our worship on feelings, not His truth. God's direction is clear: listen to my prophets, particularly the great Prophet, my Son, and find life. God provides the Law and the Prophets so that we may recognize His character and know His will in our circumstances.

The false prophets lead us to death. They speak presumptuously in God's name, seeking worship for themselves rather than the One True God. The false prophets attempt to evoke fear in people, but God directs us to not fear man. Wisdom comes from fearing the Lord.

God gives us great dignity in sending His Son as the Prophet to teach us His ways. God reveals that we too can be raised up with this prophet by listening to His loving voice and trusting in His sacrificial care. We are a blessed people, equipped by God to see His provision of life in contrast to those who succumb to the false teachings of the enemy.

Week 5, Day 4

Read It All: Deuteronomy 27-30
Read a Bit: Deuteronomy 29-30, Good review!

Unity

Deuteronomy 30:19-20 — *I call heaven and earth to witness against you today, that I have set before you life and death, the blessing and the curse. So choose life in order that you may live, you and your descendants, by loving the Lord your God, by obeying His voice, and by holding fast to Him; for this is your life and the length of your days, that you may live in the land which the Lord swore to your fathers, to Abraham, Isaac, and Jacob, to give them.*

Every person has options set before them by their Creator. We have the option to express our thoughts, to choose our friends, to be thankful or not. Based on our social standing, we may have more or fewer options than another, but we all have the option to choose whom we love. Love is an act of the will more than an emotion. The horribly oppressed still has the option to love.

God acknowledges that He gave us options. He presents the most important of decisions we make in Moses' call to the people to choose life by obeying God. This is the culmination of Moses' teaching to the next generation. Will you, will I, choose to love the Lord, to hold fast to Him? Moses clearly directs that we should.

Moses also acknowledges that we will not love consistently. He records that we tend to cycle through life. We commit ourselves to God, and then the day-to-day bears down on us and we tend to forget God. This existence (common to mankind) leads us into trouble and ultimately to the judgment of God. In our enslaved circumstances, we remember God and return (repent) to Him, crying out for His help. God mercifully responds to the repentant sinner time after time. God delivers. Although we tend to repeat these cycles of evil, judgment, repentance, and deliverance, ultimately God delivers us into His eternal kingdom, and the child of God finally experiences rest in Him as they receive a new heart consistent in their choice of God.

Thank you Lord, for the Greater Prophet who lays down His life so that I may have life in You forever!

Week 5, Day 5

Read It All: Deuteronomy 31-34
Read a Bit: Deuteronomy 32, The Song of Moses

Priority

Deuteronomy 33:29 — *Blessed are you, O Israel; Who is like you, a people saved by the Lord, Who is the shield of your help and the sword of your majesty! So your enemies will cringe before you, and you will tread upon their high places.*

I have fallen in love with Moses through spending time with him from Exodus to Deuteronomy. Through Moses' life, I see the faithfulness of God. I am comforted in knowing that imperfect leaders can lead many to our perfect Savior. Moses is not the longed-for Messiah, but he provides direction to Messiah and preserves the Word of God for our lost world.

I know we learn more about Moses at the transfiguration of Christ when he stands in the Promised Land with the Deliverer he anticipated. I smile, thinking of him there. I also know from Jude that the archangel Michael has guarded the body of Moses. God honors His child.

I close the Pentateuch devotional section by reading again the eulogy of Moses at the end of Deuteronomy. I am forever grateful for the Law of Moses that granted me the revelation of God's character and my great need of Him.

Deuteronomy 34 — *Now Moses went up from the plains of Moab to Mount Nebo, to the top of Pisgah, which is opposite Jericho. And the Lord showed him all the land, Gilead as far as Dan, and all Naphtali and the land of Ephraim and Manasseh, and all the land of Judah as far as the western sea, and the Negev and the plain in the valley of Jericho, the city of palm trees, as far as Zoar. Then the Lord said to him, "This is the land which I swore to Abraham, Isaac, and Jacob, saying, 'I will give it to your descendants'; I have let you see it with your eyes, but you shall not go over there." So Moses the servant of the Lord died there in the land of Moab, according to the word of the Lord. And He buried him in the valley in the land of*

Moab, opposite Beth-peor; but no man knows his burial place to this day. Although Moses was one hundred and twenty years old when he died, his eye was not dim, nor his vigor abated. So the sons of Israel wept for Moses in the plains of Moab thirty days; then the days of weeping and mourning for Moses came to an end.

Now Joshua the son of Nun was filled with the spirit of wisdom, for Moses had laid his hands on him; and the sons of Israel listened to him and did as the Lord had commanded Moses. Since that time no prophet has risen in Israel like Moses, whom the Lord knew face to face, for all the signs and wonders which the Lord sent him to perform in the land of Egypt against Pharaoh, all his servants, and all his land, and for all the mighty power and for all the great terror which Moses performed in the sight of all Israel.

Rest in His peace.

REST TIME

Week 6, Days 1-5

Genesis 2:2 — *By the seventh day God completed His work which He had done, and He rested on the seventh day from all His work which He had done.*

In your study of the Pentateuch, you read that God created man and woman in His image to rule, to bless others with His merciful character. You also learned about God representing Himself through His chosen people Israel and His desire that Israel would lead in blessing all the nations through proclaiming the anticipated Deliverer, the Passover Lamb. God equipped Israel with descendants, the law, and His promises so that Israel could announce His great worth to the nations. These first five books reveal that God is involved in the lives of mankind and provides a way for His children to lead others into His great promises.

Journal any thoughts you wish to record at this point in your reading.

Your Throne
Shall Be Established
Forever
2 Samuel 7:16

OLD TESTAMENT HISTORY

G od's national representative Israel is the subject of the Old Testament History books. These are Joshua, Judges, Ruth, 1 & 2 Samuel, 1 & 2 Kings, 1 & 2 Chronicles, Ezra, Nehemiah, and Esther. Many of these stories are told from the perspective of the prophets during these historical periods. God's history with His chosen nation Israel reveals mankind's struggle with self-righteousness and rebellion against God in contrast to Holy God's faithfulness to discipline His children and provide a way for them to eventually inherit the Kingdom of God. The hope in these books is the continued promise of Messiah, the Seed of the woman anticipated because of the teachings in the Pentateuch. Some of Israel's leaders represent the Seed-line well and provide indicators or pictures that help the reader prepare to recognize Messiah when He comes to reside with mankind. Moses commanded the people to listen to the Greater Moses, Joshua pointed to an eternal Leader, and King David prepared us for His worship. There are many lessons for God's people in this Old Testament History. Hopefully, we can learn from the history how to better know and represent Messiah today.

JOSHUA

Week 7, Day 1

Read It All: Joshua 1-4
Read a Bit: Joshua 1-2

The Revelation in Summary

Joshua 1:6 — *Be strong and courageous, for you shall give this people possession of the land which I swore to their fathers to give them.*

The name Joshua is the same name as Jesus in Greek and means "God saves." Joshua is the new "Moses" for the people. While Moses was still alive, Joshua was identified by God as Israel's leader. Joshua is known for his courage, a trait that Moses confessed he lacked. Courage involves trusting God more than fearing mankind.

The Book of Joshua starts with a view into the Promised Land by a people tired of wandering in the dessert and now convinced that God is able to deliver them from their enemies. The tribes of Israel are camped on the east side of the Jordan River and set to enter the land. The time is believed to be around 1000 BC.

In the Book of Joshua, the man Joshua depicts the willingness of a Savior to fight the enemy for a people, the compassion of a Savior for those considered unclean, the focus of a Savior on the plan of God, the sorrow of a Savior regarding unfaithful creation, and the commitment of a Savior to deliver Life. Under Joshua's leadership, Israel is said to have served the Lord all the days of Joshua and the elders who survived him. This is in contrast to the former days of Israel, when they were known for complaints and rebellion. For a people seeking Messiah, Joshua provided great hope, but Joshua was not the ultimate Seed of the woman. He died at 110 years old and was buried in the hill country of Ephraim. The Kingdom of God is yet to come.

Week 7, Day 2

Read It All: Joshua 5-10
Read a Bit: Joshua 6-7

Integrity

Joshua 7: 20-21 — *So Achan answered Joshua and said, "Truly, I have sinned against the Lord, the God of Israel, and this is what I did: when I saw among the spoil a beautiful mantle from Shinar and two hundred shekels of silver and a bar of gold fifty shekels in weight, then I coveted them and took them; and behold, they are concealed in the earth inside my tent with the silver underneath it."*

Have you ever seen something that you just flat out wanted? Wanted so much that acquiring the thing started consuming your thoughts? I remember as a young bride seeing ladies at church with really expensive purses and seeing myself as unsuccessful unless I had such a purse. I heard how a group of women went to New York each year to get their purses at designer pop-up shops and of course at amazing discounts. I started not only coveting the purses but also the trips to New York. Later in years, after purchasing a few of the coveted purses, I was confronted with how quickly a purse can fall apart or go out of style. The obsession upon possession proved unsatisfying.

I've witnessed women covet a particular relationship. I talked with one lady who was stalking a lady at church because she thought the other lady should be her best friend. This freaked out the subject of the obsession and caused a huge riff in their Bible Fellowship class. I've seen women so obsessed with a certain man or having children that they just can NOT be happy without him or them, and the women belittle the relationships they have. Obsessions are mean.

Achan's obsession with the Canaanite spoil becomes an integrity issue that causes defeat for an entire nation. The anger of the Lord burned against the people because in the midst of a huge victory, they just wanted more. They didn't believe God's plan was the best plan. The people were already acquiring land and buildings that another nation had worked to develop (Deuteronomy 6:10-15), yet the people desired much more. Achan's household is destroyed because of their disregard for God's instructions. Achan is a strong warning for me to set my desires on what God has revealed as good and to believe He really does know what is best. Moral of the story: Don't go "achaning" for what spoils.

Week 7, Day 3

Read It All: Joshua 11-14
Read a Bit: Joshua 14

Dignity

Joshua 14:5 — *Thus the sons of Israel did just as the Lord had commanded Moses, and they divided the land.*

Bible readers can get easily confused by the twelve sons of Jacob, the twelve tribes, and the division of the land. God makes numerous promises involving the tribes, so it is good to have some clarity on the topic.

The twelve sons of Jacob were Reuben, Simeon, Levi, Judah, Issachar, Zebulun, Joseph, Benjamin, Dan, Naphtali, Gad and Asher. Jacob, instead of blessing his first-born with a double portion of the inheritance, gave Joseph a double portion, including Joseph's sons Manasseh and Ephraim. Each son represents a tribe in Israel except that Joseph's sons are half-tribes, and Joseph is not listed as a tribe. The tribal genealogies are also important because of the promises of God. When Joshua divides the conquered land among the tribes, he is commanded by God to not designate a portion for the Levites, as they were to live among all the territories as mediators (priests) for the people. The Levites didn't inherit land like the other tribes, but they inherited a calling—the priesthood. Manasseh designates the tribe that Joseph would have had, and Ephraim designates the tribe for Levi's portion. The land divisions or territories are listed by the twelve: Reuben, Simeon, Judah, Issachar, Zebulun, Benjamin, Dan, Naphtali, Gad, Asher, Manasseh, and Ephraim.

There are many stories of Jacob's sons doing evil. Judah is known for endangering the Seed-line of Messiah by his treatment of Tamar (Genesis 38), and yet God faithfully honors His promises to Judah and preserves a land and great lineage for Judah's descendants. Israel eventually goes into exile for years of rebellion by the tribes against God, but as soon as the exile is over, the prophet Ezekiel gives specific details of the full restoration of the people back to the land and the territories to be restored to their original designations. God is continually building the dignity of His people. He sees His children as worthy of a great inheritance.

Week 7, Day 4

Read It All: Joshua 15-19
Read a Bit: Joshua 15:1-19

Unity

Joshua 19:49 — *When they finished apportioning the land for inheritance by its borders, the sons of Israel gave an inheritance in their midst to Joshua the son of Nun.*

The house next door to me is for sale. I wish I had the means to buy it for my mother. I'd love to have her living close to me without living with me. She likes her space too. Having the authority and means as a community to set aside an inheritance for loved ones is a great joy. God equipped the sons of Israel to bless their great leader, Joshua. What a privilege for the people!

Israel's unity was key in their conquering of the land and in establishing the nation as a leader among nations. Finally, Israel is in a position to represent God to all other nations, to be the refuge God desires for all people. Our unity in Him equips us to bless others on a great level. My church sets up regular service days where as a group we can basically swoop in and clean up, fix up, and build up. We focus a lot on area schools and support them with backpacks and supplies for children in need, yard work, and goodies for celebrations. It is a privilege to serve others in very tangible ways that say "You matter to us and, more importantly, you matter to the Lord God Almighty."

Week 7, Day 5

Read It All: Joshua 20-24
Read a Bit: Joshua 24

Priority

Hebrews 4:8 — *For if Joshua had given them rest, He would not have spoken of another day after that.*

I know why I do not sleep some nights; it's because I can be fearful. Rest escapes me when I forget who I am in the great I AM.

Fear is the opposite of faith. The same heart that has a tremendous capacity for fear can be purified and emptied of its fears by a grand dose of faith. Oftentimes in Scripture, the first word the Angel of the Lord, God, or Christ speak when they "arrive on the scene" is "Do not fear." There is much in this world that can be overwhelmingly fear-inducing. God provides some insights into why we do not need to be consumed by fear. Pray through these passages while asking God to replace your fears with faith in the God Who joyfully chose you.

> *"Have I not commanded you? Be strong and courageous! Do not tremble or be dismayed, for the Lord your God is with you wherever you go"* Joshua 1:9

> *"For I am the Lord your God, who upholds your right hand, Who says to you, 'Do not fear, I will help you'"* Isaiah 41:13

> *"But now, thus says the Lord, your Creator, O Jacob, and He who formed you, O Israel, Do not fear, for I have redeemed you; I have called you by name; you are Mine!'"* Isaiah 43:1

> *"Fear not, for you will not be put to shame; and do not feel humiliated, for you will not be disgraced; but you will forget the shame of your youth, and the reproach of your widowhood you will remember no more"* Isaiah 54:4

"Do not fear those who kill the body, but are unable to kill the soul; but rather fear Him who is able to destroy both soul and body in hell" Matthew 10:28

"Do not be afraid, little flock, for your Father has chosen gladly to give you the kingdom" Luke 12:32

"Do not fear what you are about to suffer. Behold, the devil is about to cast some of you into prison, so that you will be tested, and you will have tribulation for ten days. Be faithful until death, and I will give you the crown of life" Revelation 2:10

JUDGES AND RUTH

There are 66 Bible books to cover, and if we are going to do that in one year we will have to cover more than one book in some of the weeks. When we do that, we will include the Revelation in Summary topic for each book covered so that the general flow of the story is maintained. Judges and Ruth are the first books that will be collectively addressed in one week, as I appreciate these books more when I study them together. They stand in sharp contrast to one another. Judges tells the history of the Israelite tribes as they decide to do what is right in their own eyes. The book is a tragedy. Ruth reveals a life overwhelmingly enriched as a result of her valuing identity with God's people. Ruth demonstrates how an outsider to Israel who clings to a representative of God in the midst of great loss is adopted into the covenant promises of God and subsequently is greatly blessed. Ruth meets the Kinsman Redeemer, and we learn from her that God's provisions are much bigger than our feeble dreams. Have faith!

Week 8, Day 1

Read It All: Judges 1-5
Read a Bit: Judges 2:1-17; 4

The Revelation in Summary

Judges 2:16-17 — *Then the Lord raised up judges who delivered them from the hands of those who plundered them. Yet they did not listen to their judges, for they played the harlot after other gods and bowed themselves down to them. They turned aside quickly from the way in which their fathers had walked in obeying the command-ments of the Lord; they did not do as their fathers.*

Israel was created to be God's nation that would embrace the message of Messiah and bring the blessing of life in Messiah to all the nations. Joshua led Israel courageously in breaking the back of the Canaanite enemies to equip Israel with a land and people that would rule for God. As Joshua dies, the twelve tribes under the authority of judges are to take the tribal lands and establish a nation devoted to the One True God.

The reader of Judges can evaluate the historical judges based on their love and obedience to the Word of God. In doing so, the reader is keenly aware of the decline of this young nation. God's character escapes God's people. The Book of Judges is an account of Israel's leaders selfishly doing what is right in their own eyes, provoking the anger of God, crying out to God for help, experiencing times of deliverance, enjoying God's peace, and then cycling back to sin. Read Judges and know wrong and right matter. Repentance is desperately needed.

Week 8, Day 2

Read It All: Judges 6-12
Read a Bit: Judges 6-8

Integrity

Judges 11:30-31 — *Jephthah made a vow to the Lord and said, "If You will indeed give the sons of Ammon into my hand, then it shall be that whatever comes out of the doors of my house to meet me when I return in peace from the sons of Ammon, it shall be the Lord's, and I will offer it up as a burnt offering."*

In ministry, a common question from many is, "What is the will of God for me?" Usually this is asked in regard to whether one should take a certain job, break off a frustrating relationship, or move. Rarely is the question regarding attitude, the stance of the heart. God's will focuses on the heart. God cares about the heart, and so many of the other decisions in life will work out (whatever you have, whomever you are with, wherever you go) if the heart is right.

In Scripture, the heart is our thought life, our mind, will and emotions, not the beating instrument that transfers blood throughout the body. A right thought life is linked to discerning the will of God. Romans 12:1-2 states, *"Therefore I urge you, . . .do not be conformed to this world, but be transformed by the renewing of your mind, so that you may prove what the will of God is, that which is good and acceptable and perfect."*

God reveals some specifics on His will for those sincerely seeking to delight Him. Right heart responses and attitudes are the target of God's will. 1 Thessalonians 5:16-18 commands, *"Rejoice always; pray without ceasing; in everything give thanks; for this is God's will for you in Christ Jesus."* A joyful, prayerful, thankful heart is God's will.

In Judges, Jephthah's tragedy in victory jars the reader. Jephthah has mixed motives in leading the people. He receives the help of God as the

Spirit of the Lord comes upon him, but he continues to value his own reasoning and directly disregards God's covenant by making a vow and then carrying it out regardless of what God has revealed about the value of human life. Jephthah's warped reasoning overrides his seeking the will of God. Jephthah doesn't understand the heart of God or His integrity in consistently being merciful.

We are created for God, knowing and doing His will requires heart change, His integrity in us. Lord, You are incomprehensible apart from Your revelation of Yourself. Thank You God for allowing us to know anything about Your will by supernaturally preserving Your Word through the ages. Help us be sensitive to Your Holy Spirit's leading as we study Your Word. Help us to realize Your ways are best and that doing Your will involves gratefulness, prayer, and faith. Thank You for Your Truth and Your loving patience with all Your children.

Week 8, Day 3

Read It All: Judges 13-16
Read a Bit: Judges 14-16 if you want to spend time with Samson

Dignity

Judges 16:4 — *After this it came about that he loved a woman in the valley of Sorek, whose name was Delilah.*

I am a "to do list" girl. I enjoy setting goals for the day and checking them off as I conquer the world. I like to think I am in control, mainly because I like to think I am brilliant. The years have taught me that this is utter stupidity.

Case in point: I picked February 15, 2017, as the day to paint lanterns in preparation for my daughter's wedding in early April. Lantern painting had been hanging over my head, so the accomplishment of this task was going to relieve me. I was looking forward to the painting. I love doing something crafty. I ignored several key factors as I pushed through to lantern painting: I only had two cans of spray paint, the weather was incredibly windy with a chance of rain, and my daughter was home with the flu. You would think these factors might make me amend my plans. . . .

Here is how I took control. I placed a thin sheet of plastic in the yard so that I wasn't painting the yard itself or anything in the house or garage (this is in deference to my dear husband, because I have been known to thoughtlessly grab paint and spray, not realizing I've painted the dog). I knew we needed to decontaminate my sick daughter's room, so we put her bedding in the wash on hot while I positioned her on the back porch to breath in paint fumes and so we could bond over this wedding prep moment. I proceeded to take the glass out of lanterns with no know-how or proper tools. I planned 67 minutes for this project. I got schooled in stubbornness.

Several of our lanterns would forever be permanently missing glass on some sides. I was also continually running all over the yard to grab stuff to drop on the plastic as it blew all over and mainly onto freshly painted lanterns (oh, and a bicycle that I thought was also cute to paint). I came to accept that yard debris, leaves, and minuscule dirt particles might add character to otherwise perfectly flat paint. I quickly scrambled through garage chaos to find a couple old spray paint cans when I ran out of fresh cans due to wind blowing most of the paint on anything other than the lanterns. Three hours later, I humbly received the fiancée's help (who came to check on the sick daughter) in moving said lanterns as a huge rainstorm finally shut down my project. I prayed for the right heart attitude regarding some additional craftwork that I would need to schedule for those wedding lanterns.

The good news is not merely that I had on my Fitbit during this ordeal (adding up burned calories and steps like crazy), but that God knows my stubborn ways and continues to provide Light apart from these temporary little lanterns in my life. Stubbornness really can be destructive; it diminishes our dignity and belittles the dignity of others as it prioritizes my agenda before people. A mind set against God and in love with self is ultimately death. Enter Delilah and Samson's propensity to place their desires first.

> *"Or do you think lightly of the riches of His kindness and toler-*
> *ance and patience, not knowing that the kindness of God leads you*
> *to repentance? But because of your stubbornness and unrepentant*
> *heart you are storing up wrath for yourself in the day of wrath and*
> *revelation of the righteous judgment of God, who will render to*
> *each person according to his deeds to those who by perseverance in*
> *doing good seek for glory and honor and immortality, eternal life;*

but to those who are selfishly ambitious and do not obey the truth, but obey unrighteousness, wrath and indignation." Romans 2:4-8

Week 8, Day 4

Read It All: Judges 17-21
Read a Bit: Judges 19; 20:43-47; 21:25

Unity

Judges 19:25 — *But the men would not listen to him. So the man seized his concubine and brought her out to them; and they raped her and abused her all night until morning, then let her go at the approach of dawn.*

This is raw evil, the outcome of many united in hate. Think about the implications: civil wars and families fighting on opposite sides. The annihilation of our fellow citizens is preceded by the hardening of many hearts. There are never enough museums to remind us of the impact of a Holocaust, yet genocides continue. We are a forgetful people.

The Book of Judges sums it all up. Judges 19:30 – *"All who saw it said, 'Nothing like this has ever happened or been seen from the day when the sons of Israel came up from the land of Egypt to this day. Consider it, take counsel and speak up!'"*

We cannot say enough. Doing what is right in our own eyes is destructive to others and consequently to ourselves. This divides those that should be united as His family. We are created to worship and follow a loving, merciful God. To resist His character is to snuff out life.

In this same time period of the judges, a woman in Moab named Ruth values the covenant of God and clings to it. She meets God's Kinsman Redeemer. I look forward to reading Ruth, as Judges is a dark, hard read.

Week 8, Day 5

Read It All: Ruth 1-4
Read a Bit: Ruth 1-4 (you just gotta Read It All)

The Revelation in Summary

Ruth 3:11 — *Now, my daughter, do not fear. I will do for you whatever you ask, for all my people in the city know that you are a woman of excellence.*

The Book of Ruth is a biblical phenomenon—an ancient book focused on a woman's faith, a Moabitess who lives out the righteousness of God while the Israelites are "doing what is right in their own eyes," and a widow aligning herself with another widow who is also her mother-in-law. Ruth the woman amazes me.

Many see this book as a romance. I'm a Jane Austen and Hallmark girl and do enjoy a touch of romance. I think the whole Bible is one big love story: my Creator making a way for me and you to be wedded to His amazing Son. But if you think romance is only for the young and restless, you cannot understand Ruth. The romance in Ruth is based on the character of God, mature longings for His righteousness. Ruth doesn't go for the man necessarily "easy on the eyes." She has biblical standards. I have realized through the years that biblical standards lead to real joy, rest, and yes—deep love.

Four short chapters reveal the priority of identifying with the covenant people of God, from bitterness to loveliness. In Ruth, I realize the provision of God, from famine to harvest. I enjoy the unique humor of God, from roadway to threshing floor to city gate. I sense the power of God, from barrenness to legacy. I appreciate the faithfulness of God, a covenant of redemption. I am overwhelmed by the love of God, a Kinsman Redeemer.

You and I need a Redeemer. You and I hope for the Redeemer. You and I have a Redeemer who is willing, available, and able. There is no greater love than the love of God in Christ.

> *Blessed is the LORD who has not left you without a redeemer today.* Ruth 4:14

1 SAMUEL

Week 9, Day 1

Read It All: 1 Samuel 1-7
Read a Bit: 1 Samuel 1; 3; 7:15-17

The Revelation in Summary

1 Samuel 2:1-3 —

Then Hannah prayed and said,
"My heart exults in the Lord;
My horn is exalted in the Lord,
My mouth speaks boldly against my enemies,
Because I rejoice in Your salvation.
"There is no one holy like the Lord,
Indeed, there is no one besides You,
Nor is there any rock like our God."

God created mankind to rule on this earth. 1 and 2 Samuel are records of God establishing His rule through Israelite kings. The books were originally one book but were divided into parts by the Septuagint translators.[6] 1 Samuel narrates the lives of Israel's great prophet Samuel, who anointed Israel's first king, Saul, and second king, David.

Saul and David portray disobedience and obedience to the Lord. Saul epitomizes a crazy fear of mankind and obsession with position. David reflects the value of an obedient life and the impact obedience has on others. The weaknesses of Saul and David are included in these historical accounts, as is their willingness to listen to the Word of God and repent.

"Those who contend with the Lord will be shattered;
Against them He will thunder in the heavens, The Lord
will judge the ends of the earth; And He will give strength
to His king, And will exalt the horn of His anointed."
1 Samuel 2:10

---

[6]   The Septuagint is the Greek translation of the Old Testament.

Week 9, Day 2

Read It All: 1 Samuel 8-15
Read a Bit: 1 Samuel 8; 15

Integrity

1 Samuel 15:35 — *Samuel did not see Saul again until the day of his death; for Samuel grieved over Saul. And the Lord regretted that He had made Saul king over Israel.*

As we read about Saul, we see why the Lord would regret making Saul king. Saul's physical height endeared him to the people, but his heart was short on goodness. Saul lacked integrity. Saul cannot adequately represent God without a change in heart. Thinking about God's revelation of the regrets He has in the biblical story moved my heart. I searched the Scriptures to find more about what grieves God. His Word opens up His heart:

> *"Then the Lord saw that the wickedness of man was great on the earth, and that every intent of the thoughts of his heart was only evil continually. The Lord was sorry that He had made man on the earth, and He was grieved in His heart."* Genesis 6:5-6

> *"You shall not behave thus toward the Lord your God, for every abominable act which the Lord hates they have done for their gods; for they even burn their sons and daughters in the fire to their gods."* Deuteronomy 12:31

> *"The Lord tests the righteous and the wicked, and the one who loves violence His soul hates."* Psalm 11:5

> *"There are six things which the Lord hates, Yes, seven which are an abomination to Him: Haughty eyes, a lying tongue, and hands that shed innocent blood, A heart that devises wicked plans, Feet that run rapidly to evil, A false witness who utters lies, and one who spreads strife among brothers."* Proverbs 6:16-19

John 11:34-36 — *"Where have you laid him?" They said to Him, "Lord, come and see." Jesus wept. So the Jews were saying, "See how He loved him!"*

God regrets violence and death and a lack of righteous living, integrity. He has a better plan for His creation, and we groan for His way. The love of God delights in the safety and joy of His children. What the Lord hates most reveals that He does not want anyone selfishly hurting another. We are created for righteousness. Pride makes me impatient with others, and it makes me think I should have what another has. Humility helps me rejoice when another is blessed. God hates pride in how it opposes love. The person of integrity realizes their need for God's character and how their self-centeredness breeds discord and struggles.

Week 9, Day 3

Read It All: 1 Samuel 16-20
Read a Bit: 1 Samuel 16-17

Dignity

1 Samuel 17:57 — *So when David returned from killing the Philistine, Abner took him and brought him before Saul with the Philistine's head in his hand.*

Sometimes our self perception, our dignity, is injured as we question how "spiritual" we really are. To everyone who thinks they aren't "spiritual" because they don't often have a "word from God" or they aren't "the emotional type," please consider the biblical basis for spirituality: faith. Faith in the faithfulness of God and what He says should motivate our actions. Spiritual maturity is believing that we need a Savior and that Jesus is the Savior. Walk in that truth. Here is one of my favorite discussions on spirituality, an excerpt from Total Church by Tim Chester and Steve Timmis[7]:

"We teach new Christians to pray and read their Bibles, but mature spirituality, it is said, takes us into new realms-the realms of "contemplation, silence and solitude.

---

7   Tim Chester and Steve Timmis, *Total Church: A Radical Reshaping around Gospel and Community* (Carol Stream, IL: Crossway, 2008), 142-143

. . .what struck me as I pondered those words is that they describe the exact opposite of biblical spirituality. Biblical spirituality is not about contemplation; it is about reading and meditating on the word of God. It is not about detached silence; it is about passionate petition. It is not about solitude; it is about participation in community. . . It is centered on the gospel and rooted in the context of the Christian community.

God reveals Himself by His Spirit through His word. We do not meet God in the stillness: we meet Him in His word. We are not nearer to God in a garden: we draw near to God through His word (Deuteronomy 30:14). It is Scripture breathed by the Spirit of God that is "useful for teaching, rebuking, correcting and training in righteousness. "This is what makes us "thoroughly equipped for every good work" (2 Timothy 3:16-17). And it is the word of God that brings hope and change to the human heart. . .

Biblical spirituality is a spirituality of the word. One of the central rhythms of true spirituality is therefore reading and meditating on the Bible. Meditation is not emptying your mind, but filling your mind with God's word. There is much talk of listening to God today, and we are encouraged to hear God through stillness, contemplation, dreams, and special words. There are indeed times when God graciously guides in extraordinary ways (Acts 16:6-10), but we do not need these for godly living, and we should not make them normative. The reason is that God has already spoken. He has spoken through His Son and through His word. . .

The old word is also the contemporary word. And this revelation of God is wholly adequate. It is not deficient or lacking in any way. . .the Son is the exact representation of God's being, and His word is powerful, sustaining all things. How can we act as if God's revelation in God's Son recorded by God's Spirit in God's word needs to be supplemented?

In the mystical and contemplative traditions, the goal of spirituality is union with Christ. Union with Christ is attained through a pattern of spiritual disciplines or a series of spiritual stages. . .Gospel spirituality is the exact opposite. Union with Christ is not the goal of spirituality; it is the foundation of spirituality. It is not attained through disciplines or stages; it is given through childlike faith."

I particularly like the last paragraph, as I know "the righteous will live by faith." And I have learned that God is so good that He makes it possible for any who call on Him to be fully righteous, fully spiritual because of His own graciousness and not my "mystical efforts and works."

The law of the Lord is perfect, restoring the soul; The testimony of the Lord is sure, making wise the simple. The precepts of the Lord are right, rejoicing the heart; The commandment of the Lord is pure, enlightening the eyes. The fear of the Lord is clean, enduring forever; The judgments of the Lord are true; they are righteous altogether. They are more desirable than gold, yes, than much fine gold; sweeter also than honey and the drippings of the honeycomb. Moreover, by them Your servant is warned; In keeping them there is great reward. Psalm 19:7-11

Week 9, Day 4

Read It All: 1 Samuel 21-26
Read a Bit: 1 Samuel 22; 24; 25:1

Unity

1 Samuel 26:9 — *Regarding Saul, but David said to Abishai, "Do not destroy him, for who can stretch out his hand against the Lord's anointed and be without guilt?"*

As Israel journeys to be God's covenant blesser to the nations, they are thwarted by inconsistencies in character: Hannah is righteous, but Eli's sons are evil; Samuel is favored by God, but Eli is judged and taken from service; Saul is disobedient, but Jonathon is faithful; Abigail is honoring, but Michal ridicules. The people are not united for God. David, the anointed ruler, is living in hiding with a bunch of ruffians; we also learn that David has taken several wives. In Deuteronomy 16, the kings were instructed to not amass gold or wives or horses, yet they did. These details of specific covenant violations forewarn of sorrows to come. Israel is called to stand out from the other nations, but Israel values looking like those nations.

There are moments of hope in the story when we see the people unite to obediently defeat an enemy or to sacrificially follow the covenant though another way would be less difficult. We hear the cries of a contrite David in the wilderness and his longing for God's righteousness to overcome all his distress.

I have a few friends who have moved away from the area yet return for visits. Sometimes our catching up with one another covers a gap of several years. The temptation is to focus on what we consider the negative things regarding family, particularly our children, when we gather. As the years go by, we are learning that we continue to unite over the value of prayer and our need to continually pray for one another. We are more readily acknowledging our lack of control but God's faithful deliverance. God sees our chaos, our lack of unity, and understands our longing for His kingdom and reign.

> *Answer me when I call, O God of my righteousness! You have relieved me in my distress; Be gracious to me and hear my prayer. O sons of men, how long will my honor become a reproach? How long will you love what is worthless and aim at deception? But know that the Lord has set apart the godly man for Himself; the Lord hears when I call to Him. Tremble, and do not sin; Meditate in your heart upon your bed, and be still. Offer the sacrifices of righteousness, and trust in the Lord. Many are saying, "Who will show us any good?" Lift up the light of Your countenance upon us, O Lord! You have put gladness in my heart, more than when their grain and new wine abound. In peace I will both lie down and sleep, for You alone, O Lord, make me to dwell in safety. Psalm 4:1-8*

Week 9, Day 5

Read It All: 1 Samuel 27-31
Read a Bit: 1 Samuel 28; 31

Priority

1 Samuel 31:12-13 — *. . . all the valiant men rose and walked all night, and took the body of Saul and the bodies of his sons from the wall of Beth-shan, and they came to Jabesh and burned them there. They took their bones and buried them under the tamarisk tree at Jabesh, and fasted seven days.*

> *He will swallow up death for all time, And the Lord God will wipe tears away from all faces, And He will remove the reproach of His people from all the earth; For the Lord has spoken. Isaiah 25:8*

I cannot tell you how many women I have cried with over the years. I never thought to make a list or count. We would start talking and without even realizing it at times, there were tears. I rarely go through a Bible study session without some hint of tears. God's Word softens the heart, and tears seem to purify. Amazingly, I think there have been as many happy tears as there have been grief-laden waters. Sisters in Christ tear up when they share memories of God's tender care at just the right moment. Laughter can coincide with tears. Sometimes the tears are part of sharing in the realization that He is overwhelmingly good. Tears indicate life.

I can tell you how many times I've gut-bellied sobbed with another . . . never. I tend to do this with God alone. My husband hasn't even seen me ugly-cry very many times, and we've been married over thirty years. When my grandmother was dying of cancer, I hid in my car and cried. When I am scared silly for one of our children, I wait until the house is empty and lie on my floor and cry alone. Sometimes while hearing a particularly heavy life story, I remain neutral while listening, but when finally alone, I pray and cry. I've never been so shocked by someone's story to be shocked out of loving them, but I have been shocked by how little we cry. I realize that not many are comfortable wailing with an audience they can see looking back at them. Tears can clear a room.

I know I do not cry enough. Mourning openly is rather foreign to our culture. We are overwhelmed, as we have so much to mourn: poverty, oppression, trafficking, prodigal children, broken relationships. We are better at denial and escape. It was years before I attended my first funeral, as I dreaded the mourning. Now I make funerals a priority. People need friends and family near as they grieve.

It has been a privilege to share some strong emotions with others. I'm thankful for those who have walked with me through heartache and incredible joy. When I started learning about God's character, my emotions intensified. He raises the dead. He encourages His children to be self-controlled, as He knows real life in Him is highly emotional. It means engaging the heart, reviving passion, feeling again. Our tears are precious. They express our belief that something is entirely wrong or so wonderfully spot on. They are the essence of knowing there is something better, Someone yet to come who will restore the dark heart to glorious life.

> *I am weary with my sighing; Every night I make my bed swim, I dissolve my couch with my tears.* Psalm 6:6

> *My tears have been my food day and night, while they say to me all day long, "Where is your God?"* Psalm 42:3

> *Those who sow in tears shall reap with joyful shouting.* Psalm 126:5

Then I looked again at all the acts of oppression which were being done under the sun. And behold I saw the tears of the oppressed and that they had no one to comfort them; and on the side of their oppressors was power, but they had no one to comfort them. Ecclesiastes 4:1

In their streets they have girded themselves with sackcloth; On their housetops and in their squares Everyone is wailing, dissolved in tears. Isaiah 15:3

Thus says the Lord, "Restrain your voice from weeping and your eyes from tears; for your work will be rewarded," declares the Lord, "and they will return from the land of the enemy." Jeremiah 31:16

She weeps bitterly in the night and her tears are on her cheeks; She has none to comfort her Among all her lovers. All her friends have dealt treacherously with her; They have become her enemies. Lamentations 1:2

Turning toward the woman, He said to Simon, "Do you see this woman? I entered your house; you gave Me no water for My feet, but she has wet My feet with her tears and wiped them with her hair." Luke 7:44

Therefore be on the alert, remembering that night and day for a period of three years I did not cease to admonish each one with tears. Acts 20:31

For out of much affliction and anguish of heart I wrote to you with many tears; not so that you would be made sorrowful, but that you might know the love which I have especially for you. 2 Corinthians 2:4

In the days of His flesh, He offered up both prayers and supplications with loud crying and tears to the One able to save Him from death, and He was heard because of His piety. Hebrews 5:7

2 SAMUEL

Week 10, Day 1

Read It All: 2 Samuel 1-5
Read a Bit: 2 Samuel 1; 5

Of Interest: The Psalms are believed to have been written during the period of 2 Samuel. 1 Chronicles will recount the history of 2 Samuel from a perspective of Israel's worship.

The Revelation in Summary

2 Samuel 5:3 — *So all the elders of Israel came to the king at Hebron, and King David made a covenant with them before the Lord at Hebron; then they anointed David king over Israel.*

2 Samuel narrates David's reign as king over Judah and king over all of Israel. Under David's rule the Lord fulfills many of the covenant promises to Abraham. Israel has people, a kingdom, victory over its enemies, worship leaders, and hope of a permanent dwelling place for God. David is established as the true, though imperfect, representative of the Lord God Almighty. In 2 Samuel 7 the Lord continues His covenant relationship with the people with specific promises that David's rule will endure forever in Messiah. Chapter 7 is known for the Davidic Covenant text.

The narrative of David's life provides many intimate details on David and his relationship with others under the covenant. The remnants of Saul's dynasty are evident in Mephibosheth, Michal, and Abner. We read of David's murderous disobedience to the covenant as we meet Bathsheba, Uriah, and the prophet Nathan. We witness the sad breakdown of David's dysfunctional family through his children Amnon, Tamar, and Absalom. Joab, David's commander, reveals the conflict on the field and within the palace that a military leader feels in defending his king. Servants are identified as some who would most strongly rebuke the anointed of God, as Shimei, Abishai, and Ziba are interwoven into the personal accounts.

The relationship between David and His Lord reminds the reader that the Lord's chastisement is good. A heart for God isn't a perfect heart, flawless in executing life, but one that is reflected in a person who will respond to the judgment of Righteous God with repentance and restoration.

Week 10, Day 2

Read It All: 2 Samuel 6-9
Read a Bit: 2 Samuel 7

Integrity

2 Samuel 7:16 — *Your house and your kingdom shall endure before Me forever; your throne shall be established forever.*

At this point in Israel's history, the nation is fully equipped to represent the Lord. Some commentators say Israel is at its pinnacle. God gives David promises in the Davidic Covenant that reiterate the Abrahamic Covenant, with inclusion of specifics to the covenant with David. God has not forgotten His promises to Abraham. He reveals that Abraham's descendant David will establish the great nation that will be forever. His lovingkindness will continue for the family of David, and His Seed will sit on the throne from this great family. Essentially, this guarantees the Messiah of Genesis 3:15 will come from David's line.

In thanksgiving, David acknowledges the mercy and grace of God and accepts God's promises. Because of God's integrity, not David's, David will experience the fulfillment of the Davidic Covenant as he is established as king, makes a great name for himself, fills the land with God's people, and experiences rest from his enemies. We know from the biblical text that the following promises are fulfilled after David's death: rightful heirs from the Davidic line on the throne, a remnant of Jews to continue through the ages, and the authority to rule for the Jewish people.

Knowing the propensity of humanity to fail, the Davidic Covenant would be meaningless to us were it not that we can depend on God to fulfill His Word—we can depend on his integrity. The covenant gives us hope in a continuing relationship between God and His children, even knowing that the relationship will require discipline at times. The ultimate fulfillment of the covenant is in the Lord Jesus Christ, the Seed of the woman and the heir of David. The Gospel writer Matthew acknowledges this significant connection when he conveys the genealogy of Christ in Matthew 1. Come, Lord Jesus, come.

Week 10, Day 3

Read It All: 2 Samuel 10-12
Read a Bit: 2 Samuel 11-12

Dignity

2 Samuel 12:22-23 — *He said, "While the child was still alive, I fasted and wept; for I said, 'Who knows, the Lord may be gracious to me, that the child may live.' But now he has died; why should I fast? Can I bring him back again? I will go to him, but he will not return to me."*

Even the tile looked distressed. I was lying on the kitchen floor, watching myself cry. I had nobly made it through the doctor appointment. I had gently and calmly put my children, Samuel and Sarah, down for naps after reading a few stories. Now I was in the kitchen to prepare dinner and I was falling apart. I just couldn't keep standing. I guessed I would outlive a child.

I was eleven weeks pregnant. My obstetrician had some extra time at the appointment that morning and thought it would be fun to do an impromptu sonogram. But it showed that our baby had anencephaly, an absence of the brain and skull. This sobered up the morning quickly. So later, I was lying on the floor wondering if I had somehow damaged the baby within me. I was overwhelmed with the miracle of Samuel's and Sarah's healthy births and the knowledge that life is sacred.

My doctor, who doesn't perform abortions, wanted me to have a D&C. There had been complications with Sarah's birth, and my doctor had some very valid concerns. I thought my pastors would be very clear on our case, but they weren't. This was a rare scenario to many. A pastor's wife mercifully accompanied me everywhere I went Sunday morning while my husband Scott played in the orchestra. I think she was shielding me from additional hurt as much as she could. I respect those who did contact me, seeing it all as rather black and white. A friend would tell me later that another friend who didn't contact me knew she would see the pregnancy through. I was overwhelmed. Scott wanted me safe.

I had the D&C.

I thought this would change my relationship with God. It did, but not in the way I had thought. I encountered the most merciful, tender Father I could ever imagine. As I beat myself up, my precious Scott, the church, and especially our two children helped me to heal. Dignity has to do with our worth. We rely on others to help us feel worthy. I felt so unworthy after the loss of this child. I felt that I wasn't strong enough to carry her. I thought people wouldn't respect me anymore as I had made a moral decision that might not agree with what others believed I should do. Then, in the midst of T.W. Hunt's study on The Mind of Christ, I realized God's forgiveness even if I didn't know exactly what was right or wrong. I looked at the living in a new light. I mourned for women who had lost children without having any in the home to keep them from total despair. I saw bravery. I purposed to treasure others. Samuel and Sarah helped me keep going, as they needed my care. When I thought I was not worthy of another child and feared being pregnant again, Scott kindly encouraged me. Susan Grace was my easiest pregnancy of all, no complications. Susan means "grace," and we have always felt we had a double portion of God's grace through her. Without our loss, we wouldn't have had such gain.

I remember when Samuel was in high school, and after the fact, he told me that he and a friend went to try to comfort a classmate who had just had an abortion. I was shocked and sad that their youth was interrupted by such harsh realities. I remember Sam's thoughts that after the abortion was not the time to confront the taking of life but rather an opportunity to validate the hurt this girl was experiencing by simply listening and agreeing that what had happened was awful and that her baby, though prematurely dead, mattered. I thanked God for the wisdom and compassion He had given Sam and prayed for Sam's friend to know God's ultimate care.

Ministry is the privilege of praying for and helping others find the rescuing power of the gospel of Jesus Christ. May we value all life as sacred to our merciful God.

> *Upon You I was cast from birth; You have been my God from my mother's womb.* Psalm 22:10

Week 10, Day 4

Read It All: 2 Samuel 13-19
Read a Bit: 2 Samuel 13-14; 18

Unity

2 Samuel 19:2 — *The victory that day was turned to mourning for all the people, for the people heard it said that day, "The king is grieved for his son."*

Again there was civil war in Israel. The chaos from the disunity and sin in David's household ruined the peace that had been established for the nation. Regardless of how the battle turned out, David would not feel victorious. God was disciplining him for his disobedience under the covenant. David nevertheless perseveres as his kingdom is removed by his son Absalom and then restored through Absalom's death. The restoration of the kingdom to David is a reflection of God's covenant faithfulness, not David's greatness. David is struggling for hope, seeing another son die due to his poor leadership. The nation witnesses their king's conflicted heart.

I like how Dr. Charles Baylis describes the situation, saying,[8]

An important note about David's inability to rectify his love for Absalom, his son, with the requirement for justice (capital punishment) as his enemy, as a murderer [is that] under the Law, Absalom had to be executed, but David longs to be able to give mercy (as he had received it after his murder of Uriah), but cannot. Here is the problem: David cannot bring the judgment for murder and the mercy of God together (as there is no basis for mercy under the Law for murder). David reflects this in his phrase, "O Absalom, my son, my son, O that I had died in your place". In Jesus Christ, these two will be brought together, that is, God will have love for His enemies and will execute justice on them while expressing His love by dying for them. David could not. Jesus will.

---

[8] Dr. Charles Baylis, "Commentary on 2 Samuel", www.thebiblicalstory.org.

Week 10, Day 5

Read It All: 2 Samuel 20-24
Read a Bit: 2 Samuel 23:1-7; 24

Priority

One of my seminary professors is also my weekly Bible Group teacher. I knew after I graduated that I still had much to learn and much more that I would forget and need to hear again . . . and again . . . So I've kept under his teaching. I'm thankful to have great Bible teachers at my church.

One Sunday, my teacher summarized all of life in one sentence, so I might just be able to remember this lesson. He said, all of life is determined by how you treat one person." It's profoundly simple.

John 3:35-36 — *The Father loves the Son and has given all things into His hand. He who believes in the Son has eternal life; but he who does not obey the Son will not see life, but the wrath of God abides on him.*

All of Scripture reveals that to align with Christ is to live, and to deny the Son of God is to die. Life in the Son is God's gracious way of rescuing mankind from ultimate destruction due to our sin in the face of Holy God. Life is summed up by how we treat the Son of God. Scripture exhorts us to believe in the promised Seed of Genesis 3, to seek the promised Davidic King of 2 Samuel 7, to take refuge in the Psalm 2 Anointed One, to ask for the righteousness of God in Matthew 5-8, to believe in the Messianic Babe of Luke 2, to abide in the True Vine of John 15, to worship the reigning Christ of Revelation 12. The Father is clear. He loves His Son. Our love for His Son should be evident in our daily priorities. The Lord Jesus Christ is our blessed hope.

Psalm 2:12

Do homage to the Son, that He not become angry, and you perish in the way, for His wrath may soon be kindled.

How blessed are all who take refuge in Him!

1 KINGS

Week 11, Day 1

Read It All: 1 Kings 1-7
Read a Bit: 1 Kings 2-3; 6

The Revelation in Summary

1 Kings 2:1-4 — *As David's time to die drew near, he charged his son Solomon, saying, "I am going the way of all the earth. Be strong, therefore, and show yourself a man. Keep the charge of the Lord your God, to walk in His ways, to keep His statutes, His commandments, His ordinances, and His testimonies, according to what is written in the Law of Moses, that you may succeed in all that you do and wherever you turn, so that the Lord may carry out His promise which He spoke concerning me, saying, 'If your sons are careful of their way, to walk before Me in truth with all their heart and with all their soul, you shall not lack a man on the throne of Israel.'"*

God's love is a jealous love, and He warns us to have no other gods or lovers. In the Books of the Kings, mankind's battle with unfaithfulness continues. The records include Israel's phenomenal growth, unfaithfulness, decline, and eventual destruction except for a remnant known as Judah, in exile. That God didn't completely wipe out the nation is a testimony of His faithfulness and merciful kindness.

The Israelites constantly struggled with admiration for their enemies when God had told them they needed to destroy their enemies. In particular, God wanted to keep His children separate from marrying into pagan beliefs. The nations that were still in the land worshipped idols and even practiced temple prostitution and child sacrifice. It is impossible to cohabit with evil and not be harmed. Israel had already showed preference for a monarchy instead of a theocracy, indicating the people's inclination to represent the nations rather than God. At the end of 2 Samuel, the kingdom is united under King David. In 1 Kings, the nation becomes great as Solomon rules, but it declines as Solomon is heavily influenced by his many wives and their worship of foreign gods. The kingdom divides under the leadership of Solomon's son Rehoboam, such that Rehoboam leads the Southern Kingdom of Judah (1 Kings 12), and Jeroboam leads the Northern Kingdom of Israel.

Week 11, Day 2

Read It All: 1 Kings 8-11
Read a Bit: 1 Kings 8; 11:1-13

Integrity

1 Kings 11:3-5 — *He had seven hundred wives, princesses, and three hundred concubines, and his wives turned his heart away. For when Solomon was old, his wives turned his heart away after other gods; and his heart was not wholly devoted to the Lord his God, as the heart of David his father had been. For Solomon went after Ashtoreth the goddess of the Sidonians and after Milcom the detestable idol of the Ammonites.*

I got a prayer request from a young lady confessing a sexual sin and asking for prayer that she would be able to stop committing the sin. She believed that she was driven to continue in this sin because of her loneliness. She recognized that the sin also caused her to isolate, and she was in this cycle of wanting relationships but avoiding people. She was experiencing the destructive consequences of sin. I thought her a brave soul to cry for help. Acknowledging our need for deliverance is something God asks of us. He calls for us to repent and turn back to Him for His righteousness and life.

The Bible reveals that many heroes of the faith struggled with sexual sin. This struggle is common to man. For many, cultural influences and the confusion defining sexual sin is pivotal in rationalizing sexual sin. My son once posted on Facebook that he believed that the Bible should be the standard for what is immoral. By the end of the day, many had de-friended him due to their strong disagreement on what the Bible says regarding homosexuality. Instead of communicating how one determines good and evil, some were angrily name-calling. Immorality is a controversial and highly personal subject.

Do you and I believe that the Bible is true when we look at what God's Word reveals as sexual sin? The list includes adultery, fornication (sex outside of marriage), homosexuality, bestiality, sexual promiscuity and sensuality, prostitution, looking at another with lust in the heart, defiling (not honoring) a marriage, depriving a spouse of conjugal rights, remarriage after divorce, lying with a father's wife, and incest. Sexual sin enslaves. It diminishes our worship of Holy God.

For freedom Christ has set us free; stand firm therefore, and do not submit again to a yoke of slavery. Galatians 5:1

Thankfully, God readily forgives all sin when we repent and ask for His forgiveness. Thankfully, God does not label His children based on their sin. Paul called David a man after God's own heart (Acts 13:22) in spite of his sins. Today, the world purposes to label people by their sin in an effort to promote acceptance of a sin. God provides the means for us to overcome sin. Our responsibility is to recognize sin and flee from it. God makes a way to restored purity through His forgiveness and ultimate freedom that is true pleasure.

But the one who joins himself to the Lord is one spirit with Him. Flee immorality. Every other sin that a man commits is outside the body, but the immoral man sins against his own body. Or do you not know that your body is a temple of the Holy Spirit who is in you, whom you have from God, and that you are not your own? 1 Corinthians 6:17-19

Another thought. If you have reconnected with a former "love" over Facebook or another way, stop and talk to someone who loves the Lord about the connection. Bring life into His Light.

Week 11, Day 3

Read It All: 1 Kings 12-16
Read a Bit: 1 Kings 12-13; 16

Dignity

I Kings 16:33 — *Ahab also made the Asherah.[9] Thus Ahab did more to provoke the Lord God of Israel than all the kings of Israel who were before him.*

At this point in the story, Israel is looking as bad as or worse than the nations they were to guide to the holiness of God. Israel had been

---

9   "Asherah," a Phoenician goddess, also an image of the same, *Strong's Concordance* 842.

equipped by God to represent Him by conquering the land, establishing a worship system, and demonstrating the blessings of being in right relationship with God. Israel had the Word of God, people to record His Word, and a means to preserve it through the centuries. They were the chosen people of God. The genealogies they protected would provide the data points for building the faith of multitudes. Israel should have been a safe place for the widow, orphan, and foreigner seeking life in the great Covenant Blesser. But they were not. The majority of the leadership rejected God and worshipped manmade idols, endangering the family, particularly the next generation. All dignity in Him was lost as Israel chose to value the nations and their gods over the One true God.

My parents gave me a heritage of hard-working farm folks with high self-esteem and a high value of education. I grew up in a home where my physical needs were lovingly addressed. I have never known a day of hunger or of feeling unloved. I have family. My parents were not united in their beliefs. My dad enjoyed going to Protestant churches on holidays, and my mom enjoyed no commitments on the weekend. Christianity was a weird subculture to me, made more strange by tales from my Mormon tennis partner in high school. I learned about a personal relationship with God from my mom's parents, Aunt Jeanne, and Uncle Tom. We are what we believe, and finding God's Truth saved me.

Throughout the Books of Kings, after the nation Israel has divided into Israel and Judah, there is a haunting phrase that summarized how the first king of Israel, Jeroboam, impacted multiple generations and entire nations. The phrase describes king after king in Israel: "He did evil in the sight of the LORD: he did not depart from the sins of Jeroboam son of Nebat, which he made Israel sin." Jeroboam's rebellion against God kept Israel from representing God and being worthy of respect, having His dignity. Oh, to lay a foundation of truth instead of influencing others with evil deceptions.

Week 11, Day 4

Read It All: 1 Kings 17-19
Read a Bit: 1 Kings 18-19

Unity

1 Kings 19:13-14 — *When Elijah heard it, he wrapped his face in his mantle and went out and stood in the entrance of the cave. And behold, a voice came to him and*

said, "What are you doing here, Elijah?" Then he said, "I have been very zealous for the Lord, the God of hosts; for the sons of Israel have forsaken Your covenant, torn down Your altars and killed Your prophets with the sword. And I alone am left; and they seek my life, to take it away."

I love it when the omnipresent, omniscient, omnipotent God asks man a question. This reveals God's tender heart in working us through our situation. I love seeing that God always knows where we are. When we are in Him, we have unity with Father, Son, and His Spirit. It's good to have someone care about our every move. I love hearing that He challenges us to think about what we are doing here." What a great parent! I learn to ask better questions of others with caring and the right distance as God models in His history with mankind.

Elijah had forgotten about God's remnant, those who refuse to bow their knee to the enemy. God comforted Elijah by telling him there were 7,000 in Israel, all the knees that had not bowed to Baal and every mouth that had not kissed him. Oftentimes, I need the reassurance of fellow sojourners that I am not alone in the wilderness. Believers are united in Him. The enemy may have sought Elijah's life, but God was with Elijah and had other plans.

Being zealous for the Lord is hard work, and there may be times of feeling intensely alone. It is important to stay connected to a group of believers and to remember to cry out to God for His peace and rest. Being zealous for the Lord can be grievous work as it makes us more sensitive to how the world has rejected the Heavenly Creator and how bent some are on tearing down His glorious presence. Being zealous for the Lord can be burdensome as we see his people suffer under angry regimes. But the child of God is never alone and our lives can never be taken from us. The believer today has so much more revelation than did Elijah. We have been given the truth that God resurrects the dead and that He is our ultimate victory over death. Being zealous for God is life at its fullest.

Week 11, Day 5

Read It All: 1 Kings 20-22
Read a Bit: 1 Kings 21

Priority

1 Kings 21:25 — *Surely there was no one like Ahab who sold himself to do evil in the sight of the Lord, because Jezebel his wife incited him.*

In the narrative surrounding King Ahab, we are confronted by the horrible influence of a wicked woman. Jezebel epitomizes angry bitterness toward God and self-centered idol worship. She has sold herself for worldly glamour over the glory of God. Graciously, God faithfully provides a prophet, a voice for God, as a means of calling the king to repentance. This is a tough role, and Elijah feels the burden of constantly rebuking the king. Elijah becomes the enemy of Jezebel and a picture of hope to the people.

When Ahab is made king of Israel, Elijah is there to minister to the remnant and call the king to repentance. Ahab chooses Baal and Jezebel. When Ahab honors the "Baals" over the Lord God Almighty, Elijah is there to challenge the prophets of Baal. Nevertheless, Ahab stays with his defeated gods, and Elijah runs. His ministry goes to a Gentile widow, as the Israelite leader has rejected the truth. Such rejection and acceptance will be replayed with the Lord Jesus Christ.

When Ahab continues to reject God's commands and frees the king of Aram, another prophet rebukes him, but Elijah is back on the scene to confront Ahab for his murder of Naboth over Naboth's vineyard. Elijah condemns Ahab and Jezebel to a horrific ending, but Elijah also conveys the mercy of God when Ahab humbles himself. Elijah seems revived and makes fearlessly speaking for God his greatest priority again. Elijah has submitted to God's call on his life to be God's covenant messenger. Sometimes God-given responsibilities are incredibly hard and confrontational. Know that God comforts His messengers in the midst of the battles. As 1 Kings closes and 2 Kings begins, the story of the prophets stands in dramatic contrast to the kings, as the prophets are our heroes while the kings are an evil influence in the land.

2 KINGS

Week 12, Day 1

Read It All: 2 Kings 1-4
Read a Bit: 2 Kings 2; 4

The Revelation in Summary

2 Kings 2:9 — *When they had crossed over, Elijah said to Elisha, "Ask what I shall do for you before I am taken from you." And Elisha said, "Please, let a double portion of your spirit be upon me."*

Elijah and Elisha's story develops in 2 Kings. They are really the hope in this narrative work, the hope that someone would have ears to hear the Word of God. The history of the Northern and Southern Kingdoms of Israel and Judah is not a happily ever after one. Israel is conquered by a brutal Assyria. Judah is taken captive by a phenomenal foe, Babylon. The battles are not short but are drawn-out years of suffering for many. Judah's captivity occurs over three deportations. As the history progresses, so does the testimony of God's faithfulness to do just what He says He will do.

There are other prophets that enter the story of the kings. The pre-exilic prophets are Amos, Hosea, Joel, Micah, Isaiah, Zephaniah, Habakkuk, and Jeremiah. These prophets faithfully gave voice to God's warnings to the wayward Israel and Judah. God also sent prophets to enemy nations. Jonah, Nahum, and Obadiah revealed to God's people that other nations would be judged by God for their treatment of His people. These messages and fulfillments would be a testimony to the people of God's active fulfillment of His Word. God lovingly provided many voices in all types of social settings so that His children would know how to walk in His truth and be saved. Give us ears to hear Your voice today.

Week 12, Day 2

Read It All: 2 Kings 5-8
Read a Bit: 2 Kings 5; 7

Integrity

2 Kings 5:1-2 — *Now Naaman, captain of the army of the king of Aram, was a great man with his master, and highly respected, because by him the Lord had given victory to Aram. The man was also a valiant warrior, but he was a leper. Now the Arameans had gone out in bands and had taken captive a little girl from the land of Israel; and she waited on Naaman's wife.*

Like Naaman was blessed and found healing through association with an Israelite servant, I experienced the humble help of servants in the Holy Land. On mission to Israel, I listened to the Arabic Christians that led us through their land. I was reliant on them keeping me safe. I appreciated their insights, deep love for God's Word, and their humble submission to others. Their respect for one another and for all others was convicting to me.

Arabic Christians are persecuted as a minority of minorities in the land of Israel, and yet they freely love. It was a blessing to spend time with them and to sit under their teaching.

One of the leaders, Andre, taught that the Torah equates to a call to repent. He asked us what God may ask us when we see Him in heaven. Andre proposed that God will ask, "How much time did you spend reading my Word?" Andre said that reading God's Word is intimacy with God; it is time with God, relationship development, our only means of getting to know God as good, as Father, as Lord. Andre said that as we read God's Word, we gain humility if we also hear God's Word. The humble are the ones who surrender to His Word; they obey their Father's teaching. The obedient of God are those who suffer for God. Those who suffer for God are blessed, as being persecuted for Him is finding contentment in Him and ultimately that is joy—to glorify God and experience life in Him.

Andre also explained the Middle Eastern mindset of family. Israel is like Isaac and Ishmael battling for their father's approval. Christ is Jewish, and those feeling the Jews' hatred in the land of Israel must learn to love Jesus the Jew. There is reconciliation for this family in Christ Jesus, but the firstborn can fight long and hard for his perceived "birthright." Genuine faith works through the conflicts and finds God's provision of peace. To be a believer is to appreciate and learn to enjoy the family.

> *Brethren, sons of Abraham's family, and those among you who fear God, to us the message of this salvation has been sent. For those who live in Jerusalem, and their rulers, recognizing neither Him nor the utterances of the prophets which are read every Sabbath, fulfilled these by condemning Him. And though they found no ground for putting Him to death, they asked Pilate that He be executed. When they had carried out all that was written concerning Him, they took Him down from the cross and laid Him in a tomb. But God raised Him from the dead; and for many days He appeared to those who came up with Him from Galilee to Jerusalem, the very ones who are now His witnesses to the people. And we preach to you the good news of the promise made to the fathers, that God has fulfilled this promise to our children in that He raised up Jesus, as it is also written in the second Psalm, "You are My Son; today I have begotten You." As for the fact that He raised Him up from the dead, no longer to return to decay, He has spoken in this way: "I will give you the holy and sure blessings of David." . . . Therefore let it be known to you, brethren, that through Him forgiveness of sins is proclaimed to you, and through Him everyone who believes is freed from all things, from which you could not be freed through the Law of Moses. Therefore take heed, so that the thing spoken of in the Prophets may not come upon you: "Behold, you scoffers, and marvel, and perish; for I am accomplishing a work in your days, A work which you will never believe, though someone should describe it to you."* Acts 13:26-41

Week 12, Day 3

Read It All: 2 Kings 9-13
Read a Bit: 2 Kings 9-10; 13

Dignity

2 Kings 9:36-37 — *Therefore they returned and told him. And he said, "This is the word of the Lord, which He spoke by His servant Elijah the Tishbite, saying, 'In*

the property of Jezreel the dogs shall eat the flesh of Jezebel; and the corpse of Jezebel will be as dung on the face of the field in the property of Jezreel, so they cannot say, 'This is Jezebel.'"

Be warned. There is no dignity apart from God's ways. His Word is fulfilled. Align with the good King.

Week 12, Day 4

Read It All: 2 Kings 14-17
Read a Bit: 2 Kings 17

Unity

2 Kings 17:1-18 — *The sons of Israel did things secretly which were not right against the Lord their God. Moreover, they built for themselves high places in all their towns, from watchtower to fortified city. They set for themselves sacred pillars and Asherim on every high hill and under every green tree, and there they burned incense on all the high places as the nations did which the Lord had carried away to exile before them; and they did evil things provoking the Lord. They served idols, concerning which the Lord had said to them, "You shall not do this thing." . . . And they followed vanity and became vain, and went after the nations which surrounded them, concerning which the Lord had commanded them not to do like them. They forsook all the commandments of the Lord their God and made for themselves molten images, even two calves, and made an Asherah and worshiped all the host of heaven and served Baal. Then they made their sons and their daughters pass through the fire, and practiced divination and enchantments, and sold themselves to do evil in the sight of the Lord, provoking Him. So the Lord was very angry with Israel and removed them from His sight; none was left except the tribe of Judah.*

This chapter reveals the sins of Israel which were ultimately punished by God as He had faithfully warned them He would do. Unity can be a good thing or it can be a hardship. All the people in Israel were united in experiencing the consequences of their national sin. All the people were brutally conquered by Assyria. They were killed, taken as slaves, and scattered in the land. The sons of Israel were united in being known to be against their God.

The anger of God is a reality. Many do not like to discuss His anger as we do not like to instill fear in one another. But godly fear has a great purpose in that it can lead some to take refuge in Christ and receive His Life. Scripture describes God's anger and although we see His long-suffering with all people, He does warn that He will judge and we do not have the sense to know when we are at the point of judgment. We live precariously when we refuse to repent of our sin.

> *"To this day they do according to the earlier customs: they do not fear the Lord, nor do they follow their statutes or their ordinances or the law, or the commandments which the Lord commanded the sons of Jacob, whom He named Israel; with whom the Lord made a covenant and commanded them, saying, "You shall not fear other gods, nor bow down yourselves to them nor serve them nor sacrifice to them."* 2 Kings 17:34-35

Week 12, Day 5

Read It All: 2 Kings 18-25
Read a Bit: 2 Kings 22:8-37; 25

Priority

2 Kings 23:2-3 — *The king went up to the house of the Lord and all the men of Judah and all the inhabitants of Jerusalem with him, and the priests and the prophets and all the people, both small and great; and he read in their hearing all the words of the book of the covenant which was found in the house of the Lord. The king stood by the pillar and made a covenant before the Lord, to walk after the Lord, and to keep His commandments and His testimonies and His statutes with all his heart and all his soul, to carry out the words of this covenant that were written in this book. And all the people entered into the covenant.*

Reform! When Hilkiah the high priest finds the book of the law in the house of the Lord, there is renewed hope for Judah. God's children are dependent on His revelation of Himself for life in Him. They cannot figure it out for themselves.

Hilkiah is blessed to be one of the few priestly leaders to value God's Word and to be under the reign of a king who also valued God's Word and made it a priority in the land. King Josiah led Judah's reform initiated by a reading of God's Word. Josiah did well in the sight of the Lord. His heart desire was to repair the house of the Lord, and in a return to the care of God's temple, God's Word was discovered. Josiah tore his clothes when he found out that the nation had sadly neglected God's word. Josiah sought the insight of the prophetess Huldah concerning disobedient Judah and learned that Judah would experience a tragic judgment because of their neglect. Josiah also learned that in God's mercy, Josiah and the nation Judah would not experience this judgment in his lifetime. As king, he fulfilled his responsibility to call the nation back to covenant relationship with the Lord. The king sent for the elders and they covenanted to follow God. Then Josiah got rid of the abominable things in Judah. The reforms in Judah resulted in a great Passover celebration that would feed a remnant with hope, as the nation was destined to experience the wrath of Holy God.

> *The LORD said, "I will remove Judah also from My sight, as I have removed Israel. And I will cast off Jerusalem, this city which I have chosen, and the temple which I said, 'My name shall be there.'"* 2 Kings 23:27

1 CHRONICLES

1 and 2 Chronicles include historical details omitted in the records of 1 & 2 Samuel and the Books of the Kings. The Chronicles are written for the Israelites that are returning to the land following exile. These inspired writings encourage the disciplined Jews that God has not forgotten them and that they are still God's chosen people to represent His glory to the world. For those wondering if God would continue to fulfill His covenant promises, Chronicles reveals His faithful, persevering love. The records open with genealogies, the necessary link to an exiled people of a Seed-line for their Davidic King.

Week 13, Day 1

Read It All: 1 Chronicles 1-9
Read a Bit: 1 Chronicles 3:1-3

The Revelation in Summary

1 Chronicles 3:1-3 — *Now these were the sons of David who were born to him in Hebron: the firstborn was Amnon, by Ahinoam the Jezreelitess; the second was Daniel, by Abigail the Carmelitess; the third was Absalom the son of Maacah, the daughter of Talmai king of Geshur; the fourth was Adonijah the son of Haggith; the fifth was Shephatiah, by Abital; the sixth was Ithream, by his wife Eglah.*

The author of Chronicles purposefully repeats Israel's history. This repetition is to emphasizes God's providential care of His remnant followers. The historical accounts in the book reveal what it means to be in covenant relationship with God and to be representing Him to the nations. The writer emphasizes the spiritual life of the Jewish people and connects this to their role in revealing the anticipated Messiah.

The spiritually rich heritage of the people in outlined in the lineage through David and the Kings of Israel and Judah. The history of Judah is emphasized as this nation preserved God's design for worshipping Him. The line of David is emphasized; the reader learns many more details than provided in the previous historical accounts on David as the Davidic Covenant established another marker for mankind to recognize God Incarnate at the right time.

Although genealogies may be a bit tedious to read, they are an amazing foundation to our faith. The names should remind us of God's past provision through His people. It is miraculous that a conquered, exiled people when still have such detailed accounts of their ancestry. The lists reveal God's specificity in doing just as He said He would do: raise up His Seed through Abraham, Judah, and David. As Israel returns to the land and again purposes to establish the tribes, the land distributions, and the worship system, these genealogies are key to helping the people attempt to restore their former presence.

Temple worship was a crucial means of representing the sacrificial requirements in drawing near to God. The Jewish sacrificial system would reveal that mankind needs a Savior to appease the just wrath of God due to mankind's sin. The temple also reminded the people that God would dwell in their midst when they purified themselves by following His Word. 1 Chronicles ends with the account of David preparing Solomon to build the temple. The hope is a nation set on loving the Lord God Almighty with all their heart, soul, and mind such that the nations surrounding them also come to love the Great I am.

Week 13, Day 2

Read It All: 1 Chronicles 10-16
Read a Bit: 1 Chronicles 10-11; 15:25-16:36

Integrity

1 Chronicles 15:29 — *It happened when the ark of the covenant of the Lord came to the city of David, that Michal the daughter of Saul looked out of the window and saw King David leaping and celebrating; and she despised him in her heart.*

It is never a wise thing to despise the anointed of God. Whether our jealous struggle or their imperfections are influencing our responses to the anointed (those in God ordained positions of authority), we need to petition God for His love of His people. King David modeled a deep respect for God's anointed when he spared Saul's life when Saul would have hunted David down. There should be a holy reverence for those in service for the Lord.

For example, there is a fine line between discussing the words of the pastor following a sermon and questioning his worthiness as pastor or his authority. Believers are to be continually taking all they hear from those preaching and teaching the Word and aligning what they hear to His revelation. Many of the New Testament epistles warn the church of false teaching in their midst. But we need to take great care to not dampen the testimony of the anointed by God by valuing traditions or appearances over truth.

I know that out of pettiness and a propensity to overanalyze, I have belittled leaders in my church and led my own children to question leadership in ways they would not have otherwise. This is an integrity issue for me. We place crazy expectations on our leaders and then struggle in recognizing God's call on their lives in ministry. We are to build up one another and show God's grace to one another. When a sermon or lesson doesn't align with God's Word then we are to talk over our concerns with our leaders and find out if there is a miscommunication or a need for growth. These opportunities should help all to serve well. Discussing a sermon or lesson shouldn't become an opportunity to talk ill of another, particularly a leader in His Body. May we be a people that are a blessed encouragement to one another as we purpose to represent the Great King.

Week 13, Day 3

Read It All: 1 Chronicles 17-20
Read a Bit: 1 Chronicles 17; 20

Dignity

17:2 — *Then Nathan said to David, "Do all that is in your heart, for God is with you."*

1 Chronicles 17 is possibly the centerpiece of this book, as it recounts the authentication of the Abrahamic Covenant with the Davidic Covenant due to God's love for King David. This is the account of the moment when God promises David a throne forever. God bestows the dignity of the royal Seed-line on David and his descendants. We see the outcome of this promise developing in David's history as God faithfully continues with David to give him victory over his enemies and to chastise him when he sins.

We learn from the intimate discussion between God and David through the prophet Nathan in chapter 17 many characteristics of God: God dwells where He wishes to dwell; God is personally aware of His people; God accomplishes His will through His people; God is concerned for the name of His child; God has not given up on Israel; God blesses His people; God may provide a home for His child; and God's promises to David will endure through the ages and will come to pass.

My faith is bolstered by knowing God's promises to David and seeing in the genealogies of the Lord Jesus, the Christ's lineage from David. God provides many details to edify our faith, to help us see and believe in His Promised Messiah.

Week 13, Day 4

Read It All: 1 Chronicles 21-23
Read a Bit: 1 Chronicles 21

Unity

1 Chronicles 21:18 — *Then the angel of the Lord commanded Gad to say to David, that David should go up and build an altar to the Lord on the threshing floor of Ornan the Jebusite.*

The threshing floor of Ornan would be the future site of Solomon's temple. This floor is significant, as David and his leaders went there to pray and mourn as the Lord dispensed His judgment in the form of a plague on the people for David's prideful disobedience in numbering the people during a time of peace. The Lord saw David and his leaders and relaxed the hand of the Angel of the Lord that was ready with sword drawn to judge David.

The temple of God in Scripture represents Holy God providing mercy to rebellious humanity, when mankind deserved judgment and death for their prideful rebellion against their Maker. God Himself provides mercy and payment for their sins to spare their lives and enrich them with fellowship with their Maker. The temple is Holy God promising to reside in unity with His unholy creation.

The plans that David is making for the temple will be handed over to his son Solomon. These plans will include placing the temple on the land purchased from Ornan at full price. The plans will provide for articles to be used in the worshipful sacrifices made to remind the people that Holy God mercifully provides victory in Him. The center of the temple was the Holy of Holies, which included the ark of God's covenant and the mercy seat of God. The ark contained the law of God, and the mercy seat covered this law with the sprinkling of blood from sacrifices. God looked down on His law through the spattering of blood. Remember, the location of the temple is also the place known as Mount Moriah, where hundreds of years earlier Abraham had arrived to sacrifice his son Isaac. God's presence was a unifying reality to His people through the ages, and the temple served to remind the nation of His great worth. In a similar way today, the Body of Christ is the church, the temple of the Lord God Almighty. May the church represent His sacrificial mercy well.

Week 13, Day 5

Read It All: 1 Chronicles 24-29
Read a Bit: 1 Chronicles 28-29

Priority

1 Chronicles 28:9-10 — "As for you, my son Solomon, know the God of your father, and serve Him with a whole heart and a willing mind; for the Lord searches all hearts, and understands every intent of the thoughts. If you seek Him, He will let you find Him; but if you forsake Him, He will reject you forever. Consider now, for the Lord has chosen you to build a house for the sanctuary; be courageous and act."

Parenting is easy and hard. It can be easy to become a parent and it appears to be easy to parent without investing in your child. This happens all the time.

Parenting is hard when you decide to care, to care deeply. The God-given responsibility in parenting is to raise your child such that they come to value God's way and will. God reveals in Deuteronomy 4:10, "Assemble the people to Me, that I may let them hear My words so they may learn to fear Me all the days they live on the earth, and that they may teach their children." God provides a way for generation after generation to know Him. Parents are to instill His name in their children.

I didn't realize this when I first had my children. I thought my family was all about me, making me feel loved and that children would enlarge the love I felt by naturally adoring me. I didn't begin parenting by seeing God's bigger plan.

Children were such an amazement to me and such a joy that I found great purpose in parenting. But again, this was building me up, and I struggled with idolizing the children. So much simply revolved around them. I liked you if you liked my children.

The year before having my first child, I had begun a weekly group Bible study. I was learning a lot about walking by faith, and over the years I began to realize the responsibility I had to teach my children God's Word. They also became Bible students, and we learned as a family how to better love God and one another.

I was on such a learning curve with Christian disciplines and the value of church that I didn't know how to always "shepherd a child's heart". I know there were times that my children suffered from my legalistic pushes to just have control. Then I would err on liberty, the firstborn had so many freedoms that were not right for his age because of my idolizing him, and all the children felt the consequences of parenting mistakes. I look back and overanalyze but also see God's great grace.

My children are adults now. I miss the parenting days, their presence in our home, but I see that God is faithful to personally reveal Himself to them, and I believe they believe in the Seed of the woman that delivers. I agree with 3 John 4: *"I have no greater joy than this, to hear of my children walking in the truth."* May they represent Him well.

2 CHRONICLES

Week 14, Day 1

Read It All: 2 Chronicles 1-9
Read a Bit: 2 Chronicles 5-7:3; 9:22-31

The Revelation in Summary

2 Chronicles 2:1 — *Now Solomon the son of David established himself securely over his kingdom, and the* LORD *his God was with him and exalted him greatly.*

2 Chronicles is very different from 2 Kings, even though they both cover the same time period. 2 Chronicles expands the history of the reigns of the good kings that were briefly mentioned in 2 Kings, and 2 Chronicles details more of the circumstances pertinent to the construction of the temple. Some of the most glorious scenes in the history of Israel are depicted, as David's thorough planning for his son to build a dwelling place for God are fulfilled and the glory of the Lord fills the house.

Almost a third of 2 Chronicles is a record of Solomon's reign. 2 Chronicles 9 closes with the riches that Solomon amassed for himself, and we learn firsthand how our successes can cause our demise. Solomon's son, Rehoboam, was not prepared with the wisdom of his father to reign, and the kingdom divides into Judah and Israel. Resentment of Solomon's house is evident, as the records indicate much of the king's success came about from the oppression of many people. The evil Jeroboam, King of Israel, sets the standard for Israel's leadership.

Since the Books of the Chronicles center around those who respect God's commandments with regard to temple worship, the focus of 2 Chronicles is the kings of Judah and the true place of worship. Highlighted moments in the book are driven by reforms by good kings. Ultimately, the kingdom does decline due to its disrespect of the worship of God, but the book ends with a hope, as a gentile king equips Israelite exiles to return to their land. Maybe these former captives will rebuild temple worship with a new heart. Funny, the Persian King believes God has appointed him to build a house of worship in Jerusalem.

Week 14, Day 2

Read It All: 2 Chronicles 10-16
Read a Bit: 2 Chronicles 10; 12; 14-15

Integrity

2 Chronicles 14:2-5 — *Asa did good and right in the sight of the Lord his God, for he removed the foreign altars and high places, tore down the sacred pillars, cut down the Asherim, and commanded Judah to seek the Lord God of their fathers and to observe the law and the commandment. He also removed the high places and the incense altars from all the cities of Judah. And the kingdom was undisturbed under him.*

Peace in the land is a mark of God's presence. Rest is promised through the covenant for those who are obedient to God. Intimacy with God results in peace, as being right with our Creator is the ultimate satisfaction.

We should learn from Asa. In these few chapters on his reign, we see his integrity in relationship to the Lord's commands. He actively confronted the evil in the land and made changes for the worship of the One True God. He turned to the Lord when enemies sought to destroy him and he valued the words of God's prophets.

We too can gain from listening to Asa's prophet Azariah today:

> *[T]he Lord is with you when you are with Him. And if you seek Him, He will let you find Him; but if you forsake Him, He will forsake you. For many days Israel was without the true God and without a teaching priest and without law. But in their distress they turned to the Lord God of Israel, and they sought Him, and He let them find Him. In those times there was no peace to him who went out or to him who came in, for many disturbances afflicted all the inhabitants of the lands. Nation was crushed by nation, and city by city, for God troubled them with every kind of distress. But you, be strong and do not lose courage, for there is reward for your work.*
> 2 Chronicles 15:1-7

Week 14, Day 3

Read It All: 2 Chronicles 17-24
Read a Bit: 2 Chronicles 17-20

Dignity

2 Chronicles 17:3-4 — *The* Lord *was with Jehoshaphat because he followed the example of his father David's earlier days and did not seek the Baals, but sought the God of his father, followed His commandments, and did not act as Israel did.*

Jehoshaphat stands out to me as one of the few sons of a good leader who continued in the name of the Lord. Usually in Scripture there is a disconnect between a righteous king and the next in line. Jehoshaphat represents the heart of his father well and thus the heart of King David and the ultimate Ruler, the Lord God Almighty.

Jehoshaphat's troubles came from his alliances with Judah's enemies. He lacked trust in God for battles. He still had an ear to hear from God's prophets, but he allowed his alliances to direct him in chaotic and confusing moments for the nation. As he gained wealth, he opened himself up to other nations, even aligning himself with the most evil King Ahab by marriage.

Sadly, Jehoshaphat's son does not walk in the dignity of God. Our introduction to Jehoram includes the account of his killing all his brothers with the sword and many other leaders of Israel, influenced by the house of Ahab.

In Women's Ministry, I regularly hear from moms who are grieving over a child or children who do not walk with God. Once a mom, always a mom. We long for our children to be blessed and to be a blessing. If you love your children and you trust in the goodness of God knowing the evil of this world, you hope that your children will find their dignity in the Lord God Almighty.

God knows the broken heartedness of watching wayward children go deeper and deeper into darkness when they could simply cry out, repent, and have Life. God has His own Jacobs and Esaus. Moms continue to pray and hope. As long as there is breath in our child, there is opportunity for His Life in them.

Week 14, Day 4

Read It All: 2 Chronicles 25-32
Read a Bit: 2 Chronicles 29-32

Unity

2 Chronicles 30:6-7 — *The couriers went throughout all Israel and Judah with the letters from the hand of the king and his princes, even according to the command of the king, saying, "O sons of Israel, return to the Lord God of Abraham, Isaac and Israel, that He may return to those of you who escaped and are left from the hand of the kings of Assyria. Do not be like your fathers and your brothers, who were unfaithful to the Lord God of their fathers, so that He made them a horror, as you see."*

2 Chronicles 25 records another disconnect, a lack of unity, in generations between the reign of Josiah, the reformer, and his son Amaziah, known for his mixed worship, which defiles temple worship. Hezekiah's reign is the bright spot in today's section of Scripture. Four chapters in 2 Chronicles are dedicated to Hezekiah's reforms of temple worship. He brings back order to worship and reinstates the celebration of Passover. Personal moments with Hezekiah are also recorded, as he does have need of confession and repentance due to pride. The prophet Isaiah is a key figure in Hezekiah's walk of faith. A very dramatic historical account in Hezekiah's reign is provided when God honors Hezekiah and the nation with a miraculous victory over the mighty Assyrian army.

Remember, at this point in the history of Israel, the Northern Kingdom had been defeated by the Assyrians following a drawn out battle in Samaria. Though very different in their allegiance to God, the Northern Kingdom's presence in the land still represented ten of the Jewish tribes and many relatives of tribal members that had migrated to align with Judah when the nation divided. The conquest of the Northern Kingdom served as a reminder to the remaining Israelites that God did judge sin and the covenant violations. He was incredibly patient with Israel, but His patience had worn out with the Northern Kingdom. How long would He continue to contend with the Southern Kingdom of Judah?

Week 14, Day 5

Read It All: 2 Chronicles 33-36
Read a Bit: 2 Chronicles 34-35; 36:10-23

Priority

2 Chronicles 36:22-23 — *Now in the first year of Cyrus king of Persia—in order to fulfill the word of the Lord by the mouth of Jeremiah—the Lord stirred up the spirit of Cyrus king of Persia, so that he sent a proclamation throughout his kingdom, and also put it in writing, saying, "Thus says Cyrus king of Persia, 'The Lord, the God of heaven, has given me all the kingdoms of the earth, and He has appointed me to build Him a house in Jerusalem, which is in Judah. Whoever there is among you of all His people, may the Lord his God be with him, and let him go up!'"*

I continue to briefly discuss the history of Israel and Judah, as God provides this detailed history to teach the reader about faith in Him. The ups and downs of the many characters in the historical accounts in the Bible may seem frustrating to the reader. We are used to having a protagonist who is more like Clark Kent, our Superman. But God knows all and portrays the reality of life on planet earth. It is the more mature reader who sees the beauty in conflicted characters because their conflicts direct us to right living.

The history of His chosen people also demonstrates the character of God. We learn that He understands His children and in His holiness also provides great mercy. The historical Bible books provide data points for our faith. The fulfilled prophesies are foundational to a stand of faith.

2 Chronicles 36 provides one of the biggest data points to me of a God Who orchestrates nations and political leads for the preservation of His Seed-line and the Deliverer. 2 Chronicles 36 introduces King Cyrus.

Remember, since Hezekiah, Judah's story is once again declining, as Manasseh and Amnon lead the people away from right worship. We have a moment of repentance for Manasseh when he is led by hooks to Babylon. Discipline can be successful in changing hearts. This is in contrast to Amnon, who dies in as evil a way as he lived.

Another hopeful moment occurs as Josiah leads and chooses reforms for the people. He followed the example of Hezekiah and repairs the temple, re-establishing temple worship as God commanded. Like Hezekiah, Josiah leads the nation in the celebration of Passover. Sadly, a time of disobedience results in his death in battle. By 2 Chronicles 36, temple worship is being literally dispersed as the contents of the temple are carried away to Babylon. Hezekiah had pridefully given Babylon a tour of "his" temple. Apparently it made too great an impression.

Judah is taken in exile through three deportations by Babylon. The Jewish people will serve in Babylon under three leading nations: Babylon, Persia, and Greece. However, 2 Chronicles doesn't end with a disobedient, hopeless nation. The book ends on a very high note for those who desire true temple worship. The captivity of the Jewish people is ending, and the Jewish people are not only allowed to return to the Promised Land, but they are encouraged by a pagan king to rebuild temple worship. God is the Great Conductor of human history.

EZRA AND NEHEMIAH

Ezra and Nehemiah are not only main characters in the history of Israel, but books in the Bible named for these historical leaders. These books were one in the earliest Hebrew manuscripts and we will cover them together this week. The author is unknown. Ezra is considered as a potential author of these books. Though Israel is returning to the land, they are still under Gentile rule and so the Times of the Gentiles continue. The books reveal Israel's dependence on pagan rulers for their return to the land and re-establishment of temple worship. Israel has still not regained their covenant right to rule that was lost by their disobedience.

Week 15, Day 1

Read It All: Ezra 1-6
Read a Bit: Ezra 1; 4-6

The Revelation in Summary

Ezra 1:1- 4 — *Now in the first year of Cyrus king of Persia, in order to fulfill the word of the Lord by the mouth of Jeremiah, the Lord stirred up the spirit of Cyrus king of Persia, so that he sent a proclamation throughout all his kingdom, and also put it in writing, saying:*

Thus says Cyrus king of Persia, "The Lord, the God of heaven, has given me all the kingdoms of the earth and He has appointed me to build Him a house in Jerusalem, which is in Judah. Whoever there is among you of all His people, may his God be with him! Let him go up to Jerusalem which is in Judah and rebuild the house of the Lord, the God of Israel; He is the God who is in Jerusalem. Every survivor, at whatever place he may live, let the men of that place support him with silver and gold, with goods and cattle, together with a freewill offering for the house of God which is in Jerusalem."

Write one sentence, at least, in your words about what the king had done for the people before writing your own experience that relates.

Have you ever had the experience of receiving help in a very specific way from a totally unexpected source? When I first started really getting into Bible study, I was seeking resources to build my own library of materials that I could use to share with others and better ground my teaching. I always knew that you learned not just for yourself, but to bring truth to others. I have experienced that we learn even more when we share what we are learning; being a blessing blesses.

There was a time when computers and software were a new thing to students. I was studying in the midst of this change. I do not think students today have any idea how computer technology opened up the world to many. Prior to the computer, my studies were limited to physical resources I could place in my hands. Going to libraries was an essential. I saw few pictures of the lands I was studying and rarely a video. Israel was so foreign to me, and yet I was reading about the land constantly. The computer put images to my pondering.

When Bible software was developed, I longed to own it. I had seen that there was software that supplemented the text with pictures and archaeological data from the Holy Land, but that software cost several hundred dollars. I had resigned from work to raise children, and we were on a tight budget. The cost seemed insurmountable to me.

My husband's family are not advocates for the Bible. Both of his parents were raised in homes where they attended churches, but they did not adopt the beliefs of their parents. Scott's parents divorced after 29 years of marriage and were focused on relationships with new loves in their lives, not their three children, at this point in time. We rarely talked with one another and didn't really celebrate one another through holidays or birthdays. Yet Scott's father reached out to his son at this very time and asked if he could give anything to our family in celebration of the collective anniversaries and birthdays, and Scott, as only a very attentive husband would do, humbly mentioned the Bible software. His dad couldn't relate to why this had such value to us, but he heard Scott. I'll never forget receiving the disk in the mail and realizing my heavenly Father fine-tuned the galaxies. I don't believe in coincidences.

Week 15, Day 2

Read It All: Ezra 7-10
Read a Bit: Ezra 7-10 (you must not miss Ezra's influence on the people)

Integrity

Ezra 7:21-24 — *I, even I, King Artaxerxes, issue a decree to all the treasurers who are in the provinces beyond the River, that whatever Ezra the priest, the scribe of the law of the God of heaven, may require of you, it shall be done diligently, even up to 100 talents of silver, 100 kors of wheat, 100 baths of wine, 100 baths of oil, and salt as needed. Whatever is commanded by the God of heaven, let it be done with zeal for the house of the God of heaven, so that there will not be wrath against the kingdom of the king and his sons. We also inform you that it is not allowed to impose tax, tribute or toll on any of the priests, Levites, singers, doorkeepers, Nethinim or servants of this house of God.*

Reading Ezra and Nehemiah causes moments of just goofy smiles for me as I see how God specifically moved the hearts of many leaders in this time to enable the Jewish people to restore temple worship. This was so important to the pagan world transitioning from the worship of many gods to the One True God.

I rejoice in the provisions of the kings to exiled Jewish leaders. I realize that the integrity of a remnant of Jews had greatly influenced mighty kings to trust in the ways of the Jewish God, to even desire and invest in the restoration of His temple.

Ezra is known for his devoted study of God's Word. He was sent to Jerusalem to lead the re-establishment of worship and he was faithful to do just that. It is remarkable how quickly the second Jewish temple was completed and dedicated. It is remarkable that the people still knew to value the celebration of former feasts and sacrifices. Their worship was so different from that observed in Babylon.

Ezra had a huge task before him and he did it through prayer, confession, weeping and prostrating himself before the house of God, before the people in the land. He united himself with the unfaithfulness of many and mourned the covenant disobedience in the land. He grieved the impact of disobedience on the marriages and homes represented. His value on God's ways redirected a nation and restored the means for the Word of God and the fulfillment of the Word to move forward. God was faithfully bringing about His salvation.

Week 15, Day 3

Read It All: Nehemiah 1-6
Read a Bit: Nehemiah 1-2; 5-6

The Revelation in Summary

Nehemiah 1:4 — *When I heard these words, I sat down and wept and mourned for days; and I was fasting and praying before the God of heaven.*

> *Wait on the Lord; be of good courage, and He shall strengthen your heart. Wait, I say, on the Lord!* Psalm 27:14

Priscilla Shirer has written many Bible studies. In preparation for the Priscilla Shirer Live Women's Conference at my church, I read her book Fervent, partly because my mom gave me a free copy and partly because it is a pretty journal. But in the midst of reading and journaling, I was not only greatly encouraged, I was greatly equipped. Fervent prayer keeps your true identity in focus. Priscilla's teaching echoes that of Nehemiah's ministry. Here are some of the biblical insights from my study of Fervent and Nehemiah.

- Nehemiah models prayer as the way of personally contacting God and taking part in His eternal plans, any hour of the day or night.
- Don't let anything keep you from prayer; particularly overcome enemies and the mystery associated with prayer.
- Prayer strategies help you protect the areas of your life that the enemy is targeting the most.
- Fervent prayer is fueled by passion, focus, and your identity in Christ. It fortifies your family, ends the reign of past shame, confronts your fears, overcomes your susceptibility to sin, reclaims lost contentment, turns bitterness to forgiveness, and unites. This is in contrast to the enemy's strategy to dim your passion, manipulate your focus, magnify your insecurities, disintegrate your family, burden you with shame and guilt, massage your fears,

tempt you to sin, make everything seem urgent, bring old wounds to mind, and create division with you and other believers.[10]
- Pray specifically against known enemies.
- Wait on the Lord!
- Enlist others in prayer.
- Combine your prayers with honest mourning of sin and repentance.
- Rebuild your walls. PRAY!

Week 15, Day 4

Read It All: Nehemiah 7-10
Read a Bit: Nehemiah 8-9

Integrity

Nehemiah 8:1 — *And all the people gathered as one man at the square which was in front of the Water Gate, and they asked Ezra the scribe to bring the book of the law of Moses which the Lord had given to Israel.*

In the first part of Nehemiah, the physical protection of Jerusalem is established. Ezra is back in the second part of Nehemiah, and the task at hand is strengthening the spiritual protection of the people. This involves bringing them into the Light via God's Word.

> *You search the Scriptures because you think that in them you have eternal life; it is these that testify about Me . . . For if you believed Moses, you would believe Me, for he wrote about Me. But if you do not believe his writings, how will you believe My words?* John 5:39, 46-47

In teaching the Bible, I am continually reminded of the importance of knowing the Old Testament in understanding the New Testament. To not begin at the beginning of a story is to miss the passionate intent of the story teller. History matters.

---

10   Priscilla Shirer, *Fervent: A Woman's Battle Plan to Serious, Specific and Strategic Prayer*, (Nashville, TN: B&H Books, 2015), 15-17.

Jesus stated that the Old Testament, particularly the Torah, was the proof of His Messianic identity, as it predicted His appearance. We see God's sovereign care of His children when we review the biblical story with its history, poetry, and prophecy. We are overwhelmed by how a book written by over forty authors from many walks of life, over a period of 1,500 to 1,600 years on three continents in three languages is so consistent in theme and presentation of the Savior. The Bible is our sustenance for life. Jesus said in Matthew 4:4, *"It is written, 'Man shall not live on bread alone, but on every word that proceeds out of the mouth of God.'"*

It has been a blessing and privilege to be in many Bible studies through the years. I have studied alongside women who are just getting to realize the love of the good Father for them through His revelation. I have enjoyed each moment of comprehending His grace together. I have learned through the years that to avoid His revelation is to be anorexic in our faith and ultimately too dehydrated to serve.

The Old is foundational in appreciating the New. Today I thank God for the scholars who, with great integrity, spent hours of preparation in study so that others could be grounded in the truth.

> *For Ezra had set his heart to study the law of the Lord and to practice it, and to teach His statutes and ordinances in Israel.* Ezra 7:10

Week 15, Day 5

Read It All: Nehemiah 11-13
Read a Bit: Nehemiah 13

Dignity

Nehemiah 13:30-31 — *Thus I purified them from everything foreign and appointed duties for the priests and the Levites, each in his task, and I arranged for the supply of wood at appointed times and for the first fruits. Remember me, O my God, for good.*

In the closing section of Nehemiah, we are confronted with a great tragedy. Even after exile, the hearts of the majority of the people are unchanged. Nehemiah has purposed to do all he can to protect the people from the enemies outside the city walls, but he has realized that spiritual protection is needed within their hearts and this is beyond his control. Only God can redirect a heart to His priorities and to life. Only God can restore His dignity to His children.

Nehemiah repeats a phrase throughout the book: *"Remember me, O my God, for good."* He longs to be separate from those bent on living by their reasoning instead of by the revelation of God. He still longs for a people who would make God known to all nations. He longs for the glory of God. Do I, do you?

ESTHER

Week 16, Day 1

Read It All: Esther 1-2
Read a Bit: Esther 1-2

The Revelation in Summary

Esther 2:5-7 — Now there was at the citadel in Susa a Jew whose name was Mordecai, the son of Jair, the son of Shimei, the son of Kish, a Benjamite, who had been taken into exile from Jerusalem with the captives who had been exiled with Jeconiah king of Judah, whom Nebuchadnezzar the king of Babylon had exiled. He was bringing up Hadassah, that is Esther, his uncle's daughter, for she had no father or mother. Now the young lady was beautiful of form and face, and when her father and her mother died, Mordecai took her as his own daughter.

I've heard too many people fashion the story of Esther into some crazy romance. Apparently, they did not read chapter 1 and get a good glimpse of King Ahasuerus. He is not attractive.

While some of the Jewish people had returned to the Land of Promise, many were still in Babylon and its provinces. Esther provides insight into the life of these Jews. They were dominated by their Gentile leaders and their worship of pagan gods. They were oppressed in service and their inability to even protect their own children is central to Esther's story. God's law would have provided for the orphan, but in Esther, we see that the orphan has enemies.

I'm horrified for this little girl when she is introduced to the king. However, in God's sovereign care, this little girl rises up to save the Jews throughout the land and, ultimately, the royal Seed. Though God's name is not mentioned in this book, it is evident that His providential hand is upholding His Truth.

Week 16, Day 2

Read It All: Esther 3-5
Read a Bit: Esther 3-5

Integrity

Esther 3:2 — *All the king's servants who were at the king's gate bowed down and paid homage to Haman; for so the king had commanded concerning him. But Mordecai neither bowed down nor paid homage.*

It's not easy being a single dad in a land where your adopted daughter is targeted for the King's harem. Mordecai is a hero.

I have a friend who is a great dad, but he dreads Father's Day church services. He feels that on Mother's Day, all women are beloved, yet on Father's Day, all men are berated. Society has a low view of dads, and maybe, pastors use Father's Day for a pep talk typical of a losing team's locker room.

My personal experience includes observing good, great, bad, and horrific dads. I thank God for my devoted husband and his commitment to our children. He is an awesome dad. He did not learn being a great dad from his dad. His dad's focus was not the family. My husband learned from others and from drawing near to God through Bible study and prayer. I know all of our children continually thank God for their dad.

Good fathers are vital because fatherhood is a very influential and key role. Fathers can hold great physical, emotional, and spiritual power in the foundation of society, the home. The abuse of such power is devastating, and so poor fathering is horrific. Absentee fathers create not just pockets or holes but craters of chaos. These are life and death issues for the family.

I want the good dads of His Body to be affirmed. I thank God for them. I acknowledge your hard work and excellent representation of our faithful Father. Your integrity influences many. I am grateful for your protection and provision of the home. I smile thinking of the fun you add to your families. I recognize the rich heritage you are establishing for the next generation. I'm amazed at your sacrificial love, valuing time with family over personal comforts. I attribute most of the many Bible lessons I've learned to the teaching of great fathers who share His Word at home and with others. You prepare us for life.

> *Listen, O my people, to my instruction; incline your ears to the words of my mouth. I will open my mouth in a parable; I will utter dark sayings of old, which we have heard and known, and our fathers have told us. We will not conceal them from their children, but tell to the generation to come the praises of the Lord, and His strength and His wondrous works that He has done.* Psalm 78:1-4

Week 16, Day 3

Read It All: Esther 6-8
Read a Bit: Esther 6-8

Dignity

Esther 6:1 — *During that night the king could not sleep so he gave an order to bring the book of records, the chronicles, and they were read before the king.*

A restless night for the king reminds us that God hears our prayers and provides specific answers at times. The king's restless night will bring about the decline of the evil enemy of the Jews and the rise of God's representatives.

"You have been on my heart and in my prayers. . ." started the note to our Women's Ministry that came with a prayer shawl embroidered with the names of God. Usually an anonymous message isn't so very dear. This was a breath of life! The writing was beautiful. The shawl itself must have taken hours to prepare. The card that contained the handwritten letter was lovely. Needless to say, I was encouraged, humbled, and felt that God used whoever did this to lift me up in the midst of an overwhelmingly busy season.

I think what touched me the most was the personal prayer that went with this shawl. The giver wrote, "I prayed continually while my machine sewed this. For your ministry, your family, your marriage, and your heart. May God hold you close and whisper His promises in your ears."

I've read this letter so many times, and when I get to this part I always tear up. I cherish those prayers. They are a part of this ministry and probably the most powerful part. My heartbeat quickens when my family is specifically mentioned as the subject of another's prayers. There is always that struggle of wondering how ministry impacts my home. My hubby is long-suffering again and again, and I do not want to take him for granted. My adult children have a very intimate look at the church through my being on staff. We value prayers for us!

The giver reminded me that the Jewish people believe that YHWH shouldn't be written out or spoken—"They believe His name can only be breathed." I know His Word commands to never make His name common. We are not to belittle the dignity of His name. Wisdom is fearing the Lord, looking to Him as the giver and sustainer of life, realizing His ways are the best. He is not common. The embroidered shawl reminds me of His majesty.

His children are blessed to be a blessing to others. Our thoughtfulness and caring kindnesses can affirm one another, at just the right time, to continue in faith. I've seen the goodness of the Lord through so many of His children through the years. Never hesitate to encourage another as you feel so led. The chosen of God are called to build up one another!

So, as those who have been chosen of God, holy and beloved, put on a heart of compassion, kindness, humility, gentleness and patience; bearing with one another, and forgiving each other. . . .Colossians 3:12-13

Week 16, Day 4

Read It All: Esther 9
Read a Bit: Esther 9

Unity

Esther 9:1 — *Now in the twelfth month (that is, the month Adar), on the thirteenth day when the king's command and edict were about to be executed, on the day when the enemies of the Jews hoped to gain the mastery over them, it was turned to the contrary so that the Jews themselves gained the mastery over those who hated them.*

God's people must act in unity to fulfill His sovereign plan. The seemingly helpless remnant of Jews in Esther are delivered from a plot to kill them through God's control of political entities and His people joining together under His provisions. The Book of Esther is an encouragement to all the Jews of this time period. They hear that, whether in exile or in the midst of returning to the land, God has not forgotten them and He preserves them despite overwhelming opposition. This is very different than their exile from Egypt brought about by supernatural means, as God reveals He also works in the natural flow of human history.

The reader will note many points of irony in the story of Esther. The supposedly powerless Jews are the major victors. The plotting Haman ultimately plots his own destruction, even building the gallows where he dies. Mordecai, the servant of Haman, gains the charge of the land that Haman coveted, including the King's signet ring. The lot that was cast to decide the day of execution becomes the name of the feast celebrating the Jews' deliverance on that very day. Haman, the king's man who had everything, is bested by Esther, the woman who appeared to have nothing as she risked her life for her people.

At a critical time in the history of the Jewish people, God equipped them to survive and to flourish by continuing their role in giving His revelation to the next generation so that ultimately all may find life in Him. God loves sharing His abundance with His children.

Week 16, Day 5

Read It All: Esther 10
Read a Bit: Esther 10

Priority

Esther 10:3 — *For Mordecai the Jew was second only to King Ahasuerus, and great among the Jews and in favor with his many kinsmen, one who sought the good of his people and one who spoke for the welfare of his whole nation.*

Today's reading is very short as I thought you might need a little break on one day and as I think we should pause a moment regarding Mordecai's significant leadership. At the heart of his leading was his relationship with his adopted daughter Esther. Their respect for one another and willingness to bravely do what needed to be done in the moment saved the Jewish nation, and provided a godly witness to the pagan leaders they served. This should again remind us of the value of good parenting. When parents make their home a priority, teaching God's truth to their children, parents strengthen their children to represent God rightly outside the home. Mordecai's little girl Esther was a baby that grew up and became a Queen that changed everything. She represents the Deliverer in this story.

A baby changes everything! I post a Christmas music video on my Facebook page daily in the month of December to start the day with consideration of the Christ child. Every year I post the song "A Baby Changes Everything." This song pretty much summarizes my heart experience. I learned of the Christ child from visiting a church Vacation Bible School with neighbors in Columbia, Missouri. I believed in the Christ child as Savior when visiting a church with my sweet Aunt Jeanne in Brandon, Florida, and I embraced the extreme love of God through the Christ child when holding my baby son for the first time. The baby Christ and our baby Samuel changed my heart and all I held to be true.

I was baby illiterate when I became pregnant with Samuel James Montgomery. I had been married six years and we had rarely discussed having children (this was partly due to a harried morning in church nursery, followed by me joking with my hubby about being pregnant and him running a red light and totaling a car, not an easy topic to bring up again). This was also due to the fact that I was insecure and felt that love was too readily abandoned and so. . . I protected myself. I didn't get too close to too many, and a family of my own seemed too precious to embrace. It meant commitment on my part. I was a workaholic because that was something I could control.

My heart began softening when I started studying God's Word. I learned that babies were precious, a blessing from the Creator. I learned I needed to trust God as the food Father and His help in equipping me to love sacrificially.

My husband has always been very patient with me. Our first child changed our priorities, our financial aspirations, our calendars, our lifetime goals. Samuel made us into a family. God used Samuel to open my eyes to the family I have in Christ. Samuel introduced me to joyful, sacrificial, committed love. Samuel acquainted me with God as a loving heavenly parent.

I celebrate babies today and thank God that He uses these precious ones to sometimes melt the hardened hearts of those running from love.

REST TIME

Week 17, Days 1-5

Ruth 1:9 — *May the Lord grant that you may find rest, each in the house of her husband." Then she kissed them, and they lifted up their voices and wept.*

Throughout the history of Israel, the reader is taught to see what walking by belief in the promises of God looks like in the lives of His people. These historical books reveal God's unconditional love for His children and His great provision of deliverance when they turn to Him in need. These accounts also convey the impact our sins, particularly the sins of His leaders, have on the people. Hope is continually present in these Biblical books through the revelation of His promised seed renewed in His Word to King David.

Journal any thoughts you wish to record at this point in your reading.

How **Blessed** are all who take refuge in Him!

Psalms 2:12

OLD TESTAMENT WISDOM WRITINGS

I did not gain an appreciation of the Bible's wisdom literature (Job, Psalms, Proverbs, Ecclesiastes, and Song of Solomon) until I had studied the historical books of the Bible. Prior to knowing a little background to the wisdom literature, I was very confused by it. I am not one to read poetry for the fun of it. I expect a story to have an introduction, plot, crisis, and resolution. I really preferred technical literature, not dwelling on sentiments or musings. The wisdom literature seemed to be a random profusion of thoughts. I didn't see the value in going through someone else's emotional roller coaster.

This thinking changed for me when I found my walk of faith in darker paths than I'd previously encountered. I turned to the wisdom literature for just that . . . wisdom. This literature has come to be my favorite portion of His revelation. It directs my path and greatly lightens it.

If you want to increase in learning, then you must dig deeply into the character of God. The wisdom writers reveal what mankind thinks about their Maker through their most significant events and relationships in life:

Job teaches the reader an attitude of acceptance toward God. Suffering is a means by which God brings glory to Himself.

The Psalms demonstrate a life of worship that involves honesty in our communication with God. I can never figure out where the worship songs end and the prayers begin in Psalms, as the life of the believer seems to be put to poetry. Mankind's need for a pure heart is the battle cry of the Psalms. Our longings for His justice and purity are voiced by the psalmists.

Proverbs teaches the right fear of the Lord and the relationship this fear has to obtaining wisdom. The proverbs are instructions for skillful learning that provide everlasting life.

Ecclesiastes is very unique to Scripture. While Proverbs gives clear, straightforward instruction to the reader as a good father would to a cherished child, Ecclesiastes portrays the discussion an older dad might have with his grown child as they anticipate the father's passing from this life. Experiences are highlighted and regrets are voiced. Life is a vapor and priorities are reviewed based on whether the father deems them vain pursuits in life in contrast to God's truth. Our days "under the sun" are meaningless apart from God. Time in Ecclesiastes makes us realists.

Song of Solomon portrays erotic love. If we didn't have Song of Solomon in Scripture, we would miss so much regarding the intimacy of marital love. We would think sex was solely about procreation. In this song, we get the intimate details of the relationship of lovers. We see the value and freedom God has for marital love and the honor the marriage bed should have in a community. Romantic love impacts all those around, as the couple's rejoicing extends to their family, co-laborers, attendants, and neighbors. We want to experience such devotion to God and to another for ourselves.

There is great beauty in the biblical wisdom literature. These books steady the thinker in the truth of His Revelation while clearly warning against relying on human reasoning for life. The books reveal that the Creator of Life wants His creation to enjoy His abundant provision with all their hearts, souls, and minds. The intensity of emotions expressed in the literature is not a surprise to God. He provides these insights into mankind's and His thinking so that His child is wondrously prepared for life on earth. After all, God created us in His image to rule with Him and for His glory. Thank you, Lord, for lighting our paths.

JOB

Week 18, Day 1

Read It All: Job 1-14
Read a Bit: Job 1-3; 8; 12

The Revelation in Summary

Job 1:20-22 — *Then Job arose and tore his robe and shaved his head, and he fell to the ground and worshiped. He said, "Naked I came from my mother's womb, and naked I shall return there. The Lord gave and the Lord has taken away. Blessed be the name of the Lord." Through all this Job did not sin nor did he blame God.*

Job is believed to be the oldest piece of Bible literature that we have. The story may correspond to the time of early Genesis accounts. The story in Job reveals several conflicts intersecting in time. Job 1-3 introduces us to God and Satan in conflict and Job being drawn into this other-realm contest. Chapters 4-37 are the detailed arguments of Job and his "friends" as they attempt to reason through God's sovereign care of Job. The book closes with God and Job resolving the conflict for all, but this final discussion is brought about by Job's insistence that God explain Himself.

The arguments of Job's friends are presented in rounds like a boxing match. Chapters 4-14 are "Round 1," in which three friends insist on Job's sinfulness, as such circumstances must be an outcome of what they perceive as God's unwavering justice. Job argues that God made a way for the repentant to be restored to Him, and so Job insists he is right with God. "Round 2" is presented in chapters 15-21, where the friends are adamant that you reap what you sow. Job knows he is wicked, but then no man is just before God unless God declares him so. Job mourns his lot in life and looks to death. Chapters 22-31, "Round 3," is a harsh read, as the accusations get more and more personal and an anguished Job purposes to clear his name.

An angry young voice speaks up starting in Chapter 32. Job's friend Elihu challenges the wisdom of his elders, particularly their conclusions that they are capable of discerning the mind of God, as God deals with men in a multiple ways. Elihu values righteousness for the sake of being God's representative apart from any blessing from our Maker. Elihu sees value in affliction that draws us closer to Almighty God and gives glory to His name.

Chapters 38-42 are the resolution of the drama, when God speaks and man is silenced. God reveals Himself in terms Job and his friends can readily understand. The lesson is clear: God is sovereign and very much aware of the condition of humanity at all times. The Lord rebukes Job's elder friends and restores Job's fortunes. God's conflict with Satan is resolved with Job's refusal to "curse God and die". The happy ending of this story is not Job's restored fortune, but it is the wisdom gained by Job and the reader when God reveals Himself and His entrusting of mankind to be faithful to Him. When I lost a child, I also took comfort in the ending of Job, seeing that God restored Job double everything but Job's children. I wondered if this meant Job's children were still around, secure in the arms of their heavenly Father.

"Sometimes people assume God is unfair, especially to those who don't live up to His standards. This is hardly the case. The fact is that God instructed His people in accordance with His nature. His holy nature demands the best from those who serve Him."[11]

Week 18, Day 2

Read It All: Job 15-21
Read a Bit: Job 15-16; 21

Integrity

Job 21:34 — *"How then will you vainly comfort me, for your answers remain full of falsehood?"*

I think it is hard to have lifelong friends apart from family members who cannot escape their relatives. It is too easy to part ways in our culture, and there are too many options for friends. I don't want to be all about my family clan, so I keep trying to figure out friendship, but between worship, home, and work, there isn't a lot of time to develop friendships. Humanity can also get in the way. Sometimes we aren't real

---

[11] Richard R. Melick, Jr., *Called to Be Holy* (Nashville, TN: Lifeway, 2014), 18.

likable; sometimes I'm not real likable. A good friend is someone with compassion and integrity.

Change occurs too. People move away, develop other interests, and get more fed up with your children than you are. For moms of middle and high school children, your friends can tend to be their friends and family, so when the kids don't get along, all relationships can be impacted.

Job in the Old Testament gives us great insight into certain friendships—and we cringe. Job's friends are the self-righteous. They lack integrity as they have fooled themselves into thinking they can have figured out God. In contrast, Jesus was known to be a friend of tax collectors and sinners. When I read about Messiah's friendships on earth, I realize that I'm not wrong in thinking friendships can be a struggle. In Matthew, Jesus rebukes the friend who is unhappy about money arrangements (20:13), the friend who arrives improperly dressed for the wedding (22:12), and his friend Judas, who betrays Him (26:50).

To have friends is to be concerned about one another's needs. Jesus teaches on this in many parables, as the friends humble themselves to get bread for one another (Luke 11:5), hunt for lost things together (Luke 15), and wait upon one another during celebrations (John 3:29).

Friendship is a means of representing the sacrificial love of God. *"Greater love has no one than this, that one lay down his life for his friends"* (John 15:13). Friendship involves great responsibility. Those who walk in truth with the Lord are known as His friends.

Proverbs explains that we destroy friendships by slander, repeating one another's transgressions, having too many friends, showing favoritism to the wealthy, being loud in the morning, and forsaking our own friends. There are many illustrations in Scripture of people forsaking their friends. The friends in Job are known for their meanness rather than their helpfulness. *"My relatives have failed, and my intimate friends have forgotten me"* (Job 19:14). Friendship can disappoint.

All that to say, let us not take sweet friends for granted. Let us be good friends and enjoy friendships as we may, remembering that our friendships give us opportunity to represent the love of the Lord today. Thank God for friends and let your friends know they are loved.

No longer do I call you slaves, for the slave does not know what his master is doing; but I have called you friends, for all things that I have heard from My Father I have made known to you. John 15:15

Week 18, Day 3

Read It All: Job 22-31
Read a Bit: Job 23; 28; 30

Dignity

Job 28:12-13 — *But where can wisdom be found? and where is the place of under-standing? Man does not know its value, nor is it found in the land of the living.*

I've been watching some wonderful women go through some very difficult times. I began to wonder if hope is most evident when the world challenges you to be hopeless. There is a dignity inherent to hopeful women in the midst of distress. So I did a little word study in the Scriptures on hope. I thought about Job and how he suffered and wondered if the Book of Job tells me anything particular about hope. Job does. But be warned, his friends also speak of hope, and they are not known for giving wise counsel or building up their friend. Still, I hope you will be encouraged with me.

Hope as a product of wise fear and integrity

> *Is not your fear of God your confidence, and the integrity of your ways your hope?* Job 4:6

Hope as a result of His care

> *But He saves from the sword of their mouth, and the poor from the hand of the mighty. So the helpless has hope, and unrighteousness must shut its mouth.* Job 5:15-17

Hope needing a friend's kindness

> *For the despairing man there should be kindness from his friend; So that he does not forsake the fear of the Almighty . . . My brothers have acted deceitfully like a wadi, like the torrents of wadis which vanish, . . . The caravans of Tema looked, the travelers of Sheba hoped for them. They were disappointed for they had trusted, they came there and were confounded.* Job 6:14-21

Hope overcome by misery

> My flesh is clothed with worms and a crust of dirt, my skin hardens and runs. My days are swifter than a weaver's shuttle, and come to an end without hope. Job 7:5-6

Hope related to confidence

> *So are the paths of all who forget God; and the hope of the godless will perish, whose confidence is fragile, and whose trust a spider's web.* Job 8:13-14

Hope wrongly promised

> *Then you would trust, because there is hope; And you would look around and rest securely.* Job 11:18

Hope of salvation

> *But the eyes of the wicked will fail, And there will be no escape for them; And their hope is to breathe their last.* Job 11:20

Hope fed by faith

> *Though He slay me, I will hope in Him. Nevertheless I will argue my ways before Him.* Job 13:15

Hope seeming lost

> *For there is hope for a tree, When it is cut down, that it will sprout again, and its shoots will not fail . . . . Water wears away stones, Its torrents wash away the dust of the earth; So You destroy man's hope.* Job 14:7, 19

Hope valued

> *Where now is my hope? And who regards my hope?* Job 17:15

Hope discouraged

> *He breaks me down on every side, and I am gone; and He has uprooted my hope like a tree.* Job 19:10

God as the only valid source of hope

> *For what is the hope of the godless when he is cut off, When God requires his life?* Job 27:8

When Job listened to man, he had no hope. When he encountered God, he saw a full future and shuddered to have been so readily deceived by man and this world.

> *And everyone who has this hope fixed on Him purifies himself, just as He is pure.* 1 John 3:3

Week 18, Day 4

Read It All: Job 32-37
Read a Bit: Job 32-33; 35

Unity

Job 32:7-9 — *I thought age should speak, and increased years should teach wisdom. But it is a spirit in man, and the breath of the Almighty gives them understanding. The abundant in years may not be wise, nor may elders understand justice.*

Discipleship is an essential part of Christian ministry. Through discipleship, two partner in their desire to grow in Christ, and one leads the way, as the disciple maker is to be someone more mature in the faith. The expectation is that the older women in the church will lead the younger; this is the Titus 2 model. Discipleship should result in greater unity in the church as the partners unite in the basic disciplines of the faith.

Sadly, I have discovered a flaw in the Titus 2 model. Sometimes the older women have forgotten or never learned their Bible and thus they have a manmade view of God. These ladies see discipleship as enforcing a code of behavior rather than loving our amazingly gracious, merciful God together. Such discipleship matches hinder gospel life.

Thankfully, I have had the joy of witnessing many great discipleship matches through the years. Discipleship has been key to many learning the disciplines of the faith that direct them to the love of God. Good discipleship matches birth disciples hungry for God's truth and excited to disciple others. Good discipleship matches save lives and homes. They edify the church body by uniting us in His truth.

Many today do not have a godly role model. They do not even realize what a sacred opportunity it is to be discipled. We can learn much about God from corporate worship and teaching, but Christ called us to disciple one another so that many would know the personal accountability of another as they walk this realm.

Week 18, Day 5

Read It All: Job 38-42
Read a Bit: Job 38-42

Priority

Job 38:2-4 — *Who is this that darkens counsel by words without knowledge? Now gird up your loins like a man, and I will ask you, and you instruct Me! Where were you when I laid the foundation of the earth? Tell Me, if you have understanding, . . .*

> *The heavens are telling of the glory of God; and their expanse is declaring the work of His hands.* Psalm 19:1

Perhaps one of the most God-honoring things you can do is plan to watch a sunset on a regular basis. Invite some friends along if you want to finalize the watch with enthusiastic applause.

Here are the basics:
Check the weather info and know the time of sunset and likelihood of clear skies.

Choose a great spot for viewing the sunset; I recommend the beach or an overlook. A place with pretty architecture is also a good option.

Throw a comfy, portable chair in your car, along with water and a light snack (or a great sandwich from an amazing deli, which also means you need a slice of cake or Seventh Wonder bar. . .)

Go to your viewing spot at least one hour before sunset, as anticipation is part of the joy, and you want to witness the heavenlies in transition.

Do not sit near any smells that distract (smell is an important sense).

Do not bring work to do or your cell phone.

Do not forget to go to the bathroom before manning your sunset post.

Breathe deeply. Rest in Him. Open your heart to His wonder.

After the sunset, do not leave immediately. Take at least another fifteen minutes to reflect on what was pretty about the sunset. This is often the time the colors get really dramatic before it goes dark.

Thank God. Our finite minds have seen a glimpse of The Infinite.

PSALMS

Week 19, Day 1

Read It All: Psalms 1-41
Read a Bit: Psalms 1-4; 11; 19-23; 39

The Revelation in Summary

Psalm 27:4 — *One thing I have asked from the Lord, that I shall seek: That I may dwell in the house of the Lord all the days of my life, to behold the beauty of the Lord and to meditate in His temple.*

The Psalms reveal the wisdom in crying out to the Lord to know Him better and for deliverance. They help us relate to our Creator by giving us guidance for worship and prayer and revealing the character of God. The Psalms were composed by those who purposed to love the Lord regardless of their circumstances. The authors are mature in their faith; they are not questioning if God is or if He is right, but rather how long until He fully reveals Himself.

David, Israel's king after God's own heart, wrote the majority of the Psalms. Other authors include Solomon, Asaph, the Sons of Korah, Moses, and unknown authors. The back stories to the various Psalms are diverse, including anguished cries in times of imminent physical danger, grieving because of the conviction of sin, planning for intentional congregational worship, overwhelming humility in the face of God's goodness or majesty, celebrating His provision, and suffering life's greatest hardships. To study the Psalms is to hear poetical echoes of thoughts you have experienced and to realize that God is in our midst.

The Psalms address many of our most difficult life questions:

Is the God of love also a God of hate?

Why is there still injustice?

Does God hide from us? Does He forget us?

Are both men and women highly emotional?

Is it wrong to long for vengeance?

Does God guarantee safety for His children?

Does God demand or despise sacrifices?

Do we need to watch what we say in prayer?

Why pray or ask for anything? Won't God just do what He wants to do?

Is life unfair? Why does God test us?

What do I need to know about myself and my heart?

Since God is in control, why are so many things wrong?

Does anything prevent God from hearing our prayers?

What does it mean to be truly joyful?

Which biblical statements are really promises of God?

What part should meditation have in the believer's life?

How evil is evil?

When does life begin?

How can I continue in faith?

The Psalms are impossible to outline. There is no systematic order of presentation. The Psalms are arranged in five books, but there are common themes throughout all the books. Reading through the Psalms is to jump into the thought-life of numerous people. Scholars have supplied categories in an effort to analyze the Psalms: worship, contrition, Messianic anticipations, complaint, occasions (typically based on feast day celebrations), wisdom, historical review, and nature (usually praise Psalms).

The Psalms are poetical, full of highly symbolic language and many metaphors. This makes for a very visual read. Hebrew poetry included parallelism, a parallel structure of verses or lines that express the same thought. The poetical methods aid the author in emphasizing the truth that is being meditated on through the Psalm.

Why is Psalm 119 so long? The poetical device in this Psalm was a memory tool using the Hebrew alphabet to reflect on the value of God's revelation of Himself. In the original language, there is a Hebrew letter at the beginning of each section in Psalm 119. The author of Psalm 119 used an acrostic[12] with a stanza for each of the 22 letters of the Hebrew alphabet to express the value of God's Word. Some of the poetical devices are lost with the translations from ancient Hebrew into modern English, but the Psalms are still an extraordinary way to express human feelings. The Bible is God's self-disclosure; without this special revelation we would know so little about our Creator. We are limited in our means of knowing God and are dependent on Him to reveal Himself to us. The Psalms reveal that God knows our heart, our concerns on this earth, and that He relates to our emotions. The Psalms are the emotional expressions through the years of sinful yet sincere people who long to walk faithfully with God and realize their utter dependence on God.

Week 19, Day 2

Read It All: Psalms 42-72
Read a Bit: Psalms 42; 46; 53; 57; 64; 67; 71

Integrity

Psalms 42:1-3 — *As the deer pants for the water brooks, so my soul pants for You, O God. My soul thirsts for God, for the living God; when shall I come and appear before God? My tears have been my food day and night, while they say to me all day long, "Where is your God?"*

Faith in the Giver isn't faith unless there is a gap between receipt of a promise and the promise itself. Faith requires waiting. One of my missionary friends said her favorite verse, as it gives great direction for life, is *"Wait on the Lord"* (Psalm 27:14). The psalmists echo this verse

---

[12] An acrostic is a poem in which the first letter of each line spells out a word, message, or the alphabet.

with a bold *"How long, Oh Lord?"*. These psalms of lament give voice to the faithful's struggle with delays. The Psalms remind us that God is delighted by our faith, so delays must be part of His glory.

Others witness our endurance based on delays. The Psalmists also mention those who ridicule us for believing when no end to our suffering is in sight. These characters are called mockers and scoffers in the Psalms (verses?) and they are enemies to the faithful. Sometimes their presence seems unbearable to the faithful, so there are imprecatory Psalms where the faithful pray for judgment on their hateful enemies.

Many of the Psalms are simple expressions of the writer's longing for the character of God to be displayed amidst the evil in this world. The Psalmists cry out for justice because they are tired of seeing the evil going unpunished and the oppressed dying. The writers know God is good and that God is able, and sometimes they get frustrated with God being long-suffering with those that do evil. When we stop and think how awful it would be to live and die apart from God, we may gain a more merciful stance with our enemies. The long-suffering of God does create opportunities for our enemies to find life in Him. In the delays, God also gives the faithful an opportunity to love their enemies in the way that He has loved all of mankind.

Week 19, Day 3

Read It All: Psalms 73-89
Read a Bit: Psalms 73; 78; 86; 89

Dignity

Psalm 85:4-5 — *Restore us, O God of our salvation, and cause Your indignation toward us to cease. Will You be angry with us forever? Will You prolong Your anger to all generations?*

God's kind restoration of humanity reflects His value of each person and births a dignity that is eternal. The means by which God delivers us from His wrath should evoke great praise for our Redeemer. Philip Yancey wrote,[13]

---

[13]   Philip Yancey, *The Bible Jesus Read* (Grand Rapids, MI: Zondervan, 1999), 127.

The psalms wonderfully solve the problem of a praise-deficient culture by providing the necessary words. We merely need to enter into those words, letting the content of the psalms realign our inner attitudes. Dietrich Bonhoeffer suggests that the psalms are God's language course. Just as infants learn the mother tongue from their parents, Christians can learn the language of prayer from Psalms.

Most of the Psalms include an element of praise. Regardless of what the psalmists are enduring, they see a hint of God demonstrating His attributes in this world. Sometimes the authors simply declare how God has greatly blessed them personally. Other times, the praise is corporate, and we learn that public confession of God unifies His people and calls for God's name to be honored by community.

Sometimes worship styles cause division in the Body of Christ. Our blessings of many talented leaders and access to many great music genres can be turned into areas of dissension. This is sadly ridiculous. Worship is at the core of experiencing our dignity in Christ. Freedom in worship comes from surrendering our idols and preferences at times in order to unify with His Body and celebrate His great care. He has given us a new song; let's worship with a focus on His glory and not always our tastes.

> *Sing praise to the Lord, you His godly ones, and give thanks to His holy name.* Psalm 30:4

Week 19, Day 4

Read It All: Psalms 90-106
Read a Bit: Psalms 93-100

Unity

Psalm 100:1-5 — *Shout joyfully to the Lord, all the earth. Serve the Lord with gladness; come before Him with joyful singing. Know that the Lord Himself is God; it is He who has made us, and not we ourselves; we are His people and the sheep of His pasture. Enter His gates with thanksgiving and His courts with praise. Give thanks to Him, bless His name. For the Lord is good; His lovingkindness is everlasting and His faithfulness to all generations.*

Thankfulness is a great unifier. God knows we need this aspect of His character, and the Psalms include many expressions of thankfulness.

I've learned over the years that in the United States, for many, Thanksgiving is the favorite holiday. The main reasons for loving this holiday are food, family, and freedom. I also love Thanksgiving and believe that we do need to set aside a day to remember to give thanks. It is cleansing. It is Scriptural to be people of gratitude. To give thanks is to recognize the worth of the gift and the kindness of the giver. It is to recognize the Source of blessings in our life. Thankfulness is a big part of enjoying a relationship. I realize that it is no little thing to be thought of by another. I realize that God is the ultimate Giver and that His gifts are continual—every breath I take is a gift from God. I thank God as I recognize His overwhelming goodness, and in expressing thanks, I typically find joy, a smile in reflecting on the lovingkindness of another.

Now therefore, our God, we thank You, and praise Your glorious name. 1 Chronicles 29:13

The LORD is my strength and my shield; my heart trusts in Him, and I am helped; therefore my heart exults, and with my song I shall thank Him. Psalms 28:7

Oh give thanks to the LORD, for He is good, for His lovingkindness is everlasting. Psalm 107:1

So they removed the stone. Then Jesus raised His eyes, and said, "Father, I thank You that You have heard Me." John 11:41

Be anxious for nothing, but in everything by prayer and supplication with thanksgiving let your requests be made known to God. Philippians 4:6

Let the peace of Christ rule in your hearts, to which indeed you were called in one body; and be thankful. Colossians 3:15

In everything give thanks; for this is God's will for you in Christ Jesus. 1 Thessalonians 5:18

Giving thanks plays out in the simple, everyday details. I went to the flea market to find an amazing, unique dining room light fixture that worked and cost a really low amount of money, preferably free. How ridiculous! What I did find was a large shed-like structure filled, actually overfilled, with lighting fixtures, lamps, lamp shades, globes, fan parts, weird paintings, and (after one and a three quarters hours of perspiration and digging through the mayhem in which the "shop" owner almost died in a pile of lampshades), a pink flamingo. I don't know how we didn't notice it earlier. Maybe it flew in behind us. The flamingo actually had an aisle perch. This was no ordinary flamingo. It was over three feet tall, shockingly pink, and had a big gold bow at its throat. The shop owner saw my raw admiration and rushed over to plug it in. I was electrified (pun intended) when the thing lit up the whole floor lamp section with a Barbie-pink glow and, wait for it, danced. The automated tail feathers were a quirky joy. I was delighted. My husband was stunned.

There is another great aspect to this tale (tail?). My mom actually has a collection of pink flamingoes because no one ever knows what to give her for her birthday and Christmas, so everyone just gets her flamingo stuff. She really has no choice but to love flamingoes, and this flea market flamingo was too special. I knew it had to go home with us for a little fun before roosting at Mom's. This bird was going to make a lot of people smile.

We bought said flamingo ($10) and, without even dusting it off, brought it home and into the family room where we plugged it in an outlet attached to a switch so that when the kids walked into the room we could switch on the flamingo and make their day. This was all a temporary arrangement until we could secret it to Mom's and surprise her with the pink glow from wherever the flamingo would perch at her house. We were giddy happy—correction, I was. I'm still not sure my hubby got the full picture. I think this giddiness may have been a precursor to heat exhaustion; I was a bit flushed from the hot flea market, not a menopause moment.

Well, it wasn't long until we had an audience. Samuel was slightly impressed. It may have been due to slight boredom from too much football and the pink glow that impacted the color of the jerseys on the current game, adding a new aura to the match. Susan was very impressed. She frequently leads flamingo hunts for gifting her grandma, and she knew this was a major find. Boyfriend of Susan didn't see the flamingo until the next day, and the viewing was during a break in Rook (ironically, a bird-themed card game) for the sole purpose of turning off the lights and watching the flamingo dance. This got weird when my husband danced a bit with the bird. It was hard to read the level of "impressed"-ness of Boyfriend of Susan when he was trying not to notice Susan's dad.

Why am I going on about such trivial matters? To remind you and to remind myself to enjoy the journey and fun on the journey unites in a way that little else does. Adding a pink glow to your day can bless you and others. Finding and sharing something that will make another feel valued is a joy. God is the Covenant Blesser, and He delights in blessing us with nice surprises even in the midst of the broken-down and neglected. He lights our way.

> *When my anxious thoughts multiply within me, Your consolations delight my soul.* Psalm 94:19

Week 19, Day 5

Read It All: Psalms 107-150
Read a Bit: Psalms 110; 119

Priority

Psalm 119:10 — *With all my heart I have sought You; do not let me wander from Your commandments.*

God reveals Himself to His creation so that we may find Him and have Life. He provides Life to mankind through the promised Seed of the woman (Genesis 3:15). God reveals much regarding this Promised Messiah in what are known as Messianic Psalms. I cannot stress enough the eternal consequences of not taking refuge in the Anointed One of God, in the Lord Jesus Christ. God became a perfect man, paid for our sins, rescued those who would accept this gift of redemption from His wrath, and then validated His plan in resurrection power. In Christ, the believer is made new by the indwelling Spirit. In Christ, the believer becomes a joint heir with Jesus in God's family. In Christ, our Father sees us as fully forgiven, fully righteous, beyond reproach, holy, and blameless. God executes His plans beautifully and vividly. To miss the Son is to miss Life. These Psalms are a gracious gift from God to those who seek Him wholeheartedly.

If you wish to read more about Messiah through the Psalms, I suggest Psalms 2, 22, 69, 78, 110, and 118. These Psalms are quoted in the New Testament as direct fulfillments in Christ, along with many other Messianic texts. Here are some highlights:

But as for Me, I have installed My King upon Zion, My holy mountain. Psalm 2:6

My God, my God, why have You forsaken me? Psalm 22:1

For zeal for Your house has consumed me, and the reproaches of those who reproach You have fallen on me. Psalm 69:9

But [He] chose the tribe of Judah, Mount Zion which He loved. Psalm 78:68

The Lord has sworn and will not change His mind, "You are a priest forever according to the order of Melchizedek." Psalm 110:4

The stone which the builders rejected has become the chief corner stone. Psalm 118:22

PROVERBS

Week 20, Day 1

Read It All: Proverbs 1-7
Read a Bit: Proverbs 1-3

The Revelation in Summary

Proverbs 1:8-9 — *Hear, my son, your father's instruction and do not forsake your mother's teaching; indeed, they are a graceful wreath to your head and ornaments about your neck.*

Proverbs is a collection of wise sayings by followers of the One True God. The book starts with the sayings of Solomon. While Solomon is known for a very unwise finish as a result of being influenced by idolatrous women, mainly his wives, Solomon began his reign asking God for wisdom, so many of the wisdom writings are thought to be in answer to that request. Solomon's sayings fill the first 21 chapters of Proverbs; chapters 22 through 25 and 30-31 are by wise men including Agur and King Lemuel; and chapters 25-30 are attributed to Solomon but compiled years later by Hezekiah's men.

There are several main characters in Proverbs. The woman "wisdom" is constantly in contrast to the woman "folly," also known as the harlot. The father and mother stand in opposition to mockers, scoffers and sinners. The naive child is the recipient of the good teachings. It is the great hope of the author that the naive child will value the way of the woman "wisdom" and the parents to become a wise man instead of following the footsteps of the foolish group, who lust after the harlot and find death.

The wife of the man's youth is held in high regard, with faithfulness to her resulting in life, whereas the adulterous woman should be avoided at all costs, as God longs for the family to be preserved and the next generation's inheritance kept intact. The topics in Proverbs cover applied biblical knowledge so that wise living is the result. The fear of God is the basis for wisdom, and God alone reveals right and wrong. God's Spirit helps His followers to choose His way. Proverbs warns humanity of the enemy's plot to deceive or destroy God's followers. Sexual purity is key to protecting oneself from the enemy, as is avoiding ungodly men, immoral women, and self-centered gain.

Some say the Book of Proverbs is all about common sense, but it is not. God's ways are not common or sensible to those bent on pleasing themselves, valuing temporal pleasures over eternal life. Wisdom is found in God's revelation of Himself and not in what is common to mankind.

Week 20, Day 2

Read It All: Proverbs 8-13
Read a Bit: Proverbs 13

Integrity

Proverbs 9:13 — *The woman of folly is boisterous, she is naive and knows nothing.*

I have served in women's ministry for several decades, and I have met a wide range of women. Some give me the chills. I fear for our young men, as the temptation to align with the wrong woman is overwhelmingly great. I've seen women demoralized by women they thought were friends. Women know how to influence and how to take a heart. Guard your heart. It takes great wisdom to discern which women to flee.

But there are also some obvious signs of potential destruction that should illicit a no-brainer flee response in us and yet don't. Someone comfortable with sharing nudity on social media has discretion issues. A poor work ethic should glaringly signal a lack of integrity. A disrespect of family without some extreme, tragic basis should indicate ingratitude and discontentment. Our friends' and families' disgust with our relationship should be evaluated. However, what seems obvious to moms isn't always clear to their youth. It's hard to witness a contentious woman destroying anyone, but she can and does. Proverbs can help each of us escape her grasp:

> For the lips of an adulteress drip honey and smoother than oil is her speech; but in the end she is bitter as wormwood, sharp as a two-edged sword. Her feet go down to death, her steps take hold of Sheol. She does not ponder the path of life; her ways are unstable; she does not know it. Now then, my sons, listen to me and do not depart from the words of my mouth. Keep your way far from her

and do not go near the door of her house, or you will give your vigor to others and your years to the cruel one; and strangers will be filled with your strength and your hard-earned goods will go to the house of an alien; and you groan at your final end, when your flesh and your body are consumed; and you say, "How I have hated instruction!" Proverbs 5:3-12

This is the way of an adulterous woman: she eats and wipes her mouth, and says, "I have done no wrong." Proverbs 30:20

Week 20, Day 3

Read It All: Proverbs 14-18
Read a Bit: Proverbs 15-17

Dignity

Proverbs 15:17 — *Better is a dinner of herbs where love is than a fattened ox and hatred with it.*

When you travel long distances, you typically are a bit worn out upon arrival at your destination. There is luggage to claim, customs to clear, and stretching out your leg muscles that are shocked from inactivity in tight spaces. The first meal can be a tiresome ordeal if not beautifully arranged for the weary traveler. My first meal in the Holy Land was a relaxing and dignified treat.

We drove into Jerusalem from Tel Aviv in a van for fifteen. The city is white, literally white, as all residents are required to paint white anything not natural stone. For a Floridian, this is a land of overwhelmingly mixed elevations. There are stairs, cliffs, mountains, and houses at various elevations. Nothing is flat. There are walls everywhere, big stone walls, and the city is sectioned off based on identity and belief systems. The Muslims have set minarets, towers usually attached to a mosque from which the call to five Islamic daily prayers is made, throughout the city. Not many blocks are passed without a view of a minaret.

I was looking forward to dinner, of sitting somewhere that wasn't moving. We walked on the outskirts of the Old City, passing tall stone walls and entering alleyways to get to a restaurant that will always be special to me, my first taste of Jerusalem. It was beautiful. There was a narrow stone passage through a lantern-lit dining area into a private garden patio. Vibrant flowers bloomed against taller white stone walls. Under canopies to shelter us from the sun, we felt a beautiful breeze. There was music from a festival in full swing in the adjacent streets.

The meal was family style. Dish after dish of hummus and spreads, fresh vegetables, and skewers of meat were served. Some Palestinian Christians joined our party and became wonderful companions. Meals are an event in the Holy Land, time to refresh relationships as well as our physical strength. Nothing was rushed. This was soothing hospitality. Envision passionate discussions of life in addition to shared enjoyment of the food. As we lingered, the lighting changed as night settled on the city. The little lights above my head grew brighter in contrast to the deepening sky. We left the restaurant thankful. There is something about little lights and family-style meals that make me feel He has invited me home.

Week 20, Day 4

Read It All: Proverbs 19-23
Read a Bit: Proverbs 22

Unity

Proverbs 23:25 — *Let your father and your mother be glad, and let her rejoice who gave birth to you.*

There are aspects of parenting that most of us would agree are essentials to unity in the home with one another and with God. How would you describe a great mom in addition to one who engages in prayer and Bible study?

Pre-pregnancy or adoption, when you are a hope: She prepares; if she is married, she encourages your dad to be a good dad and commits to love him all the days of her life; she nests.

When you are in the womb: She protects and takes care of herself for your care; she dreams.

When you are a baby: She diligently nurtures and supports your growth and well-being; she studies your development and disciplines herself to make you secure; she overcomes weariness.

When you are a toddler: She always knows where you are and makes sure you are nourished, safe, rested, and learning; she cleans.

When you are a child: She insists you learn and grow; she teaches you love of others, respectfulness; she lovingly warns; she organizes.

When you are a teen: She lets you succeed and fail; she offers comfort and new space; she welcomes your friends; she feeds.

When you move out: She helps you set up your home; she brings you a meal; she paints that wall; she makes a special ring tone just for your calls; she grieves.

When you establish your family: She minds her own business; she continues to be a little on call; she listens with interest; she honors your new loved ones; she celebrates your victories; she loves you unselfishly.

Thank God for mothers and fathers who know the value of parenting well. I thank God that I am Mom to my three and am in ministry. I thank God for the men and women who are physical and spiritual parents to me. I thank God for family. Great parents reflect His compassion and grace.

Week 20, Day 5

Read It All: Proverbs 24-31
Read a Bit: Proverbs 30-31

Priority

Proverbs 31:30 — *Charm is deceitful and beauty is vain, but a woman who fears the LORD, she shall be praised.*

I recommended a book on being an excellent wife to a woman in my Bible study who confessed she was struggling in her marriage. The book is quite detailed and draws from many Bible passages, including Proverbs 31, the proverbial woman. After a few weeks of study, the lady I gave the book to came back to me and said that she didn't believe the woman in the study existed, but if she did, then she wanted to marry her. Some ideals seem way beyond us.

The proverbial woman gets a bit of a bad rap. Verse 31:10 acknowledges that such a lady is really hard to find. We are not sure if the description that follows is of an actual woman or is the prayer request of a mother seeking just the right woman for her son. This woman defines the word industrious. She is good, hardworking, a great chef, tireless, inventive, financially adept, strong, high functioning on minimal sleep, a joy, crafty, kind, fearless, farsighted, prepared, honoring, edifying, a sewer and knitter, wise, compassionate, blessed by her children, and praised. We are overwhelmed.

Take note—the heart of this woman is what's essential. Her hard work and praiseworthiness stem from her fear of the Lord. She represents Him well and, in doing so, fulfills the promise of God to Abraham that his people would bless many. She represents the Covenant Blesser because of her identity in Him. God sees each and every godly mom as the proverbial woman to be praised.

ECCLESIASTES

Week 21, Day 1

Read It All: Ecclesiastes 1-2
Read a Bit: Ecclesiastes 1-2

The Revelation in Summary

Ecclesiastes 1:1-2 — *The words of the Preacher, the son of David, king in Jerusalem. "Vanity of vanities," says the Preacher, "Vanity of vanities! All is vanity."*

Ecclesiastes is different than the other wisdom literature books, as they see a pathway to right living, and the authors provide advice on navigating the pathway. In Ecclesiastes, the author is resigned to not being able to understand life and to the meaninglessness of life. The author sounds like a contemporary philosopher with pipe and Xanax in hand.

Ecclesiastes balances the optimistic "We can make this work" or "How long until you correct this?" of the other wisdom books with a realistic look at the monotony of living in a fallen world. Some readers label Ecclesiastes depressing. I like it for the way it cautions me to not overthink things and to dial back my attempts to control so much that I cannot. I like it because the musings resonate with me.

If you read Proverbs and then go right into Ecclesiastes, you get a jarring sense of the Bible having covered every life scenario. The books may seem incongruent, but when you consider all of life, they mesh. The clear directions in Proverbs give way to the skeptical wonderings on whether anything matters. There are no universally clear explanations for life in Ecclesiastes. Life is unpredictable, and people can rarely control anything. Humanity cannot grasp anything; life is a vapor. How can we figure life out? The only certainty is death.

The author of Ecclesiastes gives a lot of evidence on life being meaningless, but the book does not leave the reader in the pit of futility. The conclusion of the book is to fear God and to not be a control freak. Instead, enjoy all you can of what pleases God, remembering that life is fleeting and the moments are valuable.

Week 21, Day 2

Read It All: Ecclesiastes 3-5
Read a Bit: Ecclesiastes 3-5

Integrity

Ecclesiastes 3:14 — *I know that everything God does will remain forever; there is nothing to add to it and there is nothing to take from it, for God has so worked that men should fear Him.*

Foundational to understanding Ecclesiastes is looking at the big picture of God's creation. Out of His integrity, God reveals important lessons on life so that we may have His wisdom to help us in our walk of faith. From Scripture we know that what we experience now on this earth is passing away. In contrast, God resides in a heavenly realm, and He is eternal. God has placed eternity in the heart of mankind so that there is an aspect of the individual that is eternal. We shouldn't get too hung up on this life, because in the big picture we really do not have much of an understanding of life, and the reality is that life as we know it is temporal. Live with an eternal perspective. Not much of life in this world involves my interaction. My significance is in enjoying the Maker of this world, not in the minute details of my day. The minute details are where I live out God's love of me. I cannot figure God out, but I can enjoy following Him as He has given me guidance.

Sometimes I just don't lift my eyes to God, and thus I see as the majority of people around me see. I am overwhelmed by each day's sameness and brevity. I'm weary and feel empty. The hardships in life are unsettling, frustrating. Hope has vanished. Life apart from God would be meaningless, so I take great comfort in remembering that life doesn't have to be apart from God. My significance and hope is in Him.

One of my seminary professors would tell his classes that we need to live life remembering that the Grim Reaper is always right at hand. The Bible faithfully points out that death is a constant main character in everyone's story. Our only hope is in Him Who provides victory over death. Fear God and live.

Week 21, Day 3

Read It All: Ecclesiastes 6-8
Read a Bit: Ecclesiastes 6-8

Dignity

Ecclesiastes 7:2 — *It is better to go to a house of mourning than to go to a house of feasting, because that is the end of every man, and the living takes it to heart.*

Where do you get your dignity? Work? Sports? Money? Brains? Serving? Looks? Pleasure? Freedom? The philosopher in Ecclesiastes has explored many avenues in an attempt to find meaning or dignity in life. Meaning and dignity come from being told you have value. All that the philosopher explores to find value are based in other people's endorsements of him. He reasons that this is ridiculous, as others suffer the same fate as he does—we all die. What does another's evaluation of us matter? We are unified in being under a curse and having our productivity in this realm frustrated by the effects of the fall.

The value of a human life cannot be determined based on the world's estimations. Only God can supply meaning and dignity in this life. Again and again, the philosopher returns to encourage the reader to fear God and receive life. God's evaluation of you and of me matters . . . eternally.

Week 21, Day 4

Read It All: Ecclesiastes 9-12
Read a Bit: Ecclesiastes 9-12

Unity

Ecclesiastes 10:12-14 — *Words from the mouth of a wise man are gracious, while the lips of a fool consume him; the beginning of his talking is folly and the end of it is wicked madness. Yet the fool multiplies words.*

Ecclesiastes 12:13-14 — *The conclusion, when all has been heard, is: fear God and keep His commandments, because this applies to every person. For God will bring every act to judgment, everything which is hidden, whether it is good or evil.*

The "conclusion of the matter" statement at the end of Ecclesiastes strongly exhibits the great faith of the author. Life is summarized as mattering to God and is good when walked in fear of God, remembering that He is the ultimate judge of all. Evidently God knows all and will judge every aspect of our lives, including those things we think we have hidden. God, and only God, knows what is good and what is evil. The pondering in this book did not clarify life, but rather clarified Who is the Giver of Life. Knowing Who is in charge at least gives the sojourner a direction to follow.

We lament over many things that we think we could change for the better. We really don't know what would be better. Ecclesiastes exhorts us to enjoy the gifts of God. You cannot control much, but you can have a good attitude and enjoy the life you have. Enjoy your friendships, your family, even just the sunset.

> *There is nothing better for a man than to eat and drink and tell himself that his labor is good.* Ecclesiastes 2:24

It is time to accept what you cannot control and enjoy all that God provides. Only God can unite our attempts to find meaning with His provision of Life. Ecclesiastes is a wise call to the reader to continue to long for justice and God and to live knowing He will righteously judge the world, ending all its meaninglessness. Take refuge in God's Ruler, The Christ and Judge to escape life's vanities.

Week 21, Day 5

Read It All: Ecclesiastes 12:13-14
Read a Bit: Ecclesiastes 12:13-14

Priority

Ecclesiastes 5:18 — *Here is what I have seen to be good and fitting: to eat, to drink and enjoy oneself in all one's labor in which he toils under the sun during the few years of his life which God has given him; for this is his reward.*

Eat, drink and be merry today (for tomorrow we may die ;-) —couldn't help myself) Catch up on reading if you desire.

SONG OF SOLOMON

Week 22, Day 1

Read It All: Song of Solomon 1-2
Read a Bit: Song of Solomon 1-2

The Revelation in Summary

Song of Solomon 1:1 — *The Song of Songs, which is Solomon's.*

My mom would always say that the Song of Solomon was her favorite book in the Bible. This was awkward, for we all knew that the main theme of Song of Solomon is sexual love, and no one wants to relate sexual intimacy to their mom. Ugh.

The book is also a bit controversial when people discuss their views on who the author is. King Solomon, known for his many wives and concubines, is hardly a candidate for the focused relationship depicted in the Song. Scholars who discount Solomon as the lover in the Song typically propose that the first verse of the book indicates the writings are in the style of Solomon, but not by Solomon. Some believe that the love of the Shulamite and her shepherd is contrasted to the love that Solomon forced when he is described as attempting to buy love (8:11-12). The love described in the Song could never be bought; Solomon is to be pitied.

The main theme in the Song is sexual desire, erotic love. The lovers convey their passion for one another, their frustration when separated, their physical attributes, their heightened sexual attraction, and the awareness the community has of their relationship. The love of the couple is both beautiful and threatening in its ability to consume thought lives. The friends' joy for the couple is exhilarating, and the reader sees that it takes a whole community to help the couple not to awaken passionate, sexual love until the right time. Love is a powerful emotion. It is a gift of God, and it takes us back to the freedom and intimacy of man and woman when they were first placed in the Garden of Eden.

Week 22, Day 2

Read It All: Song of Solomon 3-4
Read a Bit: Song of Solomon 3-4

Integrity

Song of Solomon 3:2-3 — *On my bed night after night I sought him whom my soul loves; I sought him but did not find him. "I must arise now and go about the city; in the streets and in the squares I must seek him whom my soul loves." I sought him but did not find him.*

My daughter Sarah Kate was calling me from her college. She needed prayer. There was a young man she had been doing ministry with through a college group, and she was struggling of thinking of him as merely a brother in Christ. She was strongly attracted to him.

She was in her third year of college and purposing to focus on her studies and area ministries, but he just seemed to be everywhere she was; they were serving in so many places together. He also recognized that they were spending a lot of time together, so he addressed this specifically by inviting her to a coffee shop where he told her over a cup of coffee that he wanted to be clear that he was not interested in dating. At the time, she was relieved and expressed her relief to his surprise. But now, just a couple months later, he was consuming her thought life and she wanted prayer, but she also wanted to just talk about him with someone. As a mom, I loved that part. We covered some details amidst my challenging her to trust God with the relationship. She was all over the place in that phone call: laughter, tears, conviction, and giddiness. Men.

We learned later that the young man was having a struggle of his own. He was learning as much as he could about our daughter and processing the data. He had already gained his family's input when they had visited him and met her at a school event. He had watched her in worship. He'd had a friend give his analysis after a group rock climbing trip.

Finally, my husband got a call from the young man asking permission to date our daughter with the intent of "courting" her. We didn't know young folks still used the term "courting." We liked Gannon Thomas Wilder and used the phone call as an opportunity to have him answer a lot of questions we thought parents should ask. He was dear. After receiving our blessing, he went into turbo mode. He invited Sarah to coffee back at the place where he had told her "no" to dating, and he planned one of the most astounding first dates I have ever heard of right after the coffee. She was overwhelmed. She went from a "yes" to dating, when he recanted his first coffee shop statement and explained his current intent, to an afternoon of sailing, build-a-bear, flowers, fancy dinner, and more coffee.

They courted for a year. Five months of that year, Sarah Kate was on mission in Guatemala, and Gannon figured out how to get a huge bouquet of red roses to a remote area of Puerto Barrios for Valentine's Day. We were all very impressed. The day Sarah Kate returned from her mission trip, Gannon was at the airport to welcome her home. Sarah was thrilled to see him. The rest of us were a bit superfluous.

He waited three days to propose, three months to get married, and her smile still hasn't dimmed. He guarded her integrity, and his, as he promised he would. Their love has filled our home in a wonderful, risky, vulnerable way. May God protect their household from the enemy. May He establish their home in Your covenant truth.

Week 22, Day 3

Read It All: Song of Solomon 5
Read a Bit: Song of Solomon 5

Dignity

Song of Solomon 5:1 — *I have come into my garden, my sister, my bride; I have gathered my myrrh along with my balsam. I have eaten my honeycomb and my honey; I have drunk my wine and my milk. Eat, friends; drink and imbibe deeply, O lovers.*

After my dad's years in Viet Nam, my family lived in a few different states and never near family. In addition, I am the middle child between two brothers. I didn't experience a culture where older women or sisters spent time mentoring one another. This is something I really love now about my church family, especially when it comes to young brides.

I arrived at church one day and was greeted by three very brilliant wives with, "Hey, come see what we got for a young bride in our ministry." I discovered cute gift wrap but not the typical silverware set. My attention was drawn to the "pleasure" lubricant. I find I am very immature when it comes to talking about sex. Instead of whispering, I shout, "What is this? Have you tried this stuff?" All three started talking at once. I was learning more than I could take in, wondering if it was appropriate to take notes. I thought, I need these ladies to take me shopping.

Now, mind you, these ladies are godly women. They have amazing advice for all women. Their heart is for Christian marriages to be the best in the world: secure, passionate, honoring, and FUN. They would like to see women in church free to rightly discuss intimacy problems that hinder sexual enjoyment. They hope that their generation would encourage the next generation to have a wholesome understanding of the joys of sex. Optimizing loving intimacy is part of God's will for brides and grooms. Society deceives couples into thinking that good sex comes naturally. It doesn't. It requires great communication and loving patience.

In all purity, my friends will tell you how to enhance your sex life while honoring God and one another. They believe that sex should be reserved for marriage, and that is where the reserve ends. Get to KNOW one another. Pre-marital sex talks are one of the dearest and most important aspects of older women pouring wisdom and shared joy into the engaged or newly married.

Some of us "older married" ladies could use a refresher course from one another. I've had women tell me that they have reached a spiritual place where physical intimacy with the spouse is no longer "needed." I have talked with too many who have just given up on physical intimacy, tired of trying to figure it out. I grieve for their homes. I think of some of the widows I know who mourn the loss of such intimacy. There is a sacred purity to marital intimacy, emotionally, spiritually, and physically. Sometimes it is just a matter of listening and learning and trying. So many of us are confused by a worldview of sex that is discouraging. Our role models are from the media, nonexistent, fairy-tale couples that don't get along off screen. The "entertainment" arts cannot depict reality and cannot portray secure, loving, committed passion. We need godly encouragement.

I do wish Christian marriage was known for being romantic and pleasing. After all, it represents Christ's love for His church. Sex is a gift to the married from God. Pray we learn to appreciate this gift rightly.

Then the Lord God said, "It is not good for the man to be alone; I will make him a helper suitable for him.". . . The man said, "This is now bone of my bones, and flesh of my flesh; she shall be called Woman, because she was taken out of Man." For this reason, a man shall leave his father and his mother, and be joined to his wife; and they shall become one flesh. And the man and his wife were both naked and were not ashamed. Genesis 2:18-25

Postscript: I think women's ministries should host seminars complete with question and answer sessions featuring my buddies. I smile writing this. I think it would be a fun gathering of women. One of them suggested selling t-shirts that say, "I love sex." Under this bold proclamation would be #withmyhusband.

Week 22, Day 4

Read It All: Song of Solomon 6-7
Read a Bit: Song of Solomon 6-7

Unity

Song of Solomon 7:10 — *I am my beloved's, and his desire is for me.*

Weddings still unite massive numbers of people. According to the ratings company Nielsen, 29 million people in America tuned in to Prince Harry's and Meghan's royal wedding (this doesn't include social media followers or those who streamed the event), and 24 million United Kingdom viewers did. Weddings are a draw, particularly royal weddings.

I loved a number of things about this royal wedding (in addition to the fun of wearing a bonnet and eating orange-glazed scones while watching from home). I still think a church or huge chapels make for great venues. In this day of outdoor and barn weddings, I love the reminder that Christian marriages should be based on dwelling in Him and endorsed by His Body. The home established by the union should reflect His love for His people.

> *Husbands, love your wives, just as Christ also loved the church and gave Himself up for her.* . . . Ephesians 5:25

I loved the truth being proclaimed. Many watched a ceremony that included a sermon on the love of God and the example of Jesus Christ as sacrificially loving. This presented a high view of marriages that can exist to represent His love to many. Blessed to bless. A call to demonstrate united intimacy.

> *For this reason a man shall leave his father and his mother, and be joined to his wife; and they shall become one flesh.* Genesis 2:24

I loved the romance of it all. The groom picking flowers from the family garden for her bouquet. Hands held as the ceremony continued. Cello music in a gorgeous setting. Favorite hymns and all dressed to honor one another.

> *You have made my heart beat faster, my sister, my bride; you have made my heart beat faster with a single glance of your eyes, with a single strand of your necklace.* Song of Solomon 4:9

I loved the joy of it all. Many came out to celebrate: the children, the masses, the smiles, the waves, the escape from dreariness and struggles. God's Word mandates feasting, celebrations. Weddings should be times of great celebration, for love is a precious miracle of God.

> *The kingdom of heaven may be compared to a king who gave a wedding feast for his son.* Matthew 22:2

I loved the formality of it all. In a day when we make light of marriage and many think we should shorten the ceremony and promote the dancing over the consecration of the couple, I am convicted of the needed sacredness of ceremony. Our weddings should gather together those who will support the couple, encourage faithfulness, and build hope through the years. Our weddings should emphasize the importance of covenant marriage. All creation longs for homes set apart for Him. This is the ultimate in romance—long-term, devoted love for a lifetime. A grand wedding reminds us of the grand impact a home established in truth can have on the masses.

> *Put me like a seal over your heart, like a seal on your arm. For love is as strong as death, . . .* Song of Solomon 8:6

Get ready for your royal wedding, for one day, when the Perfect Bridegroom will return . . . for you.

> *But at midnight there was a shout, "Behold, the bridegroom! Come out to meet him."* Matthew 25:6

Week 22, Day 5

Read It All: Song of Solomon 8
Read a Bit: Song of Solomon 8

Priority

Song of Solomon 8:6-7 — *"Put me like a seal over your heart, like a seal on your arm. For love is as strong as death, jealousy is as severe as Sheol; its flashes are flashes of fire, the very flame of the Lord. "Many waters cannot quench love, nor will rivers overflow it; if a man were to give all the riches of his house for love, it would be utterly despised."*

I've been married over 35 years. That's 245 in dog years. I don't know how this happened. I must believe in miracles, as apparently I am in one. Scott Montgomery is wonderful. I don't say that enough. Note, though, that wonderful does not mean perfect. I have said at times that he has the emotional range of a wall (that's in contrast to me), that he must be struggling with forgetfulness (or I'm not feeling I'm the center of his world), that sugar is not his best friend (physique nag), and that he needs to do something now (which translates to me as "I'm worried" or "I'm bored"). He has been an excruciatingly patient spouse because I'm not nice. Us still together is shocking.

I know when the odds on our marriage changed. We were talking divorce about 6 years into the covenant agreement when we realized we wanted the marriage for much bigger reasons than ourselves. We wanted to be a part of giving others a glimpse of the faithfulness of God by being faithful to one another. We wanted to experience love as God defined it. This meant a bit of work. We were both so biblically illiterate. We committed to consistent worship, Bible study, and prayer. This was a big change, but this also saved our marriage.

Scott has grown in faithfulness to his children, his work, in teaching cello and Bible, as a mentor, in doing house repairs, to me. This is love.

I have learned the meaning of service and dedication through Scott. I'm overwhelmed.

I hurt for women who have never met a Scott, as not having a faithful man in your life can be an obstacle to receiving the love of God Who is Father and Son of Man. The Lord Jesus Christ is the perfect Bridegroom. A wedding day will come that will make all other relationships pale in light of your union with the loving Savior. Married or single, the believer points to the ultimate kingdom wedding feast and says, "Get ready for the celebration!"

> *Let us rejoice and be glad and give the glory to Him, for the marriage of the Lamb has come and His bride has made herself ready. . . . Then he said to me, "Write, 'Blessed are those who are invited to the marriage supper of the Lamb.'" And he said to me, "These are true words of God."* Revelation 19:7-9

REST TIME

Week 23, Days 1-5

Psalm 62:7 — *On God my salvation and my glory rest; the rock of my strength, my refuge is in God.*

Through the Old Testament wisdom writings, the reader discovers the believer's responses to their heavenly Father's presence in their lives and their desire to understand Him. The wisdom writings convey the inspired teachings of authors purposing to reveal the mind of God to His children. The sovereignty of God is presented in Job, the prayerful worship and submission to His glory by His children is portrayed by the Psalms, the wisdom and warnings of God are clear in Proverbs, the musings of experienced devotion are voiced in Ecclesiastes, and the power of marital love is declared in the Song of Solomon. These writings resonate with my heart.

Journal any thoughts you wish to record at this point in your reading.

One
will go forth for
Me
to be
Ruler
in
Israel

Micah 5:2

OLD TESTAMENT MAJOR & MINOR PROPHETS

There are 17 books designated the major and minor prophets in the Old Testament. The first five are labeled "major" because of their length (although Lamentations is short) and placement in the Bible, not as an indicator that they have the more major messages. The minor prophets also have God's truth but are simply placed after the major prophets, and they are shorter than most of the major prophets.

Isaiah, Jeremiah, Lamentations, Hosea, Joel, Amos, Obadiah, Jonah, Micah, Nahum, Habakkuk, and Zephaniah are all prophets during the times of the kings recorded in 2 Kings and the second half of 2 Chronicles. Ezekiel and Daniel cover the exile. Haggai, Zechariah, and Malachi cover the period when the exiles are returning to the land and purposing to rebuild the city, the walls, and the temple. Haggai and Zechariah correspond to the time of Ezra, while Malachi's warnings relate to the Book of Nehemiah.

God faithfully provided prophets to His chosen people when their kings were not rightly representing the Lord God Almighty. The prophets demonstrate a long-suffering God Who continues to warn His wayward children and to encourage His faithful remnant. The prophets supply the call to repent and remind the people that even in the midst of judging sin, God remembers them. The prophets have words of hope for God's remnant of followers, and these words of hope will give life to those suffering in the midst of exile.

ISAIAH

Week 24, Day 1

Read It All: Isaiah 1-12
Read a Bit: Isaiah 1-7; 11

The Revelation in Summary

Isaiah 7:14 — *Therefore the Lord Himself will give you a sign: Behold, a virgin will be with child and bear a son, and she will call His name Immanuel.*

Matthew 1:23-24 — *Behold, the virgin shall be with child and shall bear a Son, and they shall call His name Immanuel," which translated means "God with us." And Joseph awoke from his sleep and did as the angel of the Lord commanded him, and took Mary as his wife . . . .*

Isaiah repeatedly gives Judah's kings and people a prophecy of exile, which they reject. Their approaching exile is God's response to their unbelief, especially by their evil Davidic kings. The Book of Isaiah specifically covers Isaiah's interactions with Kings Uzziah, Jotham, Ahaz, and Hezekiah.

Isaiah chapters 1-39 focus mainly on judgment while chapters 40-66 focus on Israel's hope following their exile. Isaiah has the longest passages in Scripture on the coming Suffering Servant King. These passages provide numerous specific details on the anticipated Messiah and thus were a great encouragement to those who found their faith in the Seed of the woman being the Lord Jesus Christ. These passages also should have invoked fear in those who refused to receive His Refuge.

God was displeased with King Ahaz. God, through Isaiah, had warned Ahaz about aligning with foreign kings instead of trusting in the Lord. God had even offered a sign to Ahaz, but he refused the Lord's revelation, feigned a spiritual reason for doing so, and aligned with mere man. Ahaz was ripe for judgment.

For some, "God with us" is good news; for others, the name means judgment.

Isaiah prophesied to Ahaz that a virgin would bear Immanuel as a judgment on Ahaz for his disbelief. God was informing Ahaz that he wasn't needed for the line of Messiah, a great honor to the Jewish kings.

As a matter of fact, a little virgin girl would have more significance than the "mighty" king Ahaz. Belief in the promises, the character of God, matters.

With the same prophecy in Matthew, God's messenger comforts and guides Joseph. Immanuel, God with us, was good news to Joseph. He believed in the Seed of a woman bearing the Redeemer and Joseph was blessed. It was the same message, but rather than being cut off from Messiah, Joseph received the Word of God and had the privilege of cradling Him. God blessed Joseph with life.

Sometimes I cringe as I think about God with me. He sees my apathy. He knows my spending lusts, walking with me as I shop more for me than those on my Christmas list. He is patient while I'm angry at the lines and judge the not-so-helpful sales associates. He is even aware of my bloated condition when I've binged on my favorite foods. I'm amazed that I haven't been cut off like Ahaz, for I can be a wicked, selfish, royal mess.

But God with me is my greatest comfort. His promise of love purifies me. His reminders that sanctification is a process comfort me, and His Word that one day I will be like His Son thrills me. Worship Him with eyes open in wonder, not with surprise at His presence but in awe because He is so real. God is with us.

Week 24, Day 2

Read It All: Isaiah 13-27
Read a Bit: Isaiah 14; 25-27

Integrity

Isaiah 14:22-26 — *"I will rise up against them," declares the Lord of hosts, "and will cut off from Babylon name and survivors, offspring and posterity," declares the Lord. "I will also make it a possession for the hedgehog and swamps of water, and I will sweep it with the broom of destruction," declares the Lord of hosts. The Lord of hosts has sworn saying, "Surely, just as I have intended so it has happened, and just as I have planned so it will stand, to break Assyria in My land, and I will trample him on My mountains. Then his yoke will be removed from them and his burden removed from their shoulder. This is the plan devised against the whole earth; and this is the hand that is stretched out against all the nations. For the Lord of hosts has planned, and who can frustrate it? And as for His stretched-out hand, who can turn it back?"*

What the Lord says will happen, happens; His Word is His integrity. Isaiah had testified that Israel would suffer at the hands of Assyria and Babylon, and Isaiah lived to witness brutal Assyria defeat the Northern Kingdom of Israel and see the rise of Babylon, who would eventually take Israel into captivity. But while God allowed these nations to discipline His children, He did not forget their brutality to His family and He judged them with destruction. The words of Isaiah regarding the enemies would ring in the people's ears and remind them of God's revelation.

Week 24, Day 3

Read It All: Isaiah 28-39
Read a Bit: Isaiah 31-35

Dignity

Isaiah 35:10 — *And the ransomed of the Lord will return and come with joyful shouting to Zion, with everlasting joy upon their heads. They will find gladness and joy, and sorrow and sighing will flee away.*

There is a great change that occurs from the Old to the New Testament. All that the Old Testament anticipated in relation to our redemption happened! When Christ came, the shadows began to fall away, because Christ himself is the Reality, the fulfillment of the Promised Provision. He is our tabernacle and temple, God with us. He delivers the sinful into His dignity and grace. The Old Testament Covenant revealed our sin, our corrupt hearts. The New Testament Covenant revealed our Savior, the means of changed hearts. Christ Jesus is our Mediator and God is pleased.

> *But when Christ appeared as a high priest of the good things to come, He entered through the greater and more perfect tabernacle, not made with hands, that is to say, not of this creation; and not through the blood of goats and calves, but through His own blood, He entered the holy place once for all, having obtained eternal redemption. For if the blood of goats and bulls and the ashes of a heifer sprinkling those who have been defiled sanctify for the cleansing of the flesh, how much more will the blood of Christ, who through the eternal Spirit offered Himself without blemish to God, cleanse*

your conscience from dead works to serve the living God? For this reason, He is the mediator of a new covenant, so that, since a death has taken place for the redemption of the transgressions that were committed under the first covenant, those who have been called may receive the promise of the eternal inheritance. Hebrews 9:11-15

It is because of the great Mediator that we are able to stand before Holy God clothed in the righteousness of the Lord Jesus Christ. His mediation is the only means of salvation. We are adopted into the New Covenant by accepting the redeeming power of the blood of Christ, being sealed by the Promised Spirit and established by faith in Christ.

God is the ultimate gift-giver. He does it all. He gives His Son, as promised in the Old Testament, as the Word that He writes on our hearts so that we may receive the reality of new life. Isaiah, through his prophecies, helped prepare the way so that the hearer of the Word might recognize God's great gift in Lord Jesus.

First of all, then, I urge that entreaties and prayers, petitions and thanksgivings, be made on behalf of all men, for kings and all who are in authority, so that we may lead a tranquil and quiet life in all godliness and dignity. This is good and acceptable in the sight of God our Savior, who desires all men to be saved and to come to the knowledge of the truth. For there is one God, and one mediator also between God and men, the man Christ Jesus, who gave Himself as a ransom for all, the testimony given at the proper time. 1 Timothy 2:1-6

Week 24, Day 4

Read It All: Isaiah 40-55
Read a Bit: Isaiah 42-43; 45; 53-55

Unity

Isaiah 49:16 — *Behold, I have inscribed you on the palms of My hands; Your walls are continually before Me.*

In 2018, I was planning a conference for over 5,000 women. I enlisted the help of a group of women that I named the Core Team. I fell in love with each team member. I learned so much from these ladies, from prayer to joyful ministry. One of my favorite things that the team did was designate a Bible verse to memorize and to remind us of what we were purposing to convey to unify all the ladies attending the conference. We chose Isaiah 49:16. We even got black t-shirts with "Inscribed" in large gold letters so that others could identify us as a team and as a resource for information on the event. For me, this emphasized a really important Bible truth that greatly blesses me personally. I am reminded that I am inscribed on my Father's hands. For someone whose earthly father left her in high school, this promise is a treasure.

The passage with 49:16 in Isaiah isn't an easy passage to read. The context is the conversation between God and His people as they head into exile, fearful and doubting the possibility of ever having a restored relationship with God. God's comfort to His people is to announce the coming of His Servant, which should reinforce the hope of restoration. God's Servant would do all that those called to be servants had not. God's Servant would be the ultimate Covenant Blesser. God promises to continue to minister to a wayward, weak people because He is faithful and good. God would bring the people out of captivity and beyond that, He would always remember those "inscribed . . . in the palms of My hands" through Messiah. I think of the nail pierced hands and see my name in the wounds.

In Isaiah, the people keep voicing their doubts, and God patiently reassures them. In verse 16, He calls for them to "Behold" His truth; He will not forget them. And the best news is that eventually they really will see that He is the Lord, their Redeemer.

It is a privilege and joy to remind women of their identity in and unity with Christ. I thank God for The Core Team that directed me to a Savior that inscribes His people in the palm of His hand. I pray I will continue to tell others about this merciful and mighty Covenant Blesser from the line of David. May we open up our hands to represent His love.

Week 24, Day 5

Read It All: Isaiah 56-66
Read a Bit: Isaiah 58-59; 61; 66

Priority

Isaiah 63:9 — *In all their affliction He was afflicted, and the angel of His presence saved them; in His love and in His mercy He redeemed them, and He lifted them and carried them all the days of old.*

> *Remember the former things long past, For I am God, and there is no other; I am God, and there is no one like Me, . . .* Isaiah 46:9

So much of walking by faith is remembering whose children we are and what our Father reveals. God knows, I forget. Humanity is united in forgetfulness. So as a good Father, throughout His Word, He patiently reminds of what to remember:

> *Remember these things, O Jacob, and Israel, for you are My servant; I have formed you, you are My servant, O Israel, you will not be forgotten by Me.* Isaiah 44:21

> *Remember Lot's wife. Whoever seeks to keep his life will lose it, and whoever loses his life will preserve it.* Luke 17:32-33

> *If you were of the world, the world would love its own; but because you are not of the world, but I chose you out of the world, because of this the world hates you. Remember the word that I said to you, "A slave is not greater than his master." If they persecuted Me, they will also persecute you; if they kept My word, they will keep yours also. But all these things they will do to you for My name's sake, because they do not know the One who sent Me.* John 15:19-21

> *. . . do not be arrogant toward the branches; but if you are arrogant, remember that it is not you who supports the root, but the root supports you.* Romans 11:18

> *And concerning you, my brethren, I myself also am convinced that you yourselves are full of goodness, filled with all knowledge and able also to admonish one another. But I have written very boldly to you on some points so as to remind you again, because of the grace that was given me from God, to be a minister of Christ Jesus to the Gentiles, ministering as a priest the gospel of God, so that my offering of the Gentiles may become acceptable, sanctified by the Holy Spirit.* Romans 15:14-16

... remember that you were at that time separate from Christ, excluded from the commonwealth of Israel, and strangers to the covenants of promise, having no hope and without God in the world. But now in Christ Jesus you who formerly were far off have been brought near by the blood of Christ. Ephesians 2:12-13

Remember Jesus Christ, risen from the dead, descendant of David ... 2 Timothy 2:8

Remember those who led you, who spoke the word of God to you; and considering the result of their conduct, imitate their faith. Hebrews 13:7

... you should remember the words spoken beforehand by the holy prophets and the commandment of the Lord and Savior spoken by your apostles. 2 Peter 3:2

Therefore remember from where you have fallen, and repent and do the deeds you did at first; or else I am coming to you and will remove your lamp stand out of its place—unless you repent. Revelation 2:5

So remember what you have received and heard; and keep it, and repent. Revelation 3:3

Isaiah knew a people shocked by a message of judgment were hardening their hearts to the message of God. He called them to remember so that when his prophecies came true, they would have hope in all he said about God's redemption. Remembering God's promises would be Israel's only hope—their only source of dignity—when they went into exile. There is much to remember, as God is faithful to reveal much. The Jewish people wisely wrote down the prophet's words so that they could read them, lest we forget.

JEREMIAH

Week 25, Day 1

Read It All: Jeremiah 1-6
Read a Bit: Jeremiah 1-4

The Revelation in Summary

Jeremiah 1:4-8 — *Now the word of the Lord came to me saying, "Before I formed you in the womb I knew you, and before you were born I consecrated you; I have appointed you a prophet to the nations." Then I said, "Alas, Lord God! Behold, I do not know how to speak, because I am a youth." But the Lord said to me, "Do not say, 'I am a youth,' because everywhere I send you, you shall go, and all that I command you, you shall speak. Do not be afraid of them, for I am with you to deliver you," declares the Lord.*

Jeremiah is the longest book in Scripture and it seems like it. The book is written as a judged people, still not believing God will do what He says, refuse to listen and learn. Jeremiah's personal suffering, specifically because he is God's messenger, is a hard read . . . unless you like tragedies.

God has a very hard job for Jeremiah in a very hard time of Israel's history. Jeremiah is to continue to tell the Jewish people, particularly the leaders, that their exile is imminent. Jeremiah will suffer violently as God's messenger due to Judah's rejection of the message and frustration with the prophet. God promises Jeremiah that He will ultimately deliver Jeremiah, but this doesn't mean that he keeps silent through the suffering. Again, I think this is one of the hardest reads in the Bible. Jeremiah is not just grieving the meanness of those opposing him, but he is watching as his home and people decline and are overtaken by the evil, idol-worshipping Babylon. Jeremiah knows from God that a remnant of those who trust in God will be spared, but he is also keenly aware that many will be destroyed, as will the city he loves, Jerusalem, the city of God.

Characteristic of our loving God, the prophet Jeremiah also has moments of revealing God's abundant grace and continual intent to deliver humanity. Jeremiah predicts that the Jewish people will be exiled for 70 years (Jeremiah 25:11-12) and he gives the promise of a New Covenant with God (Jeremiah 31:31-34). This New Covenant is the culmination of God's great promises that He will provide a way for all our iniquities to truly be forgiven. His children will receive a new heart that will empower them to know God and represent Him well. Even in the darkest of times, God provides the Light.

Week 25, Day 2

Read It All: Jeremiah 7-25
Read a Bit: Jeremiah 11-12; 15-19; 23

Integrity

Jeremiah 23:5-6 — *"Behold, the days are coming," declares the Lord, "When I will raise up for David a righteous Branch; and He will reign as king and act wisely and do justice and righteousness in the land. "In His days Judah will be saved, and Israel will dwell securely; and this is His name by which He will be called, 'The Lord our righteousness.'*

Jeremiah is contemporary with several other prophets, particularly Micah, Joel, Habakkuk, and Zephaniah, who long to see Judah repent. The steadfastness of these messengers through great persecution models great integrity. They stood on God's promises as their homeland crumbled. They anticipated His restoration even as He severely disciplined His children.

> *But as for me, I will watch expectantly for the LORD; I will wait for the God of my salvation. My God will hear me. Do not rejoice over me, O my enemy. Though I fall I will rise; though I dwell in darkness, the LORD is a light for me. I will bear the indignation of the LORD because I have sinned against Him, until He pleads my case and executes justice for me. He will bring me out to the light, and I will see His righteousness. Then my enemy will see, and shame will cover her who said to me, "Where is the LORD your God?" My eyes will look on her; at that time she will be trampled down like mire of the streets. It will be a day for building your walls. On that day will your boundary be extended.* Micah 7:7 -11

I read about Jerusalem's city walls in the Bible and applauded when Nehemiah finished reconstructing them after the exile. I had heard about the wall in the area that today separates Palestinians and Israelis.

It also separates enemies and childhood friends, some family members. I knew there were disagreements about the purpose, placement, and "peace"-keeping ability of the wall. The people with integrity grieve the separation and isolation of the walls. The people without integrity are the basis of the walls. I saw that the walls are taller in some places than the Berlin Wall[14] in order to deter sniper fire. I knew there was graffiti. I knew the wall was a message of separation, of hate.

In Bethlehem, I walked along the wall. I saw the size, the concrete, the graffiti, the barbed wire, the messages—and I longed for home. There are many enemies in this world. Peacekeeping is a complex matter. It is a grievous thing to see cities segregated due to beliefs, but we are what we believe. It is a grievous thing to see machine guns at major tourist sites or anywhere, but we do need protection. It is a grievous thing to raise children to hate, but that is the core of terrorism. It is a grievous thing to not love your neighbor, but God knew that and commands love. But only God is love, and humanity struggles. We grieve God and one another.

Many Palestinians remember a time when people of differing beliefs came together in celebrations. The West Bank walls are filled with writings from authors reminiscing of moving throughout the land freely and enjoying one another's various traditions. Now there is fear and separation. Evil is the enemy, the evil witnessed in one another.

A day is promised in which God will defeat the enemy. The new walls that will be constructed then will aid in safe transport and add beauty to the land. All nations will be united in worship as the Prince of Peace takes His stand in the land. Oh, for that day. Pray for the land. Pray for the peace of Jerusalem.

---

[14] The average height of the Berlin Wall was approximately 12 feet, and the maximum height of Israel's wall is 25 feet.

Week 25, Day 3

Read It All: Jeremiah 26-33
Read a Bit: Jeremiah 27-28; 30-33

Dignity

Jeremiah 31:31-34 — *"Behold, days are coming," declares the Lord, "when I will make a new covenant with the house of Israel and with the house of Judah, not like the covenant which I made with their fathers in the day I took them by the hand to bring them out of the land of Egypt, My covenant which they broke, although I was a husband to them," declares the Lord. "But this is the covenant which I will make with the house of Israel after those days," declares the Lord, "I will put My law within them and on their heart I will write it; and I will be their God, and they shall be My people. They will not teach again, each man his neighbor and each man his brother, saying, 'Know the Lord,' for they will all know Me, from the least of them to the greatest of them," declares the Lord, "for I will forgive their iniquity, and their sin I will remember no more."*

Our son Samuel was expecting to be cut off from the household. He had blown a semester of college by playing too much, studying too little, and allowing bad relationships to keep him from his responsibilities. I shudder to think how he must have influenced others at that time. This followed a year in which he had promised to focus and had said that if he didn't have to get a job that he would do really well in school. His continued rejection of our advice and encouragement was taking a toll on the family. As parents we had to confront our son.

We sat on the back porch, and the conversation was tense and drawn out. We went over the finances with Samuel and the consequences of his self-centered lifestyle. He was so close to finishing his undergraduate studies, and it seemed that he was remorseful about how the months had caught up with him. He was realizing that his future was at stake, but we weren't sure whether he was really repentant or just sorry at having to stop going his own way because of our standing in his way. It was a long afternoon.

We allowed him to continue at his current college, but he had to leave his current roommates. He was to live alone and finish his degree. His budget would be really tight, but he wasn't being cut off. We set up some checkpoints and we prayed. We told him how much we loved him and assured him that our happiness wasn't dependent on his. The world just didn't revolve around him, even though at the moment it seemed to because of our stress levels. We smiled again, hoping for a good future, but knowing there was lots of work for now. It's hard to discipline and instill dignity at the same time.

He recognized the undeserved favor. He returned to school and learned to live alone and to study more. He finished his degree and we celebrated. We still had many struggles ahead as a family, but in the moment we thanked God for reminding us to be merciful with one another.

As the Jewish people were heading to their punishment and a time of all work and no play, God revealed how engaged He still was with them. He promised that one day they would be able to wholeheartedly love Him under the New Covenant as He would place a new heart in them which would seal them for eternal life with Him.

Week 25, Day 4

Read It All: Jeremiah 34-45
Read a Bit: Jeremiah 36-38

Unity

Jeremiah 39:11-12 — *Now Nebuchadnezzar king of Babylon gave orders about Jeremiah through Nebuzaradan the captain of the bodyguard, saying, "Take him and look after him, and do nothing harmful to him, but rather deal with him just as he tells you."*

While Jerusalem is being destroyed, Jeremiah is protected by the enemy, as promised by the Lord God when He called Jeremiah to be His messenger. The account in the Scriptures indicates that Jeremiah was actually safer with the enemy than he had been with his countrymen, who wanted to kill Jeremiah and had recently placed him in a cistern. There was no peace in the city of God.

> *Pray for the unity and peace of Jerusalem: "May they prosper who love you."* Psalm 122:6

Sometimes those who live under oppression forget what peace is like. They forget what it feels like to be securely free. Jeremiah was horribly oppressed by Jerusalem's leaders, so much so that the Babylonian invasion may have brought some relief to him.

Many are still oppressed and at war with one another in Jerusalem today. When I visited the Old City, at the same gate I left from one late afternoon, the next morning three terrorists entered and killed two Jewish police officers by the Pool of Bethsaida. The Old City was locked down for a few hours as the terrorists were pursued. Peace seemed an impossibility amidst so much hateful unrest. Those with ears to hear know these things:

Peace is truly a gift of God – Peace I leave with you; My peace I give to you; not as the world gives do I give to you. Do not let your heart be troubled, nor let it be fearful. John 14:27

Peace is not dependent on our situation – These things I have spoken to you, so that in Me you may have peace. In the world you have tribulation, but take courage; I have overcome the world. John 16:33

Peace is being right with our Maker – Therefore, having been justified by faith, we have peace with God through our Lord Jesus Christ, through whom also we have obtained our introduction by faith into this grace in which we stand; and we exult in hope of the glory of God. Romans 5:1-3

Peace is abiding in Him – Be anxious for nothing, but in everything by prayer and supplication with thanksgiving let your requests be made known to God. And the peace of God, which surpasses all comprehension, will guard your hearts and your minds in Christ Jesus. Philippians 4:6

Shalom: "peace."

Week 25, Day 5

Read It All: Jeremiah 46-52
Read a Bit: Jeremiah 50-52

Priority

Jeremiah 50:6 — *My people have become lost sheep; their shepherds have led them astray. They have made them turn aside on the mountains; they have gone along from mountain to hill and have forgotten their resting place.*

My dad passed some time shepherding sheep. He says they are really easy to lead astray. They will follow a trail grazing away without realizing they are at the cliff's edge. They will get stuck upside down, becoming easy prey. They will run right along with the herd to a slaughterhouse. They can be "sheepish," and their neurosis keeps them from following a good shepherd's lead.

The shepherd has to be incredibly patient with the foolish sheep. God pictures people as sheep and His Son as the compassionate, thoughtful Shepherd. We get the picture. I've so stubbornly gone my own way even when my human reasoning gave way to realizing I was just being stubborn and ignoring His Word. I've lost friends, money, and family fun due to disobedience. But I've been blessed by grace in spite of my stubbornness. The closest thing to exile for me have been self-imposed times of withdrawing from society.

A life-giving priority is to know the Good Shepherd so well that we can distinguish His voice from all others, that we value His voice, and that we without hesitation respond to His commands. My grandma taught me Psalm 23 at a very early age. It is one of the few Bible passages I still know by heart. I take great comfort in those verses. These Old Testament words are beautifully echoed in John 10:1-18 for the Good Shepherd. May any who are lost sheep lift up their heads and return to His fold.

LAMENTATIONS

Lamentations records Jeremiah's heartbreak over his beloved city Jerusalem's destruction and his countrymen's exile. There is a sacred dignity to suffering depicted in Lamentations and a deeper look into the heart of God's prophet.

It may surprise you to have a full week on only five chapters. I think we tend to rush through mourning, so I want to slow down the reading to give all an opportunity to mourn along with the text for those we know who are separated from God by unbelief or rebellion. Don't rush through this week. Grieving helps us to remember what is eternal, why we need a Savior, and Whose mercies are new every morning.

Week 26, Day 1

Read It All: Lamentations 1
Read a Bit: Lamentations 1

The Revelation in Summary

Lamentations 1:1 — *How lonely sits the city that was full of people! She has become like a widow who was once great among the nations! She who was a princess among the provinces has become a forced laborer!*

The theme of Lamentations is that there are consequences to sin. The city has fallen and the representative nation of God is in exile. God's angry disciplinary judgment of His people, while severe and deserved, is deeply lamented. The phrase "daughter or son of Zion" is repeated throughout the book and develops the picture of God as grieving parent.

Jeremiah writes Lamentations as a poetical acrostic. The first poem in the book is a lament for Jerusalem's misery and desolation. The second poem is a lament for Jerusalem's inhabitants that were destroyed by God's anger. The third poem reveals that the Jews, amidst their complaints, were still hoping in God because they knew of His faithfulness.[15] The

---

[15] The hymn "Great Is Thy Faithfulness" comes from Lamentations 3:23. It was written by Thomas Chisholm and composed by William M. Runyan in 1923.

fourth poem contrasts Jerusalem's past glory with her present horror. The last poem is a lament of forgiveness and petition for restoration.

This hope of restoration in Lamentations is founded in Israel's history with Covenant God, Who promises to deliver His people when they cry out to Him for help. His disciplinary judgment is not the end of their story together. Judah's loving, compassionate, and faithful God would remain the nation's source of hope and ultimate restoration. He had revealed through the ages His mercies that are new every morning, and His character comforted the people in their suffering.

Week 26, Day 2

Read It All: Lamentations 2
Read a Bit: Lamentations 2

Integrity

Lamentations 2:1 — *How the Lord has covered the daughter of Zion with a cloud in His anger! He has cast from heaven to earth the glory of Israel, and has not remembered His footstool in the day of His anger.*

Debbie is someone I have known for years. I met her through a mutual friend who was impressed with how Debbie so wisely and lovingly "nannied" another friend's child. Debbie and I crossed paths again at an area Bible study. She was still nannying, and her love for another's child was dear. She was instrumental in telling her "spiritual child" about God, and she was so proud of his kind ways.

Debbie's husband did not share her faith. I was always encouraged by time with Debbie, as her grief in her marital differences and her longing for her husband to find peace with God made her especially appreciative of the little touches of grace in the moment. I learned a lot about integrity through Debbie. She was always honest about her situation, but also kind and respectful. She clearly loved her husband. She also had a cute way of interjecting fun.

Debbie also battled cancer. For three years, she was in and out of cancer centers and chemotherapy. She would be near death and then get better, but then, she declined. Her husband watched and witnessed her sweet faith. Debbie kept praying for him. She mourned his lack of spiritual sight and hoped for his redemption. She believed he was suffering much more than she.

Everyone knew she was going to die. Hospice came to help. People kept visiting her and bringing food. Debbie was very social. If she was even remotely feeling good, she got out to see her many friends. She was one of the most faithful members of my Sunday small group. While many of us were worrying about our hair, Debbie just popped on a cap or wrap on her bald head and went out. She had a variety of wigs, so sometimes it took me a second to realize Debbie was in the house.

Debbie did die, peacefully at home. I believe she is finally free from pain and enjoying seeing her Savior. Someone told me they didn't even think Hell would want Debbie's husband, but I always thought, what an incredible man to not run in the midst of such suffering. One of our pastors thought the same thing, and he kept visiting Debbie's husband. I learned from this pastor that Debbie's husband had prayed to receive Christ before she died. Many had been praying for him in honor of Debbie, as that was always a prayer request she would share. Debbie carried a song of lament nobly and with great integrity for many years. May she rest in His peace and in His great care where there are no more tears.

Week 26, Day 3

Read It All: Lamentations 3
Read a Bit: Lamentations 3

Dignity

Lamentations 3:22-23 — *The LORD's loving kindnesses indeed never cease, for His compassions never fail. They are new every morning! Great is Your faithfulness.*

Job 17:11 — *My days are past, my plans are torn apart, even the wishes of my heart.*

I took such great care to cover so many details prior to my daughter Susan's wedding, but there were two things that happened that served to remind me of my powerlessness: illness and an accident.

I started to feel wiped out the Sunday before the wedding. By Monday, I was struggling to teach my Monday night class, and Tuesday morning I rescheduled the teaching time to be earlier than the group time so I could head home and lie down as quickly as possible. I was congested, had a pounding headache, and was sore all over. I did not want to be sick for my daughter's wedding. Oh, well. I still had a veil to finish sewing and a few errands to run, but I scheduled a doctor appointment instead and starting stitching slowly, eyes burning. Others were texting and emailing me, letting me know that because of their health issues, they would not be at the wedding. It seemed like an epidemic. I prayed for the bride and groom to remain healthy.

Tuesday night the phone rang, and it was our son-in-law Gannon. My husband was in pre-wedding mode and thought Gannon was calling to discuss details for the weekend, particularly family fun prior to the wedding. But that isn't Gannon's way, and so I knew something had happened. Our daughter, the matron of honor, had been hit by a car while bicycling. Gannon was at the hospital, two hours away from us; there were no broken bones, but they were waiting to have a CAT scan. Thankfully, she had been wearing her helmet. We knew that this was all good news in contrast to what it could have been. The emergency people were marveling at how Sarah was doing based on the hit her small frame had taken as she was thrown over the hood of the car.

Plans and people are frail things. Unknowingly, we had included bicycles in our wedding décor. Now they served as a not-so-subtle reminder to enjoy the moments without being obsessive in the planning.

I've attended too many funerals for young adults to not know that it is a very unnatural thing for a parent to outlive a child. I've attended too many funerals to not know that life is a miracle worth celebrating daily.

In reality, the illness and accident served to enrich our celebration. The incidents made it clear what mattered most at the "big event." They helped me set aside the petty for the priceless.

Our miracle matron of honor, with punctured feet and pain killers, insisted on walking the aisle with dignity and standing for her sister. This added a poignant touch to the celebration. To witness our children rejoicing for and with one another during the wedding was worth all the planning ups and downs for this mom. I recognized that, at this point in time, we were blessed with a beautiful day, a wonderful couple to celebrate, and life. I take a moment to pray for those who have received the worst news following an accident. I ask for God's peace to overpower their pain, for hope in His sovereign love, and for the courage to continue in love.

Week 26, Day 4

Read It All: Lamentations 4
Read a Bit: Lamentations 4

Unity

Lamentations 4:11 — *The LORD has accomplished His wrath, He has poured out His fierce anger; and He has kindled a fire in Zion which has consumed its foundations.*

The consequences of sin are death. This is true for everyone. We are united in that all of our futures hold death. But annually, if we live, we get to add another year to what we tell people when they ask us our age. After a while, this really doesn't impact us much, because we eventually get to an age when people hesitate to ask you how old you are, as you are obviously "old enough." I like each additional year. They represent a temporary victory over death.

I have learned that death is unbeatable, and each day older, every breath I take, is another opportunity to humbly walk by faith instead of angrily stomping at death. The faith walk is God's purpose for His children until we meet Him face to face. I get to show Him my love by believing. He is life: purposeful life on this earth, promised life post this earth, and permanent life on redeemed earth. Our faith walk represents a permanent victory over death.

I'm thinking that the opposite of living isn't the act of dying (a temporary feat), but rather the opposite of living is existing without passion, living apathetically. I talk a lot about emotions with women (go figure)— frustrations, hopes, depression, joy, grief, excitement, lack of passion, anxiety, silliness, obsession, anger, happiness, regret . . . I'm thankful for the emotions. They help us know ourselves and others better. We should be intense about life. It is a gift from God. Passionate life represents a victory over death.

Some women wonder if it is best, or even possible, to turn off emotions, as if emotions keep us from doing what is good. Other belief systems promote "nirvana," existing, numbness, unawareness. Christianity exhorts Spirit control. There are big differences between Spirit control, self-control, and emotionlessness. Lots of people have methods for enhancing numbness. This is big business in medicine. But God reveals that emotions aren't the enemy. Emotions are expressions of our heart. They help us communicate. When our emotions are out of hand, it is clearly a heart issue. We need to transform our hearts by His truth. Joyful living is directly related to being wholeheartedly His. Purifying our hearts cleanses our emotions and leads to maturity in our circumstances. Beware of apathy or numbness because this denies life. Enjoy being created in His image, emotionally relational. Give life to living. His will is that we are thankful and loving. These things are expressed, not hidden. Loving represents a victory over death.

Thank you living, faithful, passionate, loving God for life. You are our victory over death.

Week 26, Day 5

Read It All: Lamentations 5
Read a Bit: Lamentations 5

Priority

Lamentations 5:21-22 — *Restore us to You, O LORD, that we may be restored; renew our days as of old, unless You have utterly rejected us and are exceedingly angry with us.*

Sorrow is common to man. Two books in the Bible stand out for teaching much regarding sorrow, Job and Lamentations. The books both express intense emotion regarding loss, but there are some big differences. Job laments over the destruction that he is personally suffering, and Lamentations addresses suffering at a national level. Job deals with a righteous man suffering due to Satan's allowed power in this realm, while Lamentations gives us the horrendous, sorrowful consequences of our own sins or the sins of those close to us. The situations in both books are overwhelming. I would not want to belittle any of the described losses, but I do think there is a particular wrenching of the spirit that goes along with suffering due to one's own sins. When we see our choices resulting in pain for others and ourselves, there is another dimension to the suffering that can cause immobilizing regret. To overcome, we have to forgive, and to forgive ourselves requires a level of humility that we tend to resist. Even when we know we have the forgiveness of God, going through the consequences is so mentally challenging that we are continually tempted to keep going over and over what we should have done or how it all could be so different. Playback can be ugly, and our mourning keeps rewinding and playing back our hurts.

Jeremiah (or his scribes) voices the sorrow of Israel when the nation was disciplined, not abandoned, by God for their iniquity. Jeremiah likens the suffering to that of a widow and to a woman who has enjoyed her "independence" but now realizes her need.

> *She weeps bitterly in the night and her tears are on her cheeks; she has none to comfort her among all her lovers. . . . My children are desolate because the enemy has prevailed. . . . See, O Lord, for I am in distress; my spirit is greatly troubled; my heart is overturned within me, for I have been very rebellious. . . .* Lamentations 1:2

I have sat with a few widows as well as dwelt in a place of regrets; I can relate to Jeremiah. Repentance rather than obsessive regret is the way of finding His provision of a future that overcomes a sinful past. He is to be glorified, as He is the Lord and only in Him is there hope and compassion that can renew the day. In the midst of Lamentations, there is this reminder:

> *The LORD's loving kindnesses indeed never cease, for His compassions never fail. They are new every morning; great is Your faithfulness.* Lamentations 3:22-23

EZEKIEL

Week 27, Day 1

Read It All: Ezekiel 1-3
Read a Bit: Ezekiel 1-3

The Revelation in Summary

Ezekiel 3:1 — *Now it came about in the thirtieth year, on the fifth day of the fourth month, while I was by the river Chebar among the exiles, the heavens were opened and I saw visions of God.*

Let's recap some of Israel's history, as Ezekiel can seem a bit overwhelming due to its historical details and inclusion of many dates. After King Solomon, Israel had split into the Northern and Southern Kingdoms. The Northern Kingdom, called Israel and representing 10 tribes, was conquered by Assyria in 722-721 BC. The Southern Kingdom, referred to as Judah and representing 2 tribes, was exiled to Babylon in three deportations. The prophet Daniel went in the first deportation, Ezekiel in the second, and in the third invasion, around 586 BC, the temple and city of Jerusalem were destroyed.

The Book of Ezekiel represents God's great patience and His willingness to teach His children. Through Ezekiel, God reveals why Israel was punished and the judgments God is making against the nations that took part in Israel's humiliation. This story of Israel's rejection of God is graphic, and the prophet Ezekiel's visions, particularly of God's glory leaving the temple, are sad narratives of Israel's relationship with God. The analogy of Samaria and Jerusalem as harlots betraying a faithful God exposes the baseness of human nature.

God vividly portrays His glory being removed from the temple, but He grandly reveals His glory returning and a New Jerusalem being established as His Kingdom. This return is led by a new Shepherd. The pivotal point in Ezekiel is chapter 33, depicting the city of Jerusalem being taken by Babylon. Chapter 34 addresses the prophecies against the false shepherds of Israel and begins God's assurance of full restoration for His people. Ezekiel's visions of the resurrected dry bones, the man with a measuring rod, and the tribes back on their land dramatically convey the extent of God's redemptive power. Ezekiel closes his book with the phrase, "The LORD is there." The reader is reminded of a formerly devout people who would refuse to move anywhere without Him.

Week 27, Day 2

Read It All: Ezekiel 4-24
Read a Bit: Ezekiel 4-7; 12; 21-24

Integrity

Ezekiel 11:13 — *Now it came about as I prophesied, that Pelatiah son of Benaiah died. Then I fell on my face and cried out with a loud voice and said, "Alas, Lord God! Will You bring the remnant of Israel to a complete end?"*

Our group was spending the day at the Lakeland Baptist Children's Home. It was hot and we were visiting the residents for a day of fun, playing games and eating together. The house parents were happy not to be preparing another meal as we brought in sandwich rings and chips. The children, mainly middle school age, looked detached. They were not familiar with someone taking an interest in them.

I cannot imagine what it would be like to not have a safe place to call home. When the last relative tells the court that they cannot house you either, do you cry out to God and ask if your family is at a complete end? The kids at the Children's Home realize they have no control over being loved. The Children's Home, with its block walls and donated furniture, is a haven for them. The house parents who love them unconditionally are an anomaly. I thank God for the integrity of these "parents" in making a home for the homeless children.

I sat at a table and invited several to play Uno. It's a card game that differing ages can play, so this gives opportunity for siblings to be in the same game. Uno doesn't involve much skill. I do not like Uno. I think it is repetitive and boring. I want more control than Uno allows. But I got a group to play, and I gained a new appreciation for Uno as a means of connecting the detached. The children opened up as they played. Due to the simplicity of the game, they could keep up with it and tell a little about themselves at the same time. At first, they seemed surprised to be asked about their lives. They spoke up for one another more than for themselves. They liked having the power to skip players, reverse the play, and make another draw. What I thought boring, they found fun and even fulfilling. It seemed that they had very little they could control, so controlling a few play options gave them hope. Their life strategies had never worked and they had suffered much oppression by family, their peers at school, and the court system. Uno was a nice change. Uno leveled the playing field for a little while.

One day, God will bring about His holy justice. His Son will be identified, and the children will be avenged. No more orphanages, no more rejection, no more tears, as the only thing that truly will end is the evil in the land.

Week 27, Day 3

Read It All: Ezekiel 25-32
Read a Bit: Ezekiel 28

Dignity

Ezekiel 28:11-25 — *Again the word of the Lord came to me saying, "Son of man, take up a lamentation over the king of Tyre and say to him, 'Thus says the Lord God, "You had the seal of perfection, full of wisdom and perfect in beauty. You were in Eden, the garden of God; every precious stone was your covering: the ruby, the topaz and the diamond; the beryl, the onyx and the jasper; the lapis lazuli, the turquoise and the emerald; and the gold, the workmanship of your settings and sockets, was in you. On the day that you were created they were prepared. You were the anointed cherub who covers, and I placed you there. You were on the holy mountain of God; you walked in the midst of the stones of fire. You were blameless in your ways from the day you were created until unrighteousness was found in you."*

The judgment against Tyre stands out amidst the judgment of the nations that opposed Israel, as the King of Tyre takes on attributes that do not apply to a mere man. The ruler being judged is so aligned with Satan that Ezekiel's message pictures Satan and provides one of the most detailed texts in the Bible on this fallen angel.

Every person should take heed of the description Ezekiel provides on this evil ruler in chapter 28. The fall of this perfectly created being started when he believed that his own wisdom was as great as the wisdom of God. The heart of the ruler sought the place of God and actually thought he had attained it. Many followed after this evil's ruler wisdom, and many will die because of the attraction.

Humankind's dignity is sourced in the Lord God Almighty. Dignity comes from loving the Lord God Almighty with all your heart, soul, mind, and strength, as only He is worthy. To love another in such a manner, especially to love yourself as if you are God, is to defile yourself and to miss Life. Ezekiel warns all who would read the text that judgment will descend on the enemies of God and that resurrection life is through the provision of His Spirit to those who turn to God for refuge. Remember your Maker.

Week 27, Day 4

Read It All: Ezekiel 33-39
Read a Bit: Ezekiel 33-39

Unity

Ezekiel 34:7-10 7 — *Therefore, you shepherds, hear the word of the Lord: "As I live," declares the Lord God, "surely because My flock has become a prey, My flock has even become food for all the beasts of the field for lack of a shepherd, and My shepherds did not search for My flock, but rather the shepherds fed themselves and did not feed My flock; therefore, you shepherds, hear the word of the Lord: 'Thus says the Lord God, "Behold, I am against the shepherds, and I will demand My sheep from them and make them cease from feeding sheep. So the shepherds will not feed themselves anymore, but I will deliver My flock from their mouth, so that they will not be food for them."*

I just finished the online training Ministry Safe, something I do every few years to remind myself how to best serve children. You see, there are people, evil people, who target children in order to sexually abuse them. I want this to stop.

The training is chilling. Sexual abuse is common. There are some things that any wishing to protect children should know. Awareness is important. It is important that we be prepared adults and strong advocates for children.

I pass on to you some of my training[16] so that you too can pray and be on guard. The Lord detests those who are false shepherds to His children.

Child abusers cannot be identified by appearance or a "look" (forget your biases). They come from various backgrounds, and many are adept at being helpful and friendly, as that creates opportunities for alone time with children. Abusers groom children and those who manage the care of children (the gatekeepers) to gain time with children. Grooming is an intentional process of manipulating a person so that they can be readily victimized. It typically involves secrecy, using gifts/favors, or rule breaking while establishing an emotional connection to lower inhibitions.

Interviews with many of those imprisoned for sexually abusing children reveal that an abuser doesn't typically target any one child, but more a specific age and gender. I watched interview after interview where the abuser told how they would abuse and/or molest 5-6 children a week . . . for years. This means that one abuser may have many, many, many victims. The statistics are very high for adults that report having experienced child abuse and molestation. Know that ending the silence regarding abuse can prevent someone else from becoming a victim. Abuse is so defiling; it is hard to discuss without feeling shame even when you are not the culprit. Victims tend to blame themselves, and others encourage avoiding and forgetting rather than confronting abuse. This reaps more shame and suffering. Know the abuse hotline number and share it with others: 800-500-1119 or 800-96abuse (800-962-2873). There needs to be a safe way to talk about abuse, confront abuse, and overcome, yes, end it. Lord, help us.

Many of the reported abuse situations are child-to-child interactions. Good adult supervision involves great diligence and not assuming that children are safe with one another. All parents should be informed when abuse or even questionable interactions have occurred. Again, awareness is important.

Many struggle with God's sovereign care and goodness because they've suffered years of abuse. God hates abuse. God avenges all victims. God is just, but in His sovereign plan, He allows mankind to do as

---

[16] Ministry Safe, www.ministrysafe.com, 2018.

they think reasonable. I groan in longing for God's best. Know this, He doesn't forget His children.

> *At that time the disciples came to Jesus and said, "Who then is greatest in the kingdom of heaven?" And He called a child to Himself and set him before them, and said, "Truly I say to you, unless you are converted and become like children, you will not enter the kingdom of heaven. Whoever then humbles himself as this child, he is the greatest in the kingdom of heaven. And whoever receives one such child in My name receives Me; but whoever causes one of these little ones who believe in Me to stumble, it would be better for him to have a heavy millstone hung around his neck, and to be drowned in the depth of the sea."* Matthew 18:1-6

Week 27, Day 5

Read It All: Ezekiel 40-48
Read a Bit: Ezekiel 40-48

Priority

Ezekiel 1:28 — *As the appearance of the rainbow in the clouds on a rainy day, so was the appearance of the surrounding radiance. Such was the appearance of the likeness of the glory of the Lord. And when I saw it, I fell on my face and heard a voice speaking.*

Ezekiel is so caught up with the Lord God Almighty that his writing is actually a trail map of the "glory of the Lord"; he uses the phrase repeatedly. His crisis point in his message is the departing of the glory of the Lord from Jerusalem. The resolution to all his sorrow is the return of the glory of the Lord to the temple. Join me in following the trail of God's glory with Ezekiel.

> *Then the Spirit lifted me up, and I heard a great rumbling sound behind me, "Blessed be the glory of the Lord in His place."*
> Ezekiel 3:12

So I got up and went out to the plain; and behold, the glory of the Lord was standing there, like the glory which I saw by the river Chebar, and I fell on my face. Ezekiel 3:23

Then the glory of the Lord went up from the cherub to the threshold of the temple, and the temple was filled with the cloud and the court was filled with the brightness of the glory of the Lord. Ezekiel 10:4

Then the glory of the Lord departed from the threshold of the temple and stood over the cherubim. Ezekiel 10:18

When the cherubim departed, they lifted their wings and rose up from the earth in my sight with the wheels beside them; and they stood still at the entrance of the east gate of the Lord's house, and the glory of the God of Israel hovered over them. Ezekiel 10:19

The glory of the Lord went up from the midst of the city and stood over the mountain which is east of the city. Ezekiel 11:23

And the glory of the Lord came into the house by the way of the gate facing toward the east. Ezekiel 43:4

And the Spirit lifted me up and brought me into the inner court; and behold, the glory of the Lord filled the house. Ezekiel 43:5

Then He brought me by way of the north gate to the front of the house; and I looked, and behold, the glory of the Lord filled the house of the Lord, and I fell on my face. Ezekiel 44:4

Today, the believer is the temple of God. When the believer walks in the Spirit, the believer carries the glory of the Lord wherever he or she goes. May we help one another walk in the Spirit and represent Him well.

DANIEL

Week 28, Day 1

Read It All: Daniel 1-2
Read a Bit: Daniel 1-2

The Revelation in Summary

Daniel 1:9 — *Now God granted Daniel favor and compassion in the sight of the commander of the officials, . . .*

Daniel is also a post-exilic prophet; he wrote after the exile of Judah to Babylon. Daniel was taken by Babylon in their first deportation of the Jews. Nebuchadnezzar had ordered his officials to bring in the sons of Israel's royalty and nobles, perfect-looking youths and skilled. Daniel would have been assigned to teach the Babylonians his literature and language. I picture Daniel telling Nebuchadnezzar and his leaders Bible stories and all within earshot marveling at Daniel's wisdom and God's faithfulness.

The Book of Daniel reveals how the Jewish people were oppressed by their Gentile rulers. God had established Israel to be His representative nation to the world. Now, because of their rebellion against God, Israel was exiled and the Times of the Gentiles, the period when Israel would be under Gentile dominion, had begun. To this day, Israel has not been fully restored to rule in the land. Their government is dependent upon other nations for financial and military support. The history of Daniel and his friends conveys that any responsibility they gained, any authority they had, was still under the rule of a pagan leader. They were not ruling for God as His chosen nation. Their story must continue.

Daniel's life story includes repeated cycles of bold faith, persecution, deliverance, favor as a captive, and supernatural revelation to the rulers of his day. Daniel served three powerful kings: Nebuchadnezzar (Babylon), Belshazzar (Babylon), and Darius (Medes). The visions in the Book of Daniel provide an opportunity for Daniel to bless the kings of the land and to interpret details regarding the future of the nations. Throughout the book are prophecies that will encourage the exiles that Sovereign God still remembers them. Daniel is the one who reads about

God's promise of a 70-year captivity, and thus he expectantly beseeches the Lord to help Israel return to the land. The reader sees a life of prayer and fasting, as Daniel makes supplication to the Lord throughout his lifetime. The reader also learns about angels of God that supply answers to Daniel regarding the visions he has. God is faithful to reveal Himself to an exiled remnant longing for the opportunity to glorify their King.

Week 28, Day 2

Read It All: Daniel 3-4
Read a Bit: Daniel 3-4

Integrity

Daniel 3:1 — *Nebuchadnezzar the king made an image of gold, the height of which was sixty cubits and its width six cubits; he set it up on the plain of Dura in the province of Babylon.*

I get lots of questions about our annual Holiday Tables. This event always needs a little explaining. Basically (get ready for a really long sentence since that is how I explain this event), Holiday Tables is an event for women to buy a table for ladies they wish to have in their own homes for the holidays, but probably won't get around to having as that would require cleaning toilets, and besides we wish for these "guests" to get familiar with our church home; extravagantly decorating the purchased, unclothed table based on some random theme——not necessarily about Christmas; tracking the seats as ladies decide whether they can make it or not (hearing "Oh, no big deal" is so irritating); explaining why we don't do dinner at the gorgeous table (yes, no chicken, just a snack after the speaker), and actually preferring that you don't sit down during the table tour as so many are moving around; and knowing that our focus is really the speaker with a gospel message rather than our decorated tables. This event is a workout for everyone and, like most workouts, the results are often noticeable and healthy. Ladies feel loved.

I have a Holiday Tables story that makes me laugh all the more in the retelling.

Once upon a time, there was a first-time Holiday Tables decorator. She set about preparing a Dr. Seuss table: months of planning an early morning fish purchase and hours decorating. The center of her One

Fish, Two Fish, Red Fish, Blue Fish table was a round fish bowl with three goldfish. Tragically, the fish bowl exploded as the decorator was setting it mid-table. Ladies surrounded her, helped clean up the shrapnel, and saved the fish. The committed decorator ran to the store to replace soggy table decor and acquire a new fish bowl. Happily, all got set for her sweet group to enjoy that evening.

Next to the Dr. Seuss table was an Easter table, glorious with bright green paper grass and little tea lights. Both tables were filled with guests following the speaker in the sanctuary. All were settled in for the relaxing part of the event.

The lovely ladies were enjoying their snacks and the ladies at Dr. Seuss were discussing the resiliency of fish when the Easter table green paper grass caught fire. I was circling our Gatheria near enough to hear voices yelling "Fire!" and other voices yelling "Fish!" as one lady at the fire table turned around, reached over the decorator's head at the fish table, and grabbed the fish bowl (and fish) to douse the fire. She succeeded.

The fish table ladies also succeeded in saving the fish. They watched horrified as their swimming table buddies went into the flames, and when the fire was out, a crew of ladies dug through the no-longer-bright-green grass decor to discover three undercooked, living fish. The ladies affectionately named the fish Shadrach, Meshach and Abed-nego.

These difficult circumstances for the fish ultimately saved their lives. The decorator said that after such a day and such heroic survival, she didn't have the heart to flush the fish. And they lived happily . . . well you really can't tell with fish how long or how happy.

> *If it be so, our God whom we serve is able to deliver us from the furnace of blazing fire; and He will deliver us out of your hand, O king. But even if He does not, let it be known to you, O king, that we are not going to serve your gods or worship the golden image that you have set up.* Daniel 3:17-18

Week 28, Day 3

Read It All: Daniel 5-7
Read a Bit: Daniel 5-7

Dignity

Daniel 6:21-22 — *Then Daniel spoke to the king, "O king, live forever! My God sent His angel and shut the lions' mouths and they have not hurt me, inasmuch as I was found innocent before Him; and also toward you, O king, I have committed no crime."*

Daniel in the lion's den is a frequently told Bible story. My personal favorite version is VeggieTales, with Archibald Asparagus as King Darius and Larry the Cucumber as Daniel. The story show the grandeur of the palace, the power of King Darius, the persecution of Daniel by the leaders in the land, and the conflicted character of Darius in attempting to kill his "friend" by lion hunger. The music is also very jazzy, so the tale makes death peppy. Interesting effect.

I find a certain irony in life that with the right music, no matter the situation, I too can get a little peppy. I've learned when I do not want to get out of bed I just need to use my cell phone charging on my nightstand to play some Brooklyn Tabernacle Choir tracks to get me going. The night before my double mastectomy, four friends came over to sit with me. The movie Mama Mia was out at that time, and we somehow got on the subject of the musical group Abba. We decided to play "Dancing Queen" and dance around my house. I should have a cancer dance party more regularly, as a little exuberance in the midst of trials helps you sleep better.

VeggieTales does show the darkness of the lions' den, so our children don't totally think a death sentence is cute. The meanness of the enemies is portrayed even with several punny lion-lying comments. Whether it is lions or cancer or another potential death situation, our comfort and dignity comes from His overwhelming presence. Good friends often represent His presence to us. How we embrace our difficult situations and who joins us in the struggles demonstrates what we believe about Sovereign God. Our love for one another and our courage in trials are the means for Him to be glorified. Turn up the music and join the dance.

Week 28, Day 4

Read It All: Daniel 8-10
Read a Bit: Daniel 8-10

Unity

Daniel 9:2-3 — *. . . in the first year of his reign, I, Daniel, observed in the books the number of the years which was revealed as the word of the Lord to Jeremiah the prophet for the completion of the desolations of Jerusalem, namely, seventy years.*

This 70 number is greatly significant and provides a data point that can ground our faith with overwhelmingly fulfilled history. The 70 years in verse 2 refers to the 70-year exile for Israel that Daniel was experiencing. This number was provided by Jeremiah regarding Judah's captivity. The 70 years equates to the number of years Israel ignored God's command to have a Sabbath year (every 7 years, a year to rest). Daniel was seeking wisdom as to how to determine the date for the Jews' return. It was 70 years from Jeremiah's prophecy to Cyrus' edict to return. It was 70 years from Israel's King Jehoiachin's captivity to Ezra's return to the land and it was 70 years from the destruction of the temple to the edict of Darius to rebuild. It seems to me that God orchestrated several options to encourage many working on the math!

The 70 has additional significance for those in exile. God raised up prophets to continually remind the people of His Kingdom to come, far beyond their temporal struggles. Daniel repeats 70 again in 9:24 with a longer perspective:

Seventy weeks have been decreed for your people and your holy city, to finish the transgression, to make an end of sin, to make atonement for iniquity, to bring in everlasting righteousness, to seal up vision and prophecy and to anoint the most holy place.

The transgression would end with the end of the Times of the Gentiles and with the restoration of God's rule through His people. We know from other Scriptures that the end of sin, full atonement, everlasting righteousness, His fulfillment of His Words culminates in the promised New Heaven and New Earth. This is when His children are fully renewed with hearts forever like His.

Daniel further breaks down the future 70 into 7, 62, and the last week. These numbers depict the Messiah's coming, 69 weeks from the decree to rebuild the temple to Messiah's triumphant entry into Jerusalem. The text also indicates Messiah will be cut off, the temple and city destroyed, and war. There is a delay and another 7-year period of complete destruction that should be anticipated. This is a lot to study, as this can be confusing because the history encompasses many significant events in relation to the 70.

Daniel provides more details about the End Times in contrast to the Times of the Gentiles, while God the Loving Father prepares His people through the ages to recognize His deliverance. The fulfilled 70 of the return of God's remnant to the land reminds us to expectantly trust that His last 70 will come to pass just as He says. Our faith has data points.

Week 28, Day 5

Read It All: Daniel 11-12
Read a Bit: Daniel 11-12

Priority

Daniel 12:2 — *Many of those who sleep in the dust of the ground will awake, these to everlasting life, but the others to disgrace and everlasting contempt.*

Such a short verse, and yet it expresses so much. I didn't realize until years of Bible study that the resurrection was depicted in the Old Testament. I thought the concept was only in the New Testament. After seeing resurrection in Daniel, I began to search for the hope in other Old Testament passages. I found an overwhelming affirmation of God's resurrection power. Follow with me.

Resurrection is revealing God's power over death. I think of Noah and his family overcoming the flood, Sarah's dead loins bearing Isaac, Isaac surviving the sacrifice, Joseph living to reign after being deemed dead in the pit, Moses being pulled from the river, and the Jews defeating Haman's edict of sure death. You may remember other accounts of a second chance at life.

Physical resurrection occurs in 1 Kings 17 when Elijah raises the widow's son. Ezekiel has the vision of the dry bones restored to life. Isaiah promises, *"Your dead will live; their corpses will rise. You who lie in the dust, awake and shout for joy, for your dew is as the dew of the dawn, and the earth will give birth to the departed spirits"* Isaiah 26:19.

The psalmist anticipates God's power over death: *"For You will not abandon my soul to Sheol; nor will You allow Your Holy One to undergo decay"* (Psalm 16:10), *"That he should live on eternally, that he should not undergo decay. But God will redeem my soul from the power of Sheol, for He will receive me"* (Psalm 49:9, 15). And I love this verse: *"You who have shown me many troubles and distresses will revive me again, and will bring me up again from the depths of the earth"* (Psalm 71:20).

The answer to the question, *"Will You perform wonders for the dead? Will the departed spirits rise and praise You?"* (Psalm 88:10) is yes.

REST TIME

Week 29, Days 1-5

Isaiah 14:7 — *The whole earth is at rest and is quiet; they break forth into shouts of joy.*

The major prophets are God's messengers to redirect the people back to His Refuge as they have set their hearts on imitating the nations they were to rule. God is faithful to His people and continues to reveal Himself to them through the prophets and to discipline them so that they might ultimately have Life. I'm thankful for His warnings and His persistence in love.

Journal any thoughts you wish to record at this point in your reading.

OLD TESTAMENT MINOR PROPHETS

The twelve books that close out the Old Testament in the Protestant Christian Bible are known as the Minor Prophets. The messages contained in these books echo the messages of the Major Prophets, but these speakers are a little more succinct. Less emotional turmoil and historical information is encased in their preaching. The chronological order of the minor prophets (with the most ancient text being listed first) based on the Kingdoms they served is most commonly thought to be Jonah, Amos, and Hosea to the Northern Kingdom; Obadiah, Joel, Micah (primarily to Jerusalem but also to Samaria), Nahum, Habakkuk, and Zephaniah to the Southern Kingdom; and Haggai, Zechariah, and Malachi to the Jews returning to the Promised Land after the exile. The Northern Kingdom prophets are thought to fall chronologically between the Southern Kingdom prophets Joel and Micah, and thus the Book of Obadiah is believed to be the oldest minor prophet literature.

Throughout the Old Testament, there is this thread of the Seed-line that weaves through message after message. In addition to the references of Jesus as the Angel of the Lord and God, scholars list over 550 verses that have direct personal messianic predictions. The numbers vary based on prophecies being about Jesus' first or second coming or both. You don't want to forget to watch for the Anointed One as you read through these prophets. His anticipated presence is their greatest hope as they withstand intense persecution to call the people to repentance so that they will be ready to receive their Savior and live.

It helps to know the intended audiences of these prophets and the historical backgrounds of the messages in order to rightly interpret their words. Hosea and Amos preached mainly to the Northern Kingdom, Israel, with a focus on the evil King Jeroboam II and impending judgment due to the nation's idolatry. Micah, Joel, Zephaniah, and Habakkuk rebuked the Southern Kingdom, Judah, for their injustice and insensitivity to God's holy judgment. These Southern Kingdom prophets provide compelling arguments for national repentance. In the shortest book in the Old Testament, Obadiah prophesied Edom's destruction to encourage Judah that God had not forgotten His promises to avenge them as His children. The Book of Jonah tells the story of the prophet Jonah being commanded by God to show mercy to Israel's harsh enemy Nineveh by preaching a message of repentance. We learn that Jonah ran from God, repented after a near death experience in the belly of a big fish, preached to the evil city, and then became angry at God when the city repented. Nahum picks up the story of Nineveh, as Nahum predicted Nineveh's eventual demise at a time when Assyria was fiercely conquering many neighboring nations. Nahum's message would encourage Judah that God's righteousness would ultimately triumph. Nineveh fell in 612 B.C. Haggai prophesied to the exiled Jews during King Darius' reign and encouraged the building of the temple. Zechariah and Malachi also encouraged the Jewish remnant that God would continue to restore and rebuke His children as needed. I'll remind you again of this background as we read through each book in the coming days.

God faithfully raised up many voices in various areas and walks of life throughout Israel to warn His children of impending judgment, to encourage them of His restorative grace, and to prepare them to represent Him as they anticipated His promised Deliverer. When you read these messages one after another, you may see the many similarities in the themes, calls to repentance, and future promises. These similarities should remind you of the patience of a loving Father in repeatedly teaching the same lessons until His child gains understanding. God's lovingkindness stands out in these calls for His people to heed His Word and gain Life.

HOSEA

Week 30, Day 1

Read It All: Hosea 1-3
Read a Bit: Hosea 1-3

The Revelation in Summary

Hosea 1:2 — *When the LORD first spoke through Hosea, the LORD said to Hosea, "Go, take to yourself a wife of harlotry and have children of harlotry; for the land commits flagrant harlotry, forsaking the LORD."*

Hosea writes to the Northern Kingdom, Israel, during their last days just prior to the Assyrian invasion of Israel. Hosea even identified Assyria as the enemy that God would use to judge the nation. Hosea teaches God's faithful love of Israel in spite of her unfaithfulness. The evil King Jeroboam II was the primary Israelite king during Hosea's prophecy.

To dramatically convey His messages, God would have His prophets provide living illustrations of His indictment of the nations. Isaiah was told to go around stripped and barefoot for three years to demonstrate how Assyria would treat Egyptian captives (Isaiah 20). Ezekiel was told to symbolically lay siege to a brick he labeled Jerusalem and to lie on his left side for 390 days then on his right side for 40 days to model bearing the iniquity of Israel (Ezekiel 4). In the first three chapters of Hosea, we are shocked as God commands Hosea to take a wife of harlotry and have children with her. Hosea's family life would picture how Israel commits flagrant harlotry within God's household, yet God continues to love them.

Through Hosea, God clearly and repeatedly states His case against Israel and reveals their impending judgment. Ephraim is singled out in many of the accusations as Hosea calls the Northern Kingdom by its largest tribe. Hosea also refers to the people as Samaria for their capital city. Chapter 14 reveals that God still has hope for the people as He calls for their repentance and promises restoration for those that wisely discern that He is their Source of Life.

Week 30, Day 2

Read It All: Hosea 4-5
Read a Bit: Hosea 4-5

Integrity

Hosea 4:1 — *Listen to the word of the LORD, O sons of Israel, for the LORD has a case against the inhabitants of the land, because there is no faithfulness or kindness or knowledge of God in the land.*

Numerous young children and young adults have observed their mothers with boyfriends. Numerous young children and young adults have listened to their mothers entertaining and have heard the sounds of fornication through thin walls and tried to fall asleep or at least shut out the noises. Many today still live in single room dwellings with no privacy. Numerous young children and young adults have grown up wondering what love really looks and sounds like. It all seems so awkward and scary. Maybe even gross. In many situations, faithfulness or kindness are not representative of the couplings the young witness. The way of a woman with a man is confusing.

It is hard to believe that your mother would be sexually intimate with someone that she does not love. Little ones may not understand the limited options for adults, the sexual dangers and entrapments. Prostitution is mentioned in the Bible from Genesis to Revelation. According to the Bible, prostitution is a negative aspect of culture, despite what proponents of legalized prostitution assert. Prostitution is identified with God's enemies.

Sexual "freedom" where a woman may have a number of lovers is also addressed in the Bible. Most notably, in John's Gospel there is the woman at the well and the woman caught in adultery. Christ encourages them to repent and to find Life in Him. Being identified with Christ, the integrity of Christ, is the source of love. Sexual intimacy is only to be a part of covenant marriage, as it is the physical expression of the oneness inherent in the faithfulness of husband and wife. Sexual sin violates the covenant and the representation of Covenant God. Sexual sin compromises the Seed-line. Marriage is to represent Covenant God's love for His people, particularly Christ's love for the church.

Sadly, parents do not naturally take good care of their own children. And just as sadly, additional adults in the home do not necessarily improve the care. Mothering is hard work. Single parenting is hard work. Women get lonely or financially needy and forget that whomever they bring home will also be interacting with others, their children, in the home. God help us to guard Your integrity in our homes that we might provide the best place for our children to be safe and free to learn Your truth.

Week 30, Day 3

Read It All: Hosea 6-10
Read a Bit: Hosea 6-10

Dignity

Hosea 6:6-7 — *For I delight in loyalty rather than sacrifice, and in the knowledge of God rather than burnt offerings. But like Adam they have transgressed the covenant; there they have dealt treacherously against Me.*

During the summer of our sixth year of marriage, I asked Scott for a divorce. We were working long hours at different engineering firms in different parts of town and were developing different life goals. We were familiar with divorce because our parents were divorced, some multiple times, and it was the culture. I just thought better to divorce before children and before either of us would really feel bad about it. I was practical and scared.

You could say I had attachment issues. I grew up thinking my family was very close, so when I discovered my parents were having marital problems, I shifted into super-responsible and ultra-peacemaker mode. But I was a failure in controlling my realm, as my parents parted ways. I had always enjoyed activities with my dad, especially tennis and ice skating. I considered him a great friend. Then he basically disappeared. When I went away to college, leaving the state we lived in, I lost track of him. For a number of years I didn't even know where he lived or who his second and then third family were. I become a bit skeptical about love.

My husband Scott wasn't so skeptical. While I tried to break ties, he kept up our home and pampered me. While I tried to keep distant and be moody, he was considerate and seemed content . . . even happy. While I worked even longer hours, he came home and had dinner or a good snack ready for when I did finally arrive home. He didn't guilt me or overly baby me. He was just nice.

I realized after a few months that I had never really committed to Scott or to our marriage. I had married because it seemed right at the time and thought maybe Scott could make me feel secure again. I knew neither how to love nor to value covenant marriage. I didn't think about what marriage brought to others, only what it could offer me. One day after work, I was driving home, and I pulled to the side of the road and asked God to help me understand why He had made marriage. It was shortly after this that I was invited to a weekly Bible study that included personal lessons. The study was on the Gospel of Matthew, and I learned that Christ's teaching on marriage acknowledged that marriage is hard but that it is important for the community, children, church, and character. I learned that love is an act of the will more than an emotion. I discovered the value of commitment, the covenant.

I committed to represent God through the vows I had made to Scott Lewis Montgomery. This relieved a burden that I wasn't even aware existed between us, the burden I felt that we had to be perfect for one another. Shortly after that commitment, I noticed something else about our relationship. I was falling in love with my life partner.

Hosea's message is very personal to me, as I see myself in Gomer, refusing to be faithful to any one person. I see how I was missing the blessings of God for years because of my fear and detachment. I see how caught up with the culture I was. I see, as a professing Christian, what a confusion I was to others and how I belittled my husband, who was a new believer at the time. I'm surprised that God didn't destroy me right there. But God is loving. He restores. He knows my past and still loves me. This is my dignity.

Week 30, Day 4

Read It All: Hosea 11-13
Read a Bit: Hosea 11-13

Unity

Hosea 13:16 — *Samaria will be held guilty, for she has rebelled against her God. They will fall by the sword, their little ones will be dashed in pieces, and their pregnant women will be ripped open.*

Sadly, one of the things that unifies many women (university orientation programs say 1 of 4) is suffering sexual abuse. My first experience of sexual abuse was when visiting a family member and a cousin was repeatedly "inappropriate." I was young and embarrassed and never said a word. I also felt responsible, as I did like being noticed.

Some of the hardest ministry moments for me have been hearing from moms who are processing their daughters being sexually abused. You can encourage your loved ones to report abuse, but you also know how brave and hard it is to keep reliving the incident and fighting the legal battles. You also know how shaming it can be and that justice seems a rarity. Many cases involve alcohol, and that adds another level of guilt and what ifs. Please know that it is sexual abuse if there is any undesired sexual behavior by one person on another and that the abuse is wrong regardless of the alcohol factor. If you have suffered sexual abuse, you are a victim, not the culprit. The culprit is responsible for the abuse. Justice is to serve her victims.

In the Bible, God reveals tragic consequences of sexual abuse and immorality. He provides graphic, tragic details to warn His children not to belittle the dignity of another. Remember Tamar being called more righteous than Judah when Judah devalued the Seed-line and Tamar resorted to prostitution to convict Judah of his duplicity. Remember David's family disintegrating over the rape of another Tamar. Remember the murders that Jacob's sons committed following their sister Dinah's rape. In Hosea, God specifically calls the prophet to take a woman from harlotry as his wife, not only to portray God's love to those unfaithful to His character, but also to portray how horrific it is to profane the family of God with misuse, abuse, of our bodies. God reveals how the people of Israel have grossly defiled one another in choosing fleshly lusts over Holy God. Women, children, the family, a nation suffer as the people are debased.

Human trafficking has become a significant concern in our area in the last fifteen years. Statistics indicate that a neighboring city is one of the top five cities in the nation for trafficking, so our police departments are implementing task forces to address the issue, and area ministries are joining the battle. The hope is that people could be united in fighting many of the crimes linked to trafficking, such as child pornography, kidnapping, and marketing illegal drugs. But there is no unity against these evils, and the trafficking continues to be big business in our area and in many parts of the world. Awhile back I was making announcements to groups about an anti-human trafficking training when just before the announcement, the leader of the group I was visiting pulled me aside and whispered that I was not to mention pornography or to guilt his group about sexual sin. This shook me up. I get the desire to be visitor "friendly," but not at the cost of obvious truth. He was right, human trafficking and pornography are master business partners. It's hard to combat one without bringing up the other. But he was wrong, guilt (awareness of sin) isn't the enemy. Guilt is good when it leads to repentance and life change that delivers many from destruction, especially children. We don't sin in a vacuum.

God sees what is done in secret. The prophets have told us that the Day of the Lord is coming. There will be a uniting, albeit in judgment, as all bow before our Maker when He returns. God will avenge the abused. Seek refuge.

Week 30, Day 5

Read It All: Hosea 14
Read a Bit: Hosea 14

Priority

Hosea 14:2 — *Take words with you and return to the LORD. Say to Him, "Take away all iniquity and receive us graciously, that we may present the fruit of our lips."*

Hosea is called by God to love someone who is bent on destroying themselves. We see the horrific decline of Gomer over time, the impact on her children, and the cost to the family. I don't know how Hosea doesn't have his own pity party and break down when he must go and buy his wife back for half the going slave price and bring her home.

I know many today who have bought back family members that are caught up in addictions or bad relationships. I see mothers who keep praying and praying for a child to return to God. Moms are hurting as they watch their children make one bad choice after another, oftentimes developing an addiction to help them "numb out" or allowing themselves to be oppressed in a hateful relationship. Many Gomers exist today, but I'm not sure there are Hoseas that represent God's delivering love for the defiled.

I thank God for the men and women that are the Hoseas in this world. Children everywhere need to see your extraordinary faithfulness to covenant marriage and your commitment to family. We need wisdom to know how to best help our loved ones without enabling them, we need to confront sin with His good truth, and we need encouragement when there is no sign of restored life ahead. The Hoseas in this world have enough troubles without others shaming them about their loved ones or saying they would know what to do in such hard circumstances. Only God knows what is in our hearts. God is generous, faithful, and sacrificial, as well as a disciplinarian to the undeserving. We should all be thankful that He is Hosea to us.

JOEL, AMOS, & OBADIAH

Week 31, Day 1

Read It All: Joel 1-3
Read a Bit: Joel 1-3

The Revelation in Summary

Joel 2:1 — *"Blow a trumpet in Zion, and sound an alarm on My holy mountain! Let all the inhabitants of the land tremble, for the day of the LORD is coming; surely it is near, . . ."*

Have you ever experienced an invasion of insects in your house or lawn? My neighbor had a couple of big dogs, and one year her home was invaded by ticks. She kept a really clean house, but she just couldn't get ahead of the ticks. She said they were lodged in her dry wall in places. I took her word for this and didn't feel led to go see for myself.

Scott and I have had summers of locusts in the yard. They eat everything, and we go crazy running a locust safari as we keep trying to preserve the plant life. We notice the infestation when we see black crickets on the tall grasses lining the walkway in front. If we don't do something right then, the next thing we notice is that our peace lilies have huge chomp marks, and the sides of the house and screened room are covered with ginormous yellow and green grasshopper locust things. Ugh.

I'm squeamish around the locusts at first, closing my eyes as I crush them with a clay pot base on newspapers. But as I catch sight of more and more of my enemy, I get aggressive. After two or three squishes, I get out the gardening shears and start cutting them in half from a distance. One jumped on Scott's face one time when he missed it with his first attempt at a kill. This resulted in nightmares. I postponed kissing him for a week.

The locusts are horribly destructive to life. They can wipe out entire crops and thus a family's livelihood. The invasions can lead to famine. The prophet Joel had probably witnessed many such invasions in his day, as it is believed that locust plagues were frequent in the Near East for thousands of years. Joel relates the Day of the Lord, God's just judgment on unrepentant sin, to a severe locust invasion. He knew the people could relate to this analogy and should respond accordingly with repentance to escape this judgment of God. Joel knows he is delivering a message of life or death from a God Who lovingly longs for mankind to choose Life.

Week 31, Day 2

Read It All: Amos 1-2
Read a Bit: Amos 1-2

The Revelation in Summary

Amos 2:16 — *"Even the bravest among the warriors will flee naked in that day,"* declares the LORD.

The message of Amos, a herdsman from the small town of Tekoa, targets in on the Northern Kingdom of Israel's social injustice. When I write 'targets in," I mean that literally. If you took a map of the area and traced, in order named, the cities warned by Amos about their transgressions against God and their impending judgment, you would subsequently draw a target that spirals inward to finally pinpoint Israel. Reading about all your neighbors being judged and then realizing that the judgments were getting closer and closer to your door as the message continues must have been bone-chilling for Amos' audience. They had to begin to realize they could not escape the approaching storm.

I've survived several hurricanes. It amazes me how quickly I forget the absolute dread that descends on a community as everyone hovers over the weather reports waiting to see the latest hurricane track. In 2017, we survived Hurricane Irma, but I've never felt so helpless. People, that had lived in Tampa for years, were calling us asking advice on whether they should evacuate or not. You would think this would be an easy "yes," because the hurricane data was pretty straightforward, much like an Old Testament prophet's prediction, but there are so many factors to consider. Will you be able to get gas? How is the traffic? No one should ride out a hurricane on the side of the road. How far do you need to go to really get out of the way? I've had family evacuate from one side of the state only to end up in worse danger from tornadoes spawned as the hurricane made landfall. Oftentimes, the middle of the state suffers more damage than our Bay Area.

With Hurricane Irma, by the time we decided to board up and hunker down, there was no wood to purchase at all the large lumber yards and home improvement stores. This made us a little concerned. Scott cut up our ping pong table and boarded up one room so we could ride out the storm there. Neighbors loaned us some of their scraps, so one half of the house was eerily dark as we awaited our fate.

We were out of electricity almost a week. That equates to some really hot, humid days, gasoline shortages, and empty shelves at the store, as delivery trucks could not make it into the state. The greatest inconvenience at our home was no water except what we had stored in containers before the storm, as we are on a well, requiring an electric pump. I like taking a daily shower, especially when I don't have air conditioning. Oh well. Some of our friends have generators, and so we were reliant on others for basic comforts. I didn't realize how dependent I was on cell phone service and the Internet to feel secure. The storm that seemed to target us led to our turning again to the Lord God Almighty for our greatest comfort. Thank you, God, for Irma, our reminder.

Week 31, Day 3

Read It All: Amos 3-6
Read a Bit: Amos 3-6

Integrity

Amos 5:10 — *They hate him who reproves in the gate, and they abhor him who speaks with integrity.*

One of Israel's most significant transgressions is despising the wisdom of those with integrity. Amos strongly rebukes the people for the injustices they are imposing on one another as they refuse to uphold what is good. Amos tells the people that the prudent keep silent because the society is so evil. What is the point of sharing truth that will be ignored? God has targeted Israel because of their lack of integrity. He promises to deliver His grace to a remnant of people who value His character but to harshly judge the majority who are longing for darkness.

Reading the minor prophets with their continual descriptions of judgment can be convicting and tiring. God uses every communication technique—questions and answers, word pictures, unusual messengers, visions, skilled orators—to drive home His fatherly warnings. Yet no one seems to hear Him. These prophetic books can be frustrating. They are also strangely comforting as they reveal how intentional God is regarding justice. There is no love apart from justice, as justice validates the worth of each person, and love is jealous for another's worth. God's love is a main theme of these prophets, and they faithfully proclaim His love to be consuming, holy, intimate, eternal, and restorative.

Reading the prophets makes me long for the Gospels. I long for the Seed to appear and demonstrate the character of God on earth, integrity in action. I have taught the Bible straight through several times, and I can sense the tension, the anticipation for the Gospels, particularly when we are partway through the minor prophets. It is time for Messiah!

Amos readies the heart for Messiah, as His speeches beautifully contrast the character of God with the impurity of humanity. Would Messiah really reside with us? Can Messiah truly right so many wrongs? Does God love us so sacrificially? What does a rebuilt soul even resemble?

For thus says the LORD to the house of Israel, "Seek Me that you may live." Amos 5:4

Week 31, Day 4

Read It All: Amos 7-9
Read a Bit: Amos 7-9

Dignity

Amos 9:12 — *In that day I will raise up the fallen booth of David, and wall up its breaches; I will also raise up its ruins and rebuild it as in the days of old; . . .*

> *Lord, make me to know my end and what is the extent of my days;*
> *Let me know how transient I am.* Psalm 39:4

Humankind is an eternal lot. Each of us is set forever with eternity on our hearts. The great question is our afterlife address. Scripture reveals that there is a place of rest and a place of torment. Placement in His presence is through belief in His Son, His glorious redemptive plan. We acknowledge our need of peace with God and accept His merciful provision. Pride, self-righteousness, buries us in living torment. God, Your mercy is our "soul" hope.

I'm concerned for family. Just a weekend with several of my family is a grim reminder of the brevity of life shadowed by the onset of dementia. I grieve our lack of connection with so many in our family and the loss of time and resources to do anything about this distance that is due to miles in some cases and differing value systems in other relationships. I grieve that many family members do not take refuge in Christ. I thank God for loving caregivers who know that these may be the last moments of safeguarding kindness and dignity before the judgment. What else can we do?

I've been to numerous funerals where my dear friends said goodbye to the corruptible bodies of their parents. Where did the years go? My friends are comforted by affirmations of their loved one's salvation. When you peer at the end of an earthly life, the stuff in the basement and closets is irrelevant. The eternal matter is this, are you right with your Maker? Are you resting in His arms? Do you know the Psalm 3 Lifter of our heads?

> *Behold, You have made my days as handbreadths, and my lifetime as nothing in Your sight; surely every man at his best is a mere breath. Surely every man walks about as a phantom; surely they make an uproar for nothing; He amasses riches and does not know who will gather them.* Psalm 39:5-6

Hear Amos and take note. God's judgment is unavoidable.

Week 31, Day 5

Read It All: Obadiah (no chapters, only 21 verses)
Read a Bit: Obadiah

The Revelation in Summary

Obadiah 18 — *Then the house of Jacob will be a fire and the house of Joseph a flame; but the house of Esau will be as stubble. And they will set them on fire and consume them, so that there will be no survivor of the house of Esau.*

Obadiah is about feuding nations: Israel and Edom. Israel's forefather, Jacob, had cheated Edom's forefather, Esau, out of Esau's blessing from their father, Isaac. This blessing linked the young men to the Seed of the woman and the inheritance as God's children in the Seed-line. In Genesis 25:34, the reader learns that Jacob valued the Seed-line far more than his brother Esau, as Esau sold his birthright to Jacob for a bowl of stew. Valuing the Seed-line, even doing so treacherously towards your brother, indicates belief in the promises of God.

The hatred between the brothers is the subject of numerous Bible passages. God's judgment on the brothers is based on the value they place on the Seed-line of their father. Jacob valued the Seed-line even though he was known as a deceiver. He recognized that the promised Seed was his only hope before Holy God for Life. The Bible affirms that God loved Jacob but hated Esau (Romans 9:13).

Edom became the enemy of Israel, and Obadiah records God's message regarding this enemy, because they would rejoice when their brother Jacob (Israel) was defeated by other nations. The book is short and to the point. Edom is doomed.

I have two brothers who are, as people say, polar opposites. One of my brothers lives in the city in Washington, D.C. and the other in the country in Madison, Florida. They both love the outdoors, but that is where the similarity ends. One is an office executive, the other a retired police captain. One reads Forbes, the other Jeep journals. One has cats, the other dogs. . . . Diversity in the family.

My D.C. brother's birthday is in January. One year, I got to laughing at myself as I bought a card that said, "Sisters are from Venus and brothers from Uranus" and sent it to the D.C. brother signed from my other brother. Is it forgery if no one presses charges? I thought this incredibly funny, but no one ever said anything to me about it. Maybe they never figured it out.

I realize now that it probably isn't wise to instigate any tension between your brothers.

When I read about family in the Bible, I realize that it is no little thing to get along as family. Some of the most tragic Bible stories have to do with family, particularly brothers at odds. This was true even for the Lord Jesus Christ: *"For not even His brothers were believing in Him"* (John 7:5).

God created family to secure an inheritance of loving provision and transmission of truth. God created family to teach love and forgiveness, faithfulness through the generations, to reveal unity and hope. God refers to Himself as Father because the head of a family should equate to life and love. For those who do not have an earthly family that represents God's loving presence, He reveals that the body of believers can be the true family.

And it was reported to Him, "Your mother and Your brothers are standing outside, wishing to see You." But He answered and said to them, "My mother and My brothers are these who hear the word of God and do it." Luke 8:20-22

The family has been under attack for years. In America, we are redefining the family. There is a loss of reverence for the home, which equates to a loss of community and security for all people. As we celebrate members of our family, their birthdays and anniversaries, may we remember to pray for the family. God is glorified in families that love His truth and apply His teaching in their homes.

JONAH, MICAH, NAHUM, HABAKKUK, ZEPHANIAH

Week 32, Day 1

Read It All: Jonah 1-4
Read a Bit: Jonah 1-4

The Revelation in Summary

Jonah 1:1-2 — *The word of the* LORD *came to Jonah the son of Amittai saying, "Arise, go to Nineveh the great city and cry against it, for their wickedness has come up before Me."*

Jonah is a widely shared fish tale. There are so many commentaries, children's books, games, and movies on Jonah. It is an easy story to understand due to its straight-forward narrative and picturesque writing style. It is a highly relatable account too, as who hasn't run from God or pouted over their enemy's success?

Jonah is told to warn Nineveh of God's judgment. Instead, Jonah fled from the Lord's presence, going in the opposite direction of Nineveh, but God was present wherever Jonah went and sent a great storm endangering many lives to redirect Jonah back to His mission for the prophet. This redirection involved a really large fish and some time in darkness and prayer for Jonah.

Jonah did go to Nineveh after being vomited out of the belly of the great fish. Jonah preached in Nineveh, and then the people of the city repented and God relented concerning their judgment. Jonah was greatly displeased instead of rejoicing over his "successful street ministry." He confessed his own anger over God being slow to anger and abundant in lovingkindness. Jonah confessed that he wasn't pleased with God relenting about the calamity that Jonah believed Nineveh deserved.

God used a plant to give Jonah another lesson on control issues, heartlessness, and self-righteousness. The reader does not find out Jonah's response to God's teaching, but the book does reveal the extreme disparity between the heart of man and the mercy of God.

When I first started leading Women's Ministry at a large church, there was a lady who really wanted the ministry to take off quickly and to be made a greater priority for the pastors. She was so frustrated with my not changing the "male-dominated" culture fast enough. We had differing philosophies on the priority of the ministry and on leadership. I loved and admired the staff at my church and saw wisdom in the church leadership making other areas of ministry more of a priority than an official Women's Ministry. One night after an event, this lady was voicing her frustrations about me to me. I struggled not to rudely laugh uncontrollably, because her "bad" word for me that she kept repeating amidst her rebukes was "humble": "You are just too humble, Jodie!" She had no idea that what she was actually doing was reminding me that God was faithfully answering my prayers, as I had been continually praying for humility. I did not want to be this overbearing woman, ungrateful for the opportunity to serve and grow a Women's Ministry. I understood her frustration in the process of changing a culture, but my "humility" was not a bad thing. She should have jumped on another one of my character traits, like overanalyzing. Our plans and representation of God must align with His character to glorify Him.

Nineveh was the capital of Assyria, and this mighty nation did conquer the Northern Kingdom, Israel. God used the repentant Nineveh to judge His children. It is believed that if Jonah had not gone to Nineveh and preached repentance that Nineveh would have been a much crueler enemy when they defeated Israel. Years later, Nineveh's reputation was back to the wickedness noted before Jonah's mission trip. Nahum describes Assyria's evil in later years and their impending judgment. God knows the big picture and disciplines, judges, and directs in a way that is slow to anger, abundant in lovingkindness, and merciful. Praise God.

Week 32, Day 2

Read It All: Micah 1-7
Read a Bit: Micah 1-7

The Revelation in Summary

Micah 3:11 — *Her leaders pronounce judgment for a bribe, her priests instruct for a price and her prophets divine for money. Yet they lean on the LORD saying, "Is not the LORD in our midst? Calamity will not come upon us."*

Micah pronounces God's judgment on the capital cities in Judah and Israel, primarily focusing on Jerusalem. The book provides a lot of details on why God is judging the people. God hates oppressors. Verse after verse reveals the injustice of the leaders and the wealthy in the land. God exposes their covetousness, arrogance, iniquity, and sheer meanness. In God's rebukes, the reader hears His love for the oppressed. His indictments call out those who are bringing calamity on the families in the land because of greed. God promises to bring calamity fully on the oppressors' heads. There is no love without an intense commitment to justice and defense of the weak. True love is jealous for the well-being of the loved. The opposite of love isn't hate, it is apathy. Love hates those who destroy life. Love cares.

Micah 5:2 provides the prophecy of the eternal One who will be Ruler being from Bethlehem. This prophecy is quoted often at Christmas. It is another fulfilled data point that anchors our faith. The prophecy seems rather randomly placed when you are reading straight through Micah, as if the author needed a break from focusing on judgment, so he looked up and saw the eternal Hope. Micah says that this Ruler is from long ago, from the days of eternity.

God's commitment to fulfill His covenant with the line of Abraham and David is central to Micah's message. In the midst of judgment, God continues to remind the people that He will provide hope through a great future for the remnant that takes refuge in Him. The Seed will appear from Bethlehem and will shepherd His flock. God is faithful to always provide hope and direction to those who will hear and heed His Words.

> *He has told you, O man, what is good; and what does the LORD require of you but to do justice, to love kindness, and to walk humbly with your God?* Micah 6:8

Week 32, Day 3

Read It All: Nahum 1-3
Read a Bit: Nahum 1-3

The Revelation in Summary

Nahum 1:3 — *The LORD is slow to anger and great in power, and the LORD will by no means leave the guilty unpunished.*

Nahum is different from all the other minor prophets because his prophesy is totally fulfilled relatively quickly after He speaks. As you read the details of Nineveh's judgment and complete ruin, dwell on the fact that each of the prophet's words is already, completely, fully, completely accomplished. God spoke through Nahum, and about fifty years later, Nineveh fell to the Medes. God had used mighty Assyria (Nineveh) to conquer the Northern Kingdom of Israel, and then He wiped out Assyria for their cruelty in conquering the Jewish people. God will by no means leave the guilty unpunished. God controls the history of all nations.

The word "refuge" is used twice in Nahum:

> *The Lord is good, a stronghold in the day of trouble, and He knows those who take refuge in Him.* Nahum 1:7

> *You too will become drunk, You will be hidden. You too will search for a refuge from the enemy.* Nahum 3:11

In the first usage of "refuge," there is protection and deliverance, as the Lord is good to the one who takes refuge in Him. In the second usage, refuge is sought to escape an enemy by someone who is not seeking God but rather is still aligned with God's enemy, refusing to see God's goodness as the source of refuge.

Through the ages, though has God revealed Himself as good, many have doubted His Word. We look at the evil in the world and blame God. But God didn't create the evil in the world. Everything He created was good. He allowed mankind to rule on this earth, and the outcome of this rule is sometimes good but also great evil. Sometimes it seems that the evil wins.

Those of us who are Gentiles also tend to see ourselves as Nineveh instead of Judah. We recognize cruelty within our hearts, and we've had our Jonah visits that resulted in a short-lived revival. We think, like Jonah, that it is in our best interest to run from an angry God.

If we pause long enough to listen to His voice through reading His Word, we learn that He longs for us to come to Him. He promises to show mercy on those who believe in His redeeming power and His willingness to redeem. He loves us and longs for us to choose life. Our refuge awaits us.

Week 32, Day 4

Read It All: Habakkuk 1-3
Read a Bit: Habakkuk 1-3

The Revelation in Summary

Habakkuk 3:17 — *Though the fig tree should not blossom and there be no fruit on the vines, though the yield of olive should fail and the fields produce no food, though the flock should be cut off from the fold and there be no cattle in the stalls, yet I will exult in the LORD, I will rejoice in the God of my salvation.*

Even prophets feel the need to ask God questions at times. Habakkuk records his inquiries with the God of the Universe and God's frank answers that confound the prophet. I love reading this question and answer session. In summary:

Habakkuk asks, *"How long? My kinsmen are evil and the land is full of violence and strife while the law is ignored."*

God answers, *"Not long. You will get to see Me raise up the Chaldeans to discipline Judah."*

Habakkuk says, *"What!? You are Holy! Don't You see the Chaldeans are even more wicked than Judah? They hook people and drag them away."*

God responds, *"Let me give you the details so you may prepare."*

Habakkuk records the vision, listing the woes that will certainly come. As Habakkuk reviews what he has written, he then records a prayer, acknowledging that he fears God as he should. Habakkuk worships the Lord in a poetic prayer and cries out for mercy.

Habakkuk is now set to wait on the Lord, knowing the invasion will happen, but with the comfort of realizing God is fully in control and, though the prophet trembles, God gives strength and salvation such that Habakkuk also rejoices in God's plan.

Week 32, Day 5

Read It All: Zephaniah 1-3
Read a Bit: Zephaniah 1-3

The Revelation in Summary

Zephaniah 1:14 — *Near is the great day of the LORD, near and coming very quickly; listen, the day of the LORD! In it the warrior cries out bitterly.*

"The day of the Lord" is a phrase frequently used by the prophets. This day of the Lord is not a twenty-four-hour period but an event that encompasses God's judgment of His enemies and His restoration of Israel. Zephaniah describes the day as a day of wrath, trouble, distress, destruction, desolation, darkness, gloom, clouds, thick darkness, trumpet, battle cry, and distress on men. The day isn't just dark but in thick darkness.

This is when God makes a complete end of all the inhabitants of the earth. It appears that the nations will be gathered together and separated based on their humility in seeking the Lord. Most of the inhabitants are doomed to be abandoned by God. The word "abandoned" is shocking, as God has been so present with His people through years of family dysfunction.

Zephaniah pronounces woes on Jerusalem for her rebellion and defilement. She has not been teachable or trusting. Zephaniah specifically rebukes the leaders, judges, prophets, priests, and corrupt. God's wrath is burning and will devour many, but God will leave a humble and lowly remnant because they will take refuge in the name of the LORD. These verses are some of my favorite in the prophets' writings:

> *Shout for joy, O daughter of Zion! Shout in triumph, O Israel! Rejoice and exult with all your heart, O daughter of Jerusalem! The LORD has taken away His judgments against you, He has cleared away your enemies. The King of Israel, the LORD is in your midst; You will fear disaster no more. In that day it will be said to Jerusalem: "Do not be afraid, O Zion; do not let your hands fall limp. The LORD your God is in your midst, a victorious warrior. He will exult over you with joy, He will be quiet in His love, He will rejoice over you with shouts of joy.* Zephaniah 3:14-17

For a remnant, the day of the LORD is an anticipated joy. His refuge delights.

HAGGAI, ZECHARIAH, MALACHI

These are the prophets who spoke to the Jews returning to the land following the exile. These prophets supported Ezra's and Nehemiah's ministries.

Week 33, Day 1

Read It All: Haggai 1-2
Read a Bit: Haggai 1-2

The Revelation in Summary

Haggai 1:1, 7 — *In the second year of Darius the king, on the first day of the sixth month, the word of the LORD came by the prophet Haggai to Zerubbabel the son of Shealtiel, governor of Judah, and to Joshua the son of Jehozadak, the high priest, saying, "Thus says the LORD of hosts, 'This people says, "The time has not come, even the time for the house of the LORD to be rebuilt"'. . . . Thus says the LORD of hosts, "Consider your ways! Go up to the mountains, bring wood and rebuild the temple, that I may be pleased with it and be glorified," says the LORD.*

Haggai starts off by identifying the time period and that the people are still under the authority of a Gentile king. Yet the LORD is directing the people to rebuild His house in Jerusalem. We know from other Old Testament books that the Gentile king has endorsed this building, so the delay in building is due to the Israelites' heart condition. The people have prioritized building for themselves rather than as God directed. This is not going well. God is judging them, sending calamity, for forgetting His house. God values a home with them.

There is no "happily ever after" at the end of Haggai. The reader does not know what the people will do at this point in the story. Maybe Zechariah and Malachi will more fully reveal whether exile resulted in a heart change for the children of God.

The Lord sends an encouraging word to the people through Haggai. The temple may not look as glorious as the former temple, but they were to take courage and trust that if they repented and recommitted to doing His will, then He would shake the heavens and the earth to establish Israel's leadership in the land.

Week 33, Day 2

Read It All: Zechariah 1-6
Read a Bit: Zechariah 1-6

The Revelation in Summary

Zechariah 1:3 — *Therefore say to them, "Thus says the LORD of hosts, 'Return to Me,' declares the LORD of hosts, 'that I may return to you,' says the LORD of hosts."*

Zechariah is the message of spiritual renewal for Israel. This renewal is based on how willing the people are to return to God. Through visions, God guides Zechariah to encourage the people with several messages of restoration for Israel and vengeance on those who have led the people astray. God is watching to see if the people will choose to return to Him.

I tend to be a bit of a klutz. I'll open a cabinet door in front of me, drop something from the cabinet, bend down to pick up whatever I dropped, and quickly straighten back up only to hit my head on the door I left opened. I'll pull out the garden hose to water the flowers on the patio, pull hard to get its kinks out, and trip over the extra hose I have dangling from my arm. In making my bed, I'll back up and slip on the pillows I just placed on the floor. I can give example after example. Turning around for me is difficult. I tend to go in one direction, my way, which is down.

"Return" is a significant word in Scripture. We are destined to return to dust after our years on this earth are done. Throughout their history together, God promises to return to His chosen people. Israel repeatedly asks to return to Egypt when they are unhappy with God's provision in the desert. And God commands us continually to return to Him for life. He longs for us to return to Him.

To return implies that there was a previous turn in the opposite direction from the place where God and humanity first came together. The previous turn must have been away from God. This doesn't surprise God. He knows our hearts and knows that ever since the fruit in the garden, we have chosen to go our own way even when our surroundings were ideal.

In the Law, God gave insight into how we might best imitate Him and enjoy fellowship with Him. After providing all the details on what His people should do to please Him, He acknowledged that we won't do what He says. This doesn't end our relationship. Even when we run from Him, He tells us that we will eventually cry out for help. He promises to deliver us whenever we turn back, return, to Him.

As a mom, I always have an ear poised to listen for my children's calls. I do not want them to cry out for help; I'd rather their days go smoothly. But when they do cry out, I will do whatever is in my power to help them. This isn't to build me up in some self-ingratiating way, it is because I love them. It takes heart to return.

Week 33, Day 3

Read It All: Zechariah 7-8
Read a Bit: Zechariah 7-8

Integrity

Zechariah 8:3 — *Thus says the Lord, "I will return to Zion and will dwell in the midst of Jerusalem. Then Jerusalem will be called the City of Truth, and the mountain of the Lord of hosts will be called the Holy Mountain."*

God partially fulfills these words within four hundred years of Zechariah's prophecy in the birth of Christ Jesus, but there is a future aspect to the prophecy when Christ returns again and the city and mountains are renamed. Zechariah lists many prophecies regarding the coming Seed and the promised Kingdom. Clearly, this is the hope for the nation.

These prophecies would be pretty meaningless if God's character were unknown to the people. God's integrity is essential for hope to be ignited through promises of future restoration. Israel knew the faithfulness of God. They were just coming out of a 70-year exile at the instruction of a pagan king who had been moved by God to allow the people's return at just the time the prophets had stated. This wasn't the first time God had disciplined Israel just as He said He would. There had been an ark, an exodus, and a wilderness excursion for 40 years. The prophets had pinpointed seasons of drought and famine, victories and defeats, and the stops and starts of plagues. God was faithful to His word.

Strangely, there is comfort in a Father Who disciplines His children. The discipline shows the Father cares for His children and their futures. The discipline reveals the Father's presence and involvement. The Good Father raises His children to be a blessing to others. The Good Father watches, directs, and redirects. The Good Father doesn't abandon His people but dwells in their midst.

Week 33, Day 4

Read It All: Zechariah 9-14
Read a Bit: Zechariah 10, 13-14

Dignity

Zechariah 9:9 — *Rejoice greatly, O daughter of Zion! Shout in triumph, O daughter of Jerusalem! Behold, your king is coming to you; He is just and endowed with salvation, humble, and mounted on a donkey, even on a colt, the foal of a donkey.*

In Christ's sufferings, there is restored dignity to all humanity.

> *I said to them, "If it is good in your sight, give me my wages; but if not, never mind!" So they weighed out thirty shekels of silver as my wages. Then the Lord said to me, "Throw it to the potter, that magnificent price at which I was valued by them." So I took the thirty shekels of silver and threw them to the potter in the house of the Lord.* Zechariah 11:12-13

> *I will pour out on the house of David and on the inhabitants of Jerusalem, the Spirit of grace and of supplication, so that they will look on Me whom they have pierced; and they will mourn for Him, as one mourns for an only son, and they will weep bitterly over Him like the bitter weeping over a firstborn.* Zechariah 12:10

> *In that day a fountain will be opened for the house of David and for the inhabitants of Jerusalem, for sin and for impurity.* Zechariah 13:1

> *"Awake, O sword, against My Shepherd, and against the man, My Associate," declares the Lord of hosts. "Strike the Shepherd that the sheep may be scattered; and I will turn My hand against the little ones."* Zechariah 13:7

Know this:

> *As to this salvation, the prophets who prophesied of the grace that would come to you made careful searches and inquiries, seeking to know what person or time the Spirit of Christ within them was indicating as He predicted the sufferings of Christ and the glories to follow. It was revealed to them that they were not serving themselves, but you, in these things which now have been announced to you through those who preached the gospel to you by the Holy Spirit sent from heaven—things into which angels long to look.* 1 Peter 11:10-12

Thank you, God, for the prophets. Give us eyes to see and ears to hear their heart cries.

Week 33, Day 5

Read It All: Malachi 1-4
Read a Bit: Malachi 1-4

The Revelation in Summary

Malachi 1:6 — *"A son honors his father, and a servant his master. Then if I am a father, where is My honor? And if I am a master, where is My respect?" says the Lord of hosts to you, O priests who despise My name. But you say, "How have we despised Your name?"*

Malachi is the final Old Testament book. So before we close out the reading of the Old Testament, let's review His Story thus far.

The previous 16 prophetic books warned the Jewish people that they would be judged for their rejection of God. The Northern Kingdom, in fulfillment of prophecy, was conquered in 722 BC by Assyria. The Southern Kingdom was exiled in 586 BC by Babylon. Before Judah was exiled, Jeremiah predicted their return to the land after 70 years in exile. Isaiah predicted the decree that King Cyrus would make to return the Jews to the land. Daniel predicted the fall of the Babylonians and the Persian leaders that would replace Babylon.

In this period of transition for Israel, Samaritan people repopulated the area, establishing mixed religions in Israel, as Jews remaining in the land married Gentiles. Zerubbabel led the return to the land, Haggai and Zechariah encouraged rebuilding the temple that Messiah would teach in, Ezra led reforms by rebuilding the people with God's Word, and Nehemiah rebuilt the city walls.

Malachi gives God's last appeal for Judah to repent. There will be 400 years of silence, no additional prophets for years after Malachi. God's assurances of love as He questioned the people through Malachi must have been affirming as the people anticipate the Christ.

Malachi confronts the people for holding God's name in contempt, losing sight of their own sin, ignoring the teaching of God's Word, divorcing the wife of their youth, breaking three covenants (priesthood, Law, and marriage), corrupting the tithe, and forgetting that the Lord Jesus Christ is the ultimate summation of the Law. Surely it is time to repent and take His offer of refuge.

One more note on Malachi. Many know this book solely for the verse that says God hates divorce. This verse challenged me to work on my marriage, but for many, this is an overwhelmingly hard verse as they are divorced. We hear that divorce isn't the unforgivable sin, but we see so many consequences associated with the breakup of families that we hurt. Many in my family have experienced divorce and I'm very thankful for a mom who purposed, though divorced from my dad, to teach her three children to honor their father. This freed us from having constant conflict over the parents. It also modeled goodness. Mom always said our dad deserved respect for his military service and for fathering three great children. She didn't let their divorce embitter us against our dad. She taught us to respect others even when that is difficult.

There is so much all of us can do to maximize restoration in any relationship. Choosing to be a peacemaker blesses others. God's way of forgiveness restores dignity to a broken home. Divorces happen. His children may recommitment to take marriage vows very seriously, to encourage all marriages, to honor the family, and to forgive. Oftentimes, forgiveness starts with believing God has forgiven us.

REST TIME

Week 34, Days 1-5

Micah 2:10 — *Arise and go, for this is no place of rest because of the uncleanness that brings on destruction, a painful destruction.*

The minor prophets remind the reader that God uses a variety of people from diverse backgrounds to proclaim His great Word. God's strong warnings to Israel are enveloped with hope as He also conveys His plans for the Last Days. His revelation of His final judgment and ultimate peace for Israel is vital in encouraging the remnant of faithful believers to endure the dark days that Israel is experiencing due to their abandonment of the One True God. I treasure these detailed prophecies of Christ's first and second comings as I have heard about the fulfillment of the prophecies of His first coming and these fulfillments build my faith in the faithfulness of God to fulfill His Word regarding my Messiah's second coming. Come, Lord Jesus, come.

Journal any thoughts you wish to record at this point in your reading.

Grace and Truth
were realized
through
Jesus Christ
John 1:17

NEW TESTAMENT

During the almost 400 years between the Old and New Testament writings, many events happened that would ultimately better prepare the way for the transmission of the Gospel message around the world. The Greeks defeated the Persians in 331 BC and ruled for 164 years. During this time the Old Testament was translated into Greek (known as the Septuagint) by Hebrew scholars; Syrian King Antiochus Epiphanes (as prophesied by Daniel) defiled the temple and killed many Jews, causing the Jews to hide many of the ancient writings and to establish colonies of scribes to preserve God's Word; and the Romans became powerful.

The Bible was written in three languages (Aramaic, Hebrew, and Greek). The New Testament was authored in Greek, the language of the majority at the time of Christ's birth. The Hebrew religious leaders at that time were described as self-righteous and condemning rather than as messengers of God's mercy and grace. The New Testament writers changed the culture, as led by the Lord Jesus Christ, by showing the love of God to those not considered righteous by the so-called "religious." These writers reveal that to believe in Jesus is to be identified with His righteousness, which is the real fulfillment of the Law and the means of reconciliation with Holy God. Righteousness is a gift from God through the Son, not based on performance or works.

The three Herods[17], empowered by their connections to Rome, established rule in the Promised Land and initiated large building projects. Herod the Great's temple in Jerusalem became a world wonder. The Romans improved and expanded a system of roads to optimize trade, and there were numerous cultural factors that brought many to the Holy City. Unbeknownst to all but God and a few faithful believers anticipating His Word, the time was right for the incarnation and proclamation of Christ.

The New Testament or New Covenant from God compiles the writings on the life of Christ and the establishment of His Bride, the Church. The fulfillment of the Old Testament is found in the New, so the messages in the New present Jesus Christ of Nazareth as the Seed of the Woman that redeems. The New Covenant life of those who believe in Jesus as Christ is described in great detail in the New Testament. The role of the church in sharing the Gospel message and preparing His people for His return is also explained. The writings reveal a new joy resulting from God's Spirit residing in the believer and also a groaning by believers as they long for His second coming and the absolute demise of the enemy Satan. The teachings that were considered mysterious in the Old are now beginning to come to light in the New. Jesus' incarnation, life, death, and resurrection gloriously influenced the world, as humanity's means of full reconciliation with God was finished. The hope of a bodily resurrection and an eternal kingdom is more conceivable than ever. The believer is told by God to persevere and represent Him well while faithfully awaiting His second coming. May we help many be prepared to see Him face to face as we also cry, "Come, Lord Jesus, come!"

---

[17]   Herod the Great, ruler when Jesus was born; Herod Tetrarch, his son who killed John the Baptist and interrogated Jesus; and Herod Agrippa, who participated in the trial of Paul.

NEW TESTAMENT GOSPELS

The New Testament text opens with four books known as the Gospels. These writings provide biographical accounts of the Lord Jesus Christ. The books are grounded in Old Testament revelation as the authors assert that Jesus is "God with us." The Gospels introduce us to the Word made flesh and the Holy Spirit of God. We also meet the apostles, the eyewitnesses of Jesus' fulfillment of the Old Testament anticipations. The apostles are anointed to present Jesus. They represent the Jewish remnant that was preserved through the ages, ready to recognize Messiah and deliver the Good News to all that His Light had dawned.

The Gospel writers long for the hearer to realize the truth of Jesus as Savior and to believe in Him, taking refuge in His provision of life. Telling others of Christ, evangelizing, is an essential step to others receiving life eternal. The apostolic witness will change the world!

When baby Jesus arrived on this earth, everything changed. The Law was about to be fulfilled in Christ. Jesus' death on the cross brought full forgiveness of sins to all who would identify with His death. The resurrection validated the work of God's Son, the Christ in making a way for mankind to have a new character. Humanity was given hope in their own bodily resurrection, as Christ exemplified conquering physical death for them. The Gospel writers got the message; they recognized the futility of thinking they could fulfill God's Law on their own. They repented of their sins and believed in Jesus as the Promised Savior. They followed Christ, and they eventually laid down their own lives to share

His Word, knowing God would raise them up again. The Gospels record their love of the Savior.

Turning to the disciples, He said privately, "Blessed are the eyes which see the things you see, for I say to you, that many prophets and kings wished to see the things which you see, and did not see them, and to hear the things which you hear, and did not hear them." Luke 10:23-24

It is a blessing to get to experience the good things we have anticipated. I spend a lot of timing planning for future events and activities. Part of this is because of women's ministry responsibilities and the other part is having a family and loving our time together. It is a joy to experience in full what I talk about and spend months preparing. For example, my daughters and I love to watch Jane Austen movies. For a year, we planned a 12-day trip to England together to visit the sites where many of the Austen films were shot. We wanted to walk the gardens we had repeatedly viewed in the movies and visit the cliffs where Elizabeth Bennett had hiked. This was my first trip out of the United States, so when I arrived in England, the whole adventure was very surreal to me. I was overwhelmed with getting to share the culmination of our vision for the trip with my daughters. I was disconcerted by driving on the other side of the road. Somethings were not quite how I had planned or envisioned, but all things gave me a greater understanding of the Austen stories.

The disciples grew to appreciate the blessing of seeing and hearing the Anointed One in person on this earth. They were experiencing the journey of a lifetime with the long-anticipated Son of God. We are blessed by their time with Christ as they recorded those moments and, specifically, how those moments related to the roles of the Old Testament prophets and kings in God's plan of redemption. Christ is the ultimate destination for those wondering where the Old Testament should take them. Christ initiates a New Covenant with those who have ears to hear His Story.

MATTHEW

The King has come!

Week 35, Day 1

Read It All: Matthew 1-7
Read a Bit: Matthew 1-7

The Revelation in Summary

Matthew 1:1 — *The record of the genealogy of Jesus the Messiah, the son of David, the son of Abraham: . . .*

We cannot imitate God; the Law revealed that. We need the full righteousness of God given to us or we have no hope in surviving the holy wrath of mighty God. Thankfully, God has been revealing His means of reconciling mankind to Him throughout the ages and has been preparing the way so that we could fully see His good provision of refuge in His Son from the Seed of Abraham. Through the voices of the Old Testament prophets, God affirmed that His Ruler would intervene as Redeemer and Lord. Matthew proclaims that God's King is here! In Him, the Old Covenant that indicted humanity by revealing our true character gives way to a New Covenant of the Spirit that transforms. Matthew affirms that this baby Jesus is the fulfillment of the Old Testament promises by providing His genealogy, supernatural birth account, forerunner John's message, victory over Satan's temptations, and brilliant preaching on God's Kingdom. Matthew authors an account of God's birth, life, death, and resurrection that culminates in a command to Christ's disciples to *"Go therefore and make disciples of all the nations, baptizing them in the name of the Father and the Son and the Holy Spirit, teaching them to observe all that I commanded you and lo, I am with you always, even to the end of the age"* (Matthew 28:19-20) The disciples' obedience to this command resulted in you and I studying His Words today.

As I mentioned in our devotions on the prophets, for many of the national leaders and priests, "God with us" was not a comfort. Sometimes "God with us" is not a comforting thought to me either; it is intensely scary, as I know I really, really, really deserve His wrath. I realize that God is all-knowing. I don't need a reminder that He knows I struggle with selfishness, arrogance, and jealousy. We both know I am not always loving. I may even be less loving around that most blessed, and busy, celebration of my Lord and Savior's birth, Christmas. The "Holy-days" can reveal that I, too readily, become caught up in what I really want under the tree, succumb to emotionally eating every single delectable morsel available, and comparatively covet the lives summarized in lengthy Christmas letters I receive. I struggle with putting the needs of others above my own. I like getting and being the center of attention if the attention recognizes my great worth. I'm me.

I also tend to lie at Christmas. One of my biggest lies is telling my sweet husband Scott that he really doesn't have to get me anything. Not only do I expect him to give me something really nice, I also expect him to know me to the depths of my soul and reflect that knowledge in his gift. I know and he knows that my expectations are counter to the celebration and doomed to cause silly disappointments. I don't know why I can be so bent on spreading misery at Christmas. There is really nothing I even need. What drives us to self-centered obsessions? Thankfully, a powerful baby interrupts my sin.

My heart softens as I bring out old ornaments given by loving family and friends. My conscience is pricked when I start holiday baking and remember the nearby children's home that would enjoy some fresh cookies or pumpkin bread. I begin to smile and hum when the familiar carols and movies are played. God gets my attention in the convicting messages of the Incarnation, which reminds me that He sacrificed all to give the only gift I really need: His righteousness. I long for the day when I fully realize His righteousness in me, but in the meantime, I hope and rejoice in His promise that He is with us, knowing full well who we really are.

Week 35, Day 2

Read It All: Matthew 8-12
Read a Bit: Matthew 9-11

Integrity

Matthew 8:2 — *And a leper came to Him and bowed down before Him, and said, "Lord, if You are willing, You can make me clean."*

I have something I want to convey about the leper in Matthew 8, but before I do, please be patient as I give a little background to my thoughts, for much about the leper has to do with him hearing Jesus as described in Matthew 5-7. The Matthew 8 leper leads the way for those with ears to hear.

Matthew 5-7 is known as the Sermon on the Mount. I've visited the spot where it is believed Jesus stood and gave this sermon. I first heard the Sermon on the Mount from my Grandma Burns. She read Matthew 5-7 to me when I visited her home in Iowa. As I heard her reading, I got scared because I was nothing like the person described in the Sermon on the Mount. I knew that she hoped I would hear the words and want to be like the poor in spirit, the gentle and meek, the peacemaker, and the merciful. But I just wanted to be loved. I wasn't thinking about how I should treat others. The more Grandma Burns spoke, the more wretched I felt because I was nothing like the righteous One described in the sermon. What would become of me?

Jesus knows He is talking to a bunch of self-centered folk and many worriers. When He finishes describing basically only one person, Himself, He tells all those who recognize that they need a means of righteousness to *"Ask, and it will be given to you; seek, and you will find, knock, and it will be opened to you"* (Matthew 7:7), because God, the Good Father, loves to show mercy on His children. God provides a narrow way of escape from His wrath; Jesus is the foundational way. Act on His authority and on the integrity of truth He provides by building our lives on His teaching.

Here is where the leper in chapter 8 leads us. After Jesus finishes speaking and comes down from the mountain, the leper comes to Him, bows down, and asks for His cleansing. Jesus willingly cleanses Him because He is true to His Word. A centurion is our next example; he must have heard about the Sermon. The centurion goes to Jesus and asks for life for His servant, acknowledging that Jesus can heal from right where He is. Jesus does so. Who has the authority of God as the fulfillment of the righteousness expressed in the Sermon on the Mount? Only Jesus. So He explains, ask Me and I will share Myself with you. Life is available in the Son.

Week 35, Day 3

Read It All: Matthew 13-18
Read a Bit: Matthew 14-18

Dignity

Matthew 18:15 — *If your brother sins, go and show him his fault in private; if he listens to you, you have won your brother.*

There is a lot of conflict in the Gospels. The religious self righteous test Jesus repeatedly. The call to repent offends some. Conflict is a battle for dignity. If you do not believe that Jesus is the Son of God in the flesh, then the Gospel accounts should make you mad as they clearly state that Jesus is God. Jesus' presence made a bunch of people mad when He walked the earth, and the Gospel writers had a front row view of the many confrontations. Matthew 18 describes the steps a believer should take when someone sins against them. Jesus knew His children would need His teaching on conflict resolution because He knows mankind's nature.

The religious leaders, the Pharisees and Sadducees, would test Jesus. He responded in many situations by teaching in parables as a method of screening out those who were seeking an argument rather than truth. The testing oftentimes included a request for a sign because many people value a show of power. They cry, "Make it easy for us to believe!" while ignoring the glory already in their midst. Jesus responded to one request for a sign with this warning: *"An evil and adulterous generation seeks after a sign; and a sign will not be given it, except the sign of Jonah"* (Matthew 16:4).

I know what the sign of Jonah is, and you should too. Jonah was in the belly of the big fish for three days, yet he lived. Jesus would be dead in the darkness of the tomb for three days, yet He lived through His resurrection. Jesus' response to the leaders seeking a sign may seem harsh to the reader, but even in His rebukes He extends great mercy. He is giving them a great insight into what He will do—fulfill Daniel

12:1-2.[18] His resurrection should have brought back a remembrance of that moment when He referred to Jonah and saved those who inquired for a sign. For He, like Jonah, would come back from death with a message of salvation for a wicked generation.

Unlike Jonah, though, Christ rejoices at those who hear and receive God's merciful offer of life. Christ wants to restore mankind's dignity. The sign of Jonah reminds us that the judgment of God is real. Jonah went to Nineveh as God had commanded, because the people were doomed to destruction apart from repentance and reliance on God's mercy. The religious leaders of Jesus' day and all who hear His teachings since then have opportunity to escape conviction at the Judgment Seat of Christ by trusting in the Resurrected Redeemer.

In the midst of the accounts of increasing hostility toward Christ Jesus is the record of the transfiguration. What a contrast between those who are bent on unbelief, demanding a sign, and the small group of humble followers who go with Jesus up a mountain, seeing Him reveal His deity. Moses and Elijah attend this gathering, where God speaks from the cloud, something He had also done at Jesus' baptism. I'm reminded that there are many signs of His presence all around me, day after day. This Bible next to me is a supernatural work of God. So often we are just so miserable, we want to fight. God's will is that we are a thankful people. This comes from remembering the many signs we have already heard from His eyewitness accounts. Stop the conflict and enjoy His presence and merciful provision of forgiveness. His signs remind us to receive His forgiveness and extend this forgiveness to all.

And the lord of that slave felt compassion and released him and forgave him the debt. Matthew 18:27

---

[18] Now at that time Michael, the great prince who stands guard over the sons of your people, will arise. And there will be a time of distress such as never occurred since there was a nation until that time; and at that time your people, everyone who is found written in the book, will be rescued. Many of those who sleep in the dust of the ground will awake, these to everlasting life, but the others to disgrace *and* everlasting contempt.

Week 35, Day 4

Read It All: Matthew 19-25
Read a Bit: Matthew 19, 23-24

Unity

Matthew 19:14 — *But Jesus said, "Let the children alone, and do not hinder them from coming to Me; for the kingdom of heaven belongs to such as these."*

Some moms admit that they attend Bible study because there is free child care and they need a break. I get this. We are all alike in that we get weary. I hope that the church continues to realize how important it is to support moms as they purpose to lovingly raise children in His ways. But I'm concerned. I see a trend that indicates the church isn't valuing involvement in the care of its little ones. There is a valuing of comfort over caring. We are very busy people who don't prioritize children. It isn't easy to find great, joyful, purpose-driven volunteers in children's ministry, and because of today's culture, the really enthusiastic ones are, sadly, a bit suspect. It's unusual to take too great an interest in children. We pray for help.

With this in mind, I decided to sign up to help with the babies once a month on a Sunday morning. This brings back memories of when my husband and I served weekly with three-year-olds, and after a crazy morning, I teased him that I was pregnant and he ran a stop light and hit another car. Babies terrified us.

I know the volunteering routine. I get a reminder in my email of when to show up. The children's leaders supply all the resources in a bucket for the volunteer to pick up, use, and return after class. I become a monthly hero to parents and other children's leaders. I appear quite spiritual and helpful, but I'm really not.

The reality is that I still need children to teach me about God. I need to see the miraculous beauty of the little babies. I need to be entrusted with a tiny hand to hold and remember what it means to freely trust. I need to see the struggle with sin in the midst of learning self-control. I need to hear the children's questions about the Lord Jesus Christ and the honest admissions of confusion and wonder. I need to witness spontaneous praise.

There is great joy in serving where you are greatly needed. There is a softening of hardened hearts in the presence of little children. There is a reminder of how reliant humankind is on their Maker in the midst of vulnerability. I want our children at church to know the right, good love of their Father, and I want their parents to see overwhelming support of their homes. The family is being redefined today. We have an opportunity to support families, to provide sanctuary in the worldly chaos. Surely the church is united in its call to minister to children.

> *. . . and [they] said to Him, "Do You hear what these children are saying?" And Jesus said to them, "Yes; have you never read, 'Out of the mouth of infants and nursing babies You have prepared praise for Yourself'?"* Matthew 21:16

> *. . . and [He] said, "Truly I say to you, unless you are converted and become like children, you will not enter the kingdom of heaven."* Matthew 18:3

Week 35, Day 5

Read It All: Matthew 26-28
Read a Bit: Matthew 26-28

Priority

Matthew 27:37 — *And above His head they put up the charge against Him which read, "THIS IS JESUS THE KING OF THE JEWS."*

Jesus preached five sermons as recorded by Matthew. These sermons revealed how Jesus is the Christ and many things that were to come. Jesus openly taught how righteousness is imputed to the believer through the King, how Israel would respond to His truth, the delay in His Kingdom due to Israel's rejection of the King, signs of His return, lessons on impending judgment, and how to be ready for the ultimate salvation. Following all this teaching, as Matthew began to finish his account, he wrote, *"When Jesus had finished all these words, He said to His disciples, 'You know that after two days the Passover is coming, and the Son of Man is to be handed over for crucifixion'"* (Matthew 26:1-2). It was time for the teaching to be exemplified in the cross.

I've taught through the details of the week prior to the crucifixion many times. Jesus' suffering began long before He picked up the cross. Pouring out your heart in teaching that is ignored must have been excruciating. Christ had been repeatedly warning people He loved to take cover, yet they threw off His blanket of refuge. In this week before the crucifixion, He would be betrayed, ridiculed, misunderstood, beaten, left hungry, mocked some more, denied, aware of His mother's needs, arrested, tried, cried to, and believed. The prophets knew about this week. The priesthood His Father had established ironically took part in His murder. The greatest Temple known to mankind was crushed. The King of the Jews hung on a tree. The cry of Psalm 22 was fulfilled: *"My God, My God, why have You forsaken Me?"*

God came into His creation as a man to pay the debt of sin that was beyond the ability of everyone to overcome. God was rejected, beaten, and killed as a criminal. The debt was paid, the resurrection validated Jesus' claims of deity, and the recipient of this truth is granted life. When the resurrected Jesus greeted His disciples following His appearance to the women at the tomb, He wasn't yelling for the destruction of all who sent Him to the cross. He didn't avenge Himself. Instead, He said, *"Do not be afraid; go and take word to My brethren to leave for Galilee, and there they will see Me"* (Matthew 28:20). He prepared His children to get ready for His Spirit and to take His message to those that were as good as dead. God loves resurrecting Life.

MARK

Who is this Servant-King? The Son of God that bears Good News and ultimately removes the Roman rule in His return.

Day 36, Day 1

Read It All: Mark 1-7
Read a Bit: Mark 1-7

The Revelation in Summary

Mark 1:1 — *The beginning of the gospel of Jesus Christ, the Son of God.*

Mark jumps right in explaining how Jesus is the fulfillment of the prophetical writings. The Gospel of Mark presents Jesus' ministry as God's servant and Jesus' teaching on servanthood particularly for the disciples, Israel's rejection of God's Servant, Jesus' continued service to all of humanity, and the Resurrected Jesus' command to proclaim His Gospel. I love that Mark repeatedly uses the word "Gospel" and prioritizes telling all mankind the good news.

Mark is a Gospel of action. Even the writing style draws the reader along at a clipped pace: short sentences, driving from point to point in Jesus' ministry, with quick glimpses into Christ's ministry while emphasizing service. The text moves. You see phrase after phrase that relates to timing and distance: "immediately," "when evening came," "going on further," "suddenly," "time is fulfilled," "next," "in those days," . . . . Mark presents an adventure. His central character, Jesus, provides surprise after surprise in how He serves and what He says. Mark is a countercultural attack on the Roman mindset of honoring oppressive authority.

I particularly like the examples Mark gives regarding the faith of others. Those who are brilliant in their response to Lord Jesus include the paralytic with friends, a despised tax collector, a woman with a hemorrhage, and the widow with a tiny bit of change. I wonder at Mark's consideration of women in his gospel accounts. He simply states the details and includes those who would normally be ignored in the literature of his day. Jesus served all.

Week 36, Day 2

Read It All: Mark 8-10
Read a Bit: Mark 8-10

Integrity

Mark 8:35 — *For whoever wishes to save his life will lose it, but whoever loses his life for My sake and the gospel's will save it.*

Mark 10:13-16 — *And they were bringing children to Him so that He might touch them; but the disciples rebuked them. But when Jesus saw this, He was indignant and said to them, "Permit the children to come to Me; do not hinder them; for the kingdom of God belongs to such as these. Truly I say to you, whoever does not receive the kingdom of God like a child will not enter it at all." And He took them in His arms and began blessing them, laying His hands on them.*

One of my most life-changing events was becoming a mother. It was years after my marriage that I even voiced thoughts of having a child. I was motivated to address my "no kids" policy following a Bible lesson that included the thought that "children are a blessing from God." New truth to me. On to life-change.

Mothering transformed me. I want to cry just writing this, for several reasons. I know many who hurt from wanting to conceive; they have taught me to be thankful for the miracle of life. My children opened my heart to love in ways I didn't think I was capable of; they taught me to die to self. When I was pregnant with my second, sweet Sarah Kate, I voiced a concern to my mom about being able to love enough for another, but she assured me I hadn't reached my love capacity and another child would be a joy. She was right; each child taught me to enjoy simpler ways and to love more thoroughly. Through being a mom, I also gained insight into God the Father as loving, faithful and good. Family matters.

The children's bedrooms at my house are empty now. It has been wonderful to see them take flight, but this may be another life-changing transition for my hubby and me. Time to learn how to make the most of this season of life. God's kingdom is for the childlike, for those who believe in the goodness of their father. Children aren't just aware of their limitations; they readily reach for a hand up, a hand to hold, and even a hand out. They don't hesitate to ask for more of what delights them. They embrace the life-giver. We suffer if we isolate and create a childless existence for ourselves.

God entrusts His children with a message to proclaim Him to others. What we do with the message He has entrusted us is a matter of integrity. There are spiritual children to raise.

I hope to encourage all moms and dads with a houseful to enjoy these busy days as fully as possible. They pass all too quickly. I recommend that families be very intentional about time together and for women, in particular, to not adopt a culture that challenges any freedom you have to raise your own children. We need these little ones to guide the way, to reveal the Father's love and our own capacity to represent His love. This is our time to proclaim His truth to our little ones. Children are a blessing from God.

Week 36, Day 3

Read It All: Mark 11-13
Read a Bit: Mark 11-13

Dignity

Mark 13:10 — *The gospel must first be preached to all the nations.*

I spent a week in Nazareth. I went in the name of the Lord Jesus Christ to show God's love to children and their teachers at a Day Camp in Nazareth, the place where Jesus experienced rejection by those who knew him well, family and friends, and I taught reconciliation. The proclamation of Christ, through the centuries, open to reconciling descendants of many rejecters of His message. His pain enriching us all.

I stood on Mount Precipice in Nazareth, looked all around at the area Jesus grew up in, and thought about how it would be to have your hometown rejecting your teaching so angrily that they purposed to stone you. Stoning involved taking the accused to a high place, throwing them off the stony high place, and then hurling smaller stones at them if the fall didn't kill them. You can read the account in Luke 4:16-30.

And they rose up and drove him out of the town and brought him to the brow of the hill on which their town was built, so that they could throw him down the cliff. Luke 4:29

This was rejection from a view Christ must have held dear—a view of His home and countryside.

While in Nazareth, I woke up one morning and read a passage that I had never really noticed before; it stood out that morning, as I had been thinking of all Jesus suffered in His hometown.

When His own people heard of this, they went out to take custody of Him; for they were saying, "He has lost His senses." Mark 3:21

I adore my family. I would be out of my mind if I lost their respect and care. Jesus will ask later in this passage, "Who are my mother and my brothers?" And looking about at those who sat around him, he answered his own question, "Here are my mother and my brothers! For whoever does the will of God, he is my brother and sister and mother."

The rejection of Jesus by His own family revealed what Scripture means when God says, "Nor are they all children because they are Abraham's descendants" (Romans 9:7). His true family are those that believe Christ is the anticipated Messiah that fulfills God's promises to Abraham. I became a child of God when I took refuge in the Lord Jesus Christ. From Mount Precipice, a bit in the distance, is another mountain, the Mount of Transfiguration. For those who see Jesus as the Psalm 2 Christ, He is their eternal brother. Thank You, Lord, for eternal family! May the nations hear of your grace!

Week 36, Day 4

Read It All: Mark 14-15
Read a Bit: Mark 14-15

Unity

Mark 14:9 — *Truly I say to you, wherever the gospel is preached in the whole world, what this woman has done will also be spoken of in memory of her.*

Life comes in layers. I mean this literally and in a deep metaphorical way. My fingertips are often numb trying to scratch through just the surface layers of life. In the Old City, Jerusalem, the layers seem to be a bit more obvious, but still so much is hidden. The "religious" sites are typically layer upon layer of structures, and the thoughtful tourist explores with a chronological view of the site in mind. Because of the layering, sites that may have gone lost in this land of contention are believed to be identifiable due to the attempts by others to make them into something else, something not related to Jesus' presence. Many have tried to hide a Christian site by conquering and building a temple to a foreign god, and so they ultimately serve to mark the spot of the original site. History is thus traceable in the layers.

The Church of St. Peter in Gallicantu, or Caiaphas' house, is such a place. It is a church built on the slopes of Mount Zion in 1931 AD on the site of a church that was built by the Crusaders in 1102. The name dates back to 1102. A Byzantine church was built on the place believed to be Caiaphas' house in 457 AD, destroyed in 1010 and rebuilt by the Crusaders in 1102. The Crusader church sat in ruins from 1320 to 1931 AD. St. Peter in Gallicantu is beautiful in a stark, stony sense.

In the basement of this church is an array of caves cut into the rock under the houses of the ancient city. Tradition holds that these caves included a jail, a "pit," where Jesus was held after his arrest. If you remember in Mark 14, in contrast to the woman who anointed Him with perfume in recognition of His deity, Jesus was betrayed by a kiss in the garden of Gethsemane, led away to the high priest's house, interrogated by a Council set to condemn Him, spit at, blindfolded, slapped, and denied by His dear disciple Peter.

The jail/cave/pit had a hole in the top where the prisoner would be let down or thrown through for containment. The jail/cave/pit that I visited had an extra entrance at floor level added for the comfort of the visitor, so I wasn't thrown down. I stood in that pit, touched the walls of that pit, and watched my companions, including my husband, get teary-eyed in that pit. It was a hot July day in the Old City, but I felt the coldness of the cave. The layers above made me aware of how low and dark the Savior went to counter sin.

Tearing his clothes, the high priest said, "What further need do we have of witnesses? You have heard the blasphemy; how does it seem to you?" And they all condemned Him to be deserving of death.
Mark 14:63 -64

Week 36, Day 5

Read It All: Mark 16
Read a Bit: Mark 16

Priority

Mark 16:15 — *And He said to them, "Go into all the world and preach the gospel to all creation.*

My lead pastor for our Women's Ministry, Wade, holds a huddle twice a week for our family-life staff. The primary reason for the huddle is to remind one another that we are blessed to be God's messengers of reconciliation to the world. We get together and celebrate all our attempts to share the good news. We get together to encourage, not to compete, Gospel-centered living. We have realized that we struggle in sharing about our Savior. This is convicting. Do we really believe the Gospel? Do we realize that what we live for should be worth Christ dying for? Do we fear rejection so much that we forget that even death has no victory over us?

I greatly appreciate the accountability of this huddle. Because of it, my awareness of my calling from God has greatly increased, and I am being more faithful to talk about the Gospel. The kindness of this group has also helped me see that I need to be a better listener and more discerning about what to say and when. My goal isn't to defend my beliefs or to win an apologetic discussion; my goal is to help people receive His mercy and to be reconciled to their Maker.

Mark records that the resurrected Jesus appeared to the disciples and reproached them for their unbelief and hardness of heart because they did not believe those who had seen Him after He had risen. Because my pastor believes that Jesus rose from the dead, he is passionate about telling others about the Risen Redeemer. He wants our group to get the vision. I've seen him right after he has prayed with someone to receive

Christ; he is inexpressibly, wonderfully, elated by life in those moments. Glory to God in the highest!

I appreciate how patient my pastor is with us. I appreciate his reminder of the importance of sharing the Gospel meeting after meeting. I appreciate how long suffering the Lord Jesus Christ was with His disciples and with you and with me. Lord, help us with our unbelief and make us your precious messengers of life. To reproduce your Life in another is Life for all.

LUKE

Who is this LORD of the Sabbath? Finally, the One Who will bring rest to the captive.

Week 37, Day 1

Read It All: Luke 1-4
Read a Bit: Luke 1-4

The Revelation in Summary

Luke 1:1-4 — *Inasmuch as many have undertaken to compile an account of the things accomplished among us, just as they were handed down to us by those who from the beginning were eyewitnesses and servants of the word, it seemed fitting for me as well, having investigated everything carefully from the beginning, to write it out for you in consecutive order, most excellent Theophilus; so that you may know the exact truth about the things you have been taught.*

Luke is the author of more New Testament text, not books, than any other New Testament writer.[19] Luke wrote the Gospel of Luke and the Book of Acts to compile an account of the things he had witnessed so that his dear friend Theophilus would know the exact truth about what he had been taught. Luke had the heart of a great spiritual father.

Luke understood the need for humanity, specifically represented by the nation Israel, to receive the rescuing power of the Gospel of Jesus Christ. Luke knew that in Christ, God had brought Sabbath rest to the people. Luke supplies story after story about Jesus being the LORD of the Sabbath. Sadly, we witness Israel's response to their Emancipator. Israel purposes to kill their Deliverer.

Luke beautifully records the humble worship of Jesus by many who appreciate His willingness to deliver them from their sins. Luke contrasts the self-righteous with those who recognize their spiritual need. I cherish the details of Simeon, noted as righteous and devout, holding the baby

---

[19]   Mari Kaimo, "Who Wrote Most of the New Testament?" *ApoLogika* (blog), May 3, 2014, accessed September 10, 2018, https://apologika.blogspot.com/2014/05/who-wrote-most-of-new-testament.html.

Jesus and proclaiming that as God's bondservant, he, Simeon, can now depart in peace for he has seen God's salvation.

Week 37, Day 2

Read It All: Luke 5-9
Read a Bit: Luke 5-9

Integrity

Luke 5:20 — *Seeing their faith, He said, "Friend, your sins are forgiven you."*

It doesn't take much for me to remember my lack of integrity. I am quick to rationalize my sin and cover my shortcomings. You may be like me, as I reflect on my life, including sinful habits, ugly attitudes, longtime goals, lack of perseverance in prayer, relationship concerns . . . I desire change. I've learned that a key to change is reminding myself that my past sins have been forgiven. We don't have to pay penance for our sins; Christ has fully paid for all sin on the cross. We are free to move forward and, in Christ, should have great hope that change is possible. God's Word reveals that there is hope for any and all of us to change as needed to glorify God, because when we receive Christ as Savior, we receive God's forgiveness and His Spirit that sets us apart for His name's sake. Our Savior transforms His followers.

Wayne Mack's discipleship manual[20] helps in reviewing the Scriptures on how forgiveness initiates change in the believer.

Forgiveness in Christ changes us:

> *Therefore if anyone is in Christ, he is a new creature; the old things passed away; behold, new things have come.* 2 Corinthians 5:17

> *Or do you not know that the unrighteous will not inherit the kingdom of God? Do not be deceived; neither fornicators, nor idolaters, nor*

---

[20] Wayne A. Mack and Wayne E. Johnston, *A Christian Growth and Discipleship Manual, Volume 3: A Homework Manual for Biblical Living* (Bemidji, MN: Focus Publishing, 2005).

adulterers, nor effeminate, nor homosexuals, nor thieves, nor the covetous, nor drunkards, nor revilers, nor swindlers, will inherit the kingdom of God. Such were some of you; but you were washed, but you were sanctified, but you were justified in the name of the Lord Jesus Christ and in the Spirit of our God. 1 Corinthians 6:9-11

Therefore consider the members of your earthly body as dead to immorality, impurity, passion, evil desire, and greed, which amounts to idolatry. . . . But now you also, put them all aside: anger, wrath, malice, slander, and abusive speech from your mouth. Do not lie to one another, since you laid aside the old self with its evil practices, and have put on the new self who is being renewed to a true knowledge according to the image of the One who created him . . . ." Colossians 3:5-11

Forgiveness in Christ births a willingness for continual change:

So then, my beloved, just as you have always obeyed, not as in my presence only, but now much more in my absence, work out your salvation with fear and trembling; for it is God who is at work in you, both to will and to work for His good pleasure. Philippians 2:12-13

But by the grace of God I am what I am, and His grace toward me did not prove vain; but I labored even more than all of them, yet not I, but the grace of God with me. 1 Corinthians 15:10

Forgiveness in Christ provides guidance for change:

The law of the Lord is perfect, restoring the soul; The testimony of the Lord is sure, making wise the simple. The precepts of the Lord are right, rejoicing the heart; The commandment of the Lord is pure, enlightening the eyes. The fear of the Lord is clean, enduring forever; The judgments of the Lord are true; they are righteous altogether. They are more desirable than gold, yes, than much fine gold; Sweeter also than honey and the drippings of the honeycomb. Moreover, by them Your servant is warned; In keeping them there is great reward. Psalm 19:7-11

The unfolding of Your words gives light; it gives understanding to the simple. Psalm 119:130

Forgiveness in Christ builds perseverance to change:

Let us not lose heart in doing good, for in due time we will reap if we do not grow weary. Galatians 6:9

But the seed in the good soil, these are the ones who have heard the word in an honest and good heart, and hold it fast, and bear fruit with perseverance. Luke 8:15

Forgiveness in Christ unites us to promises that promote change:

No temptation has overtaken you but such as is common to man; and God is faithful, who will not allow you to be tempted beyond what you are able, but with the temptation will provide the way of escape also, so that you will be able to endure it. 1 Corinthians 10:13

Grace and peace be multiplied to you in the knowledge of God and of Jesus our Lord; seeing that His divine power has granted to us everything pertaining to life and godliness, through the true knowledge of Him who called us by His own glory and excellence. For by these He has granted to us His precious and magnificent promises, so that by them you may become partakers of the divine nature, having escaped the corruption that is in the world by lust. 2 Peter 1:2-4

And we know that God causes all things to work together for good to those who love God, to those who are called according to His purpose. For those whom He foreknew, He also predestined to become conformed to the image of His Son, so that He would be the firstborn among many brethren; and these whom He predestined, He also called; and these whom He called, He also justified; and these whom He justified, He also glorified. What then shall we say to these things? If God is for us, who is against us? He who did not spare His own Son, but delivered Him over for us all, how will He not also with Him freely give us all things? Who will bring a charge against God's elect? God is the one who justifies; who is the one who condemns? Christ Jesus is He who died, yes, rather who was raised, who is at the right hand of God, who also intercedes for us. Who will separate us from the love of Christ? Will tribulation, or distress, or persecution, or famine, or nakedness, or peril, or sword? Just as it is written, For Your sake we are being put to death all day long; we were considered as sheep to be slaughtered." But in all these things we overwhelmingly conquer through Him who loved us. For I am convinced that neither death, nor life, nor angels, nor principalities, nor things present, nor things to come, nor powers, nor height, nor depth, nor any other created thing, will be able to separate us from the love of God, which is in Christ Jesus our Lord. Romans 8:28-39

Don't underestimate His Spirit, His Body the Church, and His Word's involvement in working out the forgiveness you have received to impact change in your life. Walk in His truth.

Week 37, Day 3

Read It All: Luke 10-14
Read a Bit: Luke 10-14

Dignity

Luke 10:30 — *Jesus replied and said, "A man was going down from Jerusalem to Jericho, and fell among robbers, and they stripped him and beat him, and went away leaving him half dead.*

My children attended a weekly Bible study with me from when they were age two until they were eighteen. My two eldest children are close in age, and they would hear the same Bible story from two different teachers. It was always interesting to hear their discussions of their stories after their classes. Sometimes I would visit my grandmother after the study, and their Bible story telling would crack her up. The Good Samaritan story by Samuel and Sarah was one of Grandma's favorites.

Three-year-old Samuel announced, "Did you know that in the Bible there were these fleas who robbed and beat up this man and then left him by the roadside?"

Sarah corrected him. "No, Samuel, it was bees that did that to him."

Suppressing a smile, I jumped in, "No, children. You may have misunderstood. It was thieves. They do bad things like that to people."

Samuel, heaving a tolerant sigh, said, "Anyway, it doesn't matter who hurt him because the Good American came along and helped him."

The Story of the Good Samaritan reveals God's love for all people. It challenged the Jewish listeners that thought they were righteous to love better, like a Gentile that they typically snubbed. Jesus knocked down social barriers which were obstacles to the spread of the Gospel. He reveals mankind's dependence on Him while also revealing the dignity He bestowed on any He would help.

Week 37, Day 4

Read It All: Luke 15-19
Read a Bit: Luke 15-19

Unity

Luke 15:31-32 — *And he said to him, "Son, you have always been with me, and all that is mine is yours. But we had to celebrate and rejoice, for this brother of yours was dead and has begun to live, and was lost and has been found."*

In Luke 15, there are three stories that depict what people really value. In the first story, the shepherd values his lost sheep. He actually leaves the ninety-nine sheep he has in the pasture to go and find one that is lost. Upon finding the one sheep, he calls his friends and rejoices. Jesus teaches that in similar fashion, those in heaven rejoice when one sinner repents.

The second story also reveals the joy the angels have in the sinner that repents, as the experience is likened to a woman who finds a coin she has lost. The story depicts her careful search for the coin and again she includes her friend and neighbors in the celebration of the coin's recovery. There is no condemnation expressed of the woman or the shepherd from the first story in valuing temporal, material things, just a simple illustration of how such joy is expressed in heaven over a sinner's repentance.

The last story, often referred to as the story of the prodigal son, draws us in to someone who values the well-being of another at great cost to themselves. The good father in the story rejoices greatly over his wayward son's realization that he is better off in his father's home than on his own. The thing of value, eternal value, is the relationship between the father and the sinner son. The restoration of this relationship is celebrated by all in the household except for the older son. The older son has all the father has except for his father's value system. The self-righteous older son doesn't rejoice at a repentant sinner like those in heaven would. The older son rebukes his father and boycotts the party. Sometimes, the sons of God on this earth value the blessings from God more than God Himself. These stories challenge us to consider, is He sufficient to me? If not, do I really know the difference between life and death, the eternal and the temporal?

Week 37, Day 5

Read It All: Luke 20-24
Read a Bit: Luke 20-24

Priority

Luke 23:34 — *But Jesus was saying, "Father, forgive them; for they do not know what they are doing."*

The supernatural work of God on the cross forgiving mankind occurs just a few short passages away from a simple act of women anointing the body of Jesus with spices. It is in these distinctions that we rejoice in God's sovereign care of us and purpose to do any little thing we can to express our thankfulness for His presence.

In Nazareth of today, there is a celebrity spice guy. He has traveled all over the world doing TV special programs on his spices. My Israel mission leader, Donna, has connections with this fascinating man, which led to a little adventure of the senses for me and my traveling companions.

We had spent the morning cleaning at the school where we were serving during our mission trip. This involved scrubbing desks, painting, and removing thousands of staples from boards and walls throughout the school. There were so many staples, you couldn't paint neatly without removing them. Staples really are quite a violent, intrusive invention. After our work, we had lunch at a neighborhood restaurant that had hamburgers and onion rings and a wonderful diced-veggie salad. In the local restaurants, entire families help serve. Water is not iced and is in pitchers that were continually passed around, as the glasses were small and we were thirsty. We left the restaurant for the spice shop after lunch.

Our group stood out when walking the streets of Nazareth. For the most part, people were friendly. We were going through the narrow passageways and streets at a time when most people were avoiding the heat, so it was a quiet walk. The entrance to the spice shop, like so many in the area, was just a big metal door off the street front. I felt like I was entering a speakeasy from the times of Prohibition, as from the outside we had no idea what was inside, but when we entered, the world came alive! The entrance was a landing with stairs descending down into a large space filled with scales and open containers of all types of spices, nuts, dried fruits, and kitchen utensils. The aroma was my first impression and I was hungry again. The people inside were delighted to have us, a group of fourteen with Donna, who is special to many in this town, as her ministry enriches so many homes. The shop owner's joy was also due to seeing others of his faith. He prays for believers to fill the city.

We were given snacks and hot coffee, which was a bit overwhelming in the heat of the day. The shop is over 250 years old, passed down from generation to generation. What an inheritance! Two brothers run the shop with great enthusiasm. They told us the history of the family and the business today and asked for prayer. They long to continue a business that blesses their hometown, but opposition is growing and they need discernment.

Spices are such an integral part of so many Bible narratives. Selection and use of spices reflect care and consideration of life's moments and our desire to involve our senses in living fully. Spices attack apathy in the day-to-day routine of meal after meal. Spices can serve as money for trade. Spices are used to honor the dead. The believer is to be a spice, enticing others to God's table in the wilderness.

> *But on the first day of the week, at early dawn, they came to the tomb bringing the spices which they had prepared.* Luke 24:1

JOHN

Do you recognize the Greater Moses Who delivers eternal life?

Week 38, Day 1

Read It All: John 1-4
Read a Bit: John 1-4

The Revelation in Summary

John 1:1-3 — *In the beginning was the Word, and the Word was with God, and the Word was God. He was in the beginning with God. All things came into being though Him, and apart from Him nothing came into being that has come into being.*

John very intentionally develops the case for Jesus being the fulfillment of all the Old Testament anticipations of the Deliverer. God's love for His Son and God's love for humanity are emphasized by John. Love is a repeated theme in the book, and we see that to love Jesus is to love others, as Jesus commands Peter to demonstrate Peter's love for Messiah by tending to His sheep. It is God's desire that people find Life and learn to abide in His Life. It is God's desire that His children share the love of God with the world, even in the midst of tribulation.

John tells his purpose in writing the Gospel: "Therefore many other signs Jesus also performed in the presence of the disciples, which are not written in this book; but these have been written so that you may believe that Jesus is the Christ, the Son of God and that believing you may have life in His name" (John 20:30-31). The signs John records reveal that Jesus from Nazareth, baptized by John, and teaching about God's Kingdom, is the Psalm 2 Christ and the Deuteronomy Greater Moses that has prepared the Way for all who believe in Him to have eternal life.

My son Samuel lives in Arkansas and I am in Florida, so I don't get to see him as much as I would like, which would be every day, particularly every night, so I could sleep knowing he is tucked in safely. Sigh. Anyway, my husband and I went to visit Samuel and were a bit surprised to see his place so orderly. He has always been an organized young man, but bathrooms and kitchens were never his strong suit. We also weren't sure how much time he would have to straighten up the apartment since he seemed to be working long hours at his new job. But everything looked great. He was excited to see us, and he had not only picked up, but at his wonderful kitchen island, he gave us beautiful gifts and celebrated us as his parents. This was dear. He even had his sister's picture still sitting on the counter where she had placed it when helping him move in. His cabinets were organized and full of dishes provided by Grandma Janet, as well as odds and ends from growing up in our home. No matter how far away he moves, we are family and we are part of one another. His kitchen reflects our relationship.

One of the essentials in the kitchen, which I insist all my children own, is a great cookie sheet. Baking cookies is homey. Flour, sugar (preferably brown), and chocolate chips should always be on hand, as well as the ingredients for oatmeal raisin cookies, as these are my version of health food. Before heading back to Florida, I asked Samuel if he wanted his mom to make him some chocolate chip cookies. Of course! Funny thing though, he said, "Before you use the oven, you need to look in it and do some rehab." What? He had neatened up the kitchen before our arrival by putting all the dirty dishes that were in his sink into the oven so they weren't obvious to his visitors, i.e. the parents. I frequently learn something new from my children.

I love my son. I think of him constantly and long for God's very best for him. I'm on his side. God also loves His Son. He loves His Son with a holy jealousy for Him. Take note, God is enraged when we belittle His Son. It is good for us to honor one another's children, and it is foolish for us to ignore the Father's intense love for His Son. Honor the Son. John summarizes His message with this statement:

The Father loves the Son and has given all things into His hand. He who believes in the Son has eternal life; but he who does not obey the Son will not see life, but the wrath of God abides on him. John 3:35-36

Week 38, Day 2

Read It All: John 5-12
Read a Bit: Matthew 8, 10-12

Integrity

John 10:11-16 — *I am the good shepherd; the good shepherd lays down His life for the sheep. He who is a hired hand, and not a shepherd, who is not the owner of the sheep, sees the wolf coming, and leaves the sheep and flees, and the wolf snatches them and scatters them. He flees because he is a hired hand and is not concerned about the sheep. I am the good shepherd, and I know My own and My own know Me, even as the Father knows Me and I know the Father; and I lay down My life for the sheep. I have other sheep, which are not of this fold; I must bring them also, and they will hear My voice; and they will become one flock with one shepherd.*

I have a small group that meets at my house throughout Christmas and into January. We call ourselves a variety of names, including The Dumb Sheep Group. One member recommended a slogan for the group: "Fear not, little flock! . . . for it is your Father's good pleasure to give you the kingdom" (Luke 12:32). We like her slogan. We are thinking of getting t-shirts made. Possibly woolen. . . .

The group meets because we love studying Scripture together, but primarily at this time in the season we meet to hold one another accountable to remember the Good Shepherd through the celebration of His birth. We lambs can tend to get a bit flighty in the midst of holidays. Therefore, we are intentionally focusing on Him by committing to read and discuss His Word. We specifically talk about the prophecies and parables about the Good Shepherd. This is a joy, as we love to hear our Shepherd's voice. We are a diverse flock. Some are in marital struggles, others hurting regarding children, some lonely, others overwhelmed. The Good Shepherd knows us. He knows our needs, He knows our desires, He knows our fears, and He knows our futures. We don't have to know much for ourselves, and we don't. We just need to know Him.

I have come to appreciate the heart of the Good Shepherd. I realize He loves me even when I am a rather poor sight to behold, frail and worn. I have come to appreciate the Shepherd's staff. He guides and rescues His sheep through gentle guidance and by completely blocking a way at times. I have come to appreciate the flock. There are many in His sheepfold. This equates to much stupidity and much joy in the realization of ensures life and what endangers life in the sheepfold. We sheep are learning how to listen and safeguard our homes as His undershepherds. He gives us purpose and integrity. We are thankful for The Good Shepherd. His devotion to lowly sheep is the epitome of unconditional, sacrificial love.

Week 38, Day 3

Read It All: John 13-17
Read a Bit: John 13-17

Dignity

John 14:26 — *But the Helper, the Holy Spirit, whom the Father will send in My name, He will teach you all things, and bring to your remembrance all that I said to you.*

John introduces the followers of Christ to the third person of the Trinity, the Holy Spirit. The Spirit within the believer is in fulfillment of the New Covenant promises and affirms the believer's dignity in Christ. We have read bits and pieces about the Spirit as we have progressed through His Story. In the Pentateuch, the Spirit anointed individuals for a particular work historically. The prophets were guided in their messages by the Spirit's work in revelation and inspiration. The prophets experienced Spirit-led revelations of the future for God's people, His Kingdom to come. The Psalmist valued the Holy Spirit and prayed that God wouldn't take His Spirit away. Isaiah revealed that God may place His Spirit in our midst and warned that His people could grieve His Spirit.

In the Gospels, the reader has witnessed the power of the Holy Spirit through the words and works of the Lord Jesus Christ. The Spirit impregnated Mary, validated Jesus as Messiah at His baptism, and continued to reveal the future to New Testament writers. Now John boldly introduces us to the person and work of Spirit.

The Book of Acts will reveal the formation of God's Body, the church, by the Spirit. The Spirit was expressed in tongues at Pentecost, equipped overseers for the early church, and made the believer the temple of God by His indwelling. Believers will minister His Word by the power of the Spirit.

The New Testament letters promise believers gifts of the Spirit. In 2 Corinthians, we are reminded that the Spirit is our Helper (as John described). Additional epistles teach on the Spirit: Galatians describes the fruit of the Spirit; Ephesians portrays the Spirit as the Revealer of Truth; 2 Thessalonians identifies the Spirit as Restrainer; and Ephesians assures the believer that they are sealed by the Spirit. The believer is exhorted, continually, to walk by the Spirit without quenching or grieving the Spirit.

The work of God the Spirit in the world and in the believer's life is Christocentric. Everything He does and wants to do exalts the Son of God. The primary function of the Spirit is to help God's children believe His truth. The Spirit inspired God's revelation and He illuminates His truth to those with an ear to hear. The Spirit helps us take refuge in the Son.

Week 38, Day 4

Read It All: John 18-20
Read a Bit: John 18-20

Unity

John 20:29 — *Jesus said to him, "Because you have seen Me, have you believed? Blessed are they who did not see and yet believed."*

When reading through God's Word, it is important to sometimes park on words or phrases that are central to the author's vocabulary. "Eternal life" is such a phrase for the apostle John. John uses the phase more than any other New Testament author, and in John's Gospel, the phrase is used five times more often than in the other three gospels. John believes in eternal life.

Eternal life is the righteous character of the Father imputed to His child. It is Christ in the believer, the hope of glory. The believer receives eternal life when he or she believes in Christ as Savior (1 John 1:1-3; 5:11-13). This life reflects the holiness of God. To receive eternal life is to have Adam's mortal life replaced by the Holy Spirit, the essence of this Life, Christ.

John says the believer receives this Life when they believe in Christ:

As Moses lifted up the serpent in the wilderness, even so must the Son of Man be lifted up; so that whoever believes will in Him have eternal life. For God so loved the world, that He gave His only begotten Son, that whoever believes in Him shall not perish, but have eternal life. John 3:15-16

John is asserting that the believer has been gifted God's righteousness, which includes the bodily resurrection (Daniel 12:2). This is complete victory over death. Those who take refuge in Christ are filled with His Spirit and saved from eternal separation from God.

I love reviewing the verses on eternal life. They are a great comfort to me.

Truly, truly, I say to you, he who hears My word, and believes Him who sent Me, has eternal life, and does not come into judgment, but has passed out of death into life. John 5:24

This is eternal life, that they may know You, the only true God, and Jesus Christ whom You have sent. John 17:3

Week 38, Day 5

Read It All: John 21
Read a Bit: John 21

Priority

John 21:25 — And there are also many other things which Jesus did, which if they were written in detail, I suppose that even the world itself would not contain the books that would be written.

The Lord Jesus Christ makes it clear what the believer's priority should be—He said to follow Him. As John closes out his Gospel account of Jesus' life, he gives a very intimate look at Jesus' last instructions to His disciples. Remember, this is the resurrected Jesus, the One they knew had been crucified on a Roman cross, died, was buried for three days, and is now fishing and dining with them. This is no ordinary man.

Resurrected Jesus enjoys surprising them. When they do not recognize Him as He is on the shore and they have had a long night on the boat of not catching any fish, He directs them where to fish. They follow His directions, catch a great number of fish, and then realize it is Him. The abundance gives Him away.

After breakfast, the risen, manifested Lord directs Peter to follow Him by considering his love for Jesus and humbly shepherding His sheep. A grieved Peter learns to rely on Jesus for His love in caring for others.

Jesus cautions His followers about the hardships of following Him. Peter will go where he does not wish to go and will stretch out his own hands in death. Jesus reminds Peter to not question His authority and decisions for the other disciples, as Peter inquires about the future of the disciple Jesus loved (a phrase used to refer to John).

Believers have the Gospel message to share and life to enjoy in ministry with other followers of Jesus. We need to remember to look for Jesus' presence in the simple things, even an early breakfast meal. Following Jesus means loving His flock. A good shepherd adds to his flock regularly. In writing the his Gospel, John portrays the joy of following Messiah not because we need to earn a right standing with Him, but because He is our right standing with God. Walking with Jesus is abiding in the Light of the World, the Bread of Life, the Resurrection and the Life, the One True God. To walk with Jesus is to believe His revelation. In Him is Life.

"God has made Him both Lord and Christ- this *Jesus* whom you crucified."

Acts 2:36

NEW TESTAMENT ACTS

T he careful Scripture reader knows there is some type of gap between the first and second comings of Messiah. The prophets and the Gospel writers all allude to a delay between Christ's death and resurrection and the Kingdom. There is a mystery associated with this gap, an entity that will represent Christ to the nations. Daniel talks about "former days," while other prophets mention "latter days." In the former days, the people believed in the promises of God having a partial, symbolic, and prophetic idea of Christ's atonement for sin. Following the cross, those who believed in Christ received His real righteousness, not just a promise of righteousness, but imputed righteousness from God and His Spirit within to affirm that they were sealed until His return and the Kingdom. The delay between Christ's first and second comings is connected with Israel's rejection of Messiah and God's merciful revelation of Himself to all nations through His Body, the church. Acts introduces His church and its expansion so that all nations could be blessed by the great Covenant Blesser.

Week 39, Day 1

Read It All: Acts 1-7
Read a Bit: Acts 1-4

The Revelation in Summary

Acts 1:8 — *. . . but you will receive power when the Holy Spirit has come upon you and you shall be My witnesses both in Jerusalem, and in all Judea and Samaria, and even to the remotest part of the earth.*

Luke continues his narrative about the life of Jesus and His body of believers, the church, in the Book of Acts. The risen Savior ascends into heaven, as recorded in Acts 1, to fulfill His role as High Priest, interceding for those on earth while seated at the right hand of the Father. Jesus had revealed that He was God's Word made flesh and that He had the authority of God. Jesus imparted His Life through His Words of truth to those with ears to hear. Following the ascension of Christ, Life is still available to those who would receive the Words of God proclaimed by God's messengers, His church. In this sense, the church holds the keys to life and death for mankind.

In Acts we learn that the gift of the Holy Spirit enables those who hear the Gospel to receive it as truth. The Holy Spirit indwells the believer and helps illuminate the mind of the unbeliever to respond to God's Word. This is the power of the Holy Spirit, to reveal truth, to witness of Christ. The ongoing witness of Jesus Christ is accomplished through the work of His Spirit in His messengers going forth to the nations. There are many examples of witnessing personalities in Acts: Stephen, Philip, Saul, Barnabus, Peter, James, Samaritans, John, Aquila, Priscilla, Lydia . . . . God's message to the ends of the earth is sent via His people.

In reading Acts you will see the apostles' concentrated efforts on still reaching the Jews. The accounts of people believing start with the Word being spoken in Jerusalem and then branching out to other parts of the world. Many of the missionaries will start their witnessing in the Jewish synagogues and in cities known to have Jewish settlements. But as the historical accounts in the Book of Acts continue, the reader sees the church is expanding as a result of the Gentiles hearing and believing from Jerusalem to Judea and Samaria, through Rome, to the uttermost parts of the earth.

Week 39, Day 2

Read It All: Acts 8-9
Read a Bit: Acts 8-9

Integrity

Acts 9:31 — *So the church throughout all Judea and Galilee and Samaria enjoyed peace, being built up; and going on in the fear of the Lord and in the comfort of the Holy Spirit, it continued to increase.*

I grew up at a time when the era of believing that it was a matter of integrity to be part of the church in America was ending. When I was little, I attended a Mennonite Church in Pulaski, Iowa, where my mother taught Sunday School while my father was in Viet Nam. When my father returned home, we moved from Iowa, and my family didn't see a need for church. By the time I was in high school, I really didn't know what it looked like to be involved in a church. I had some friends who invited me to a vacation Bible School at their church, and I attended but felt very out of place, confused by their fascination with old stories and intimidated by their family-like relationships. I felt unknown. They were a big family that seemed loud to me.

About this time, some of our family moved to Florida. They became very passionate about their church there, and when I visited, I got to experience the sweet fellowship at their church. I also got to hear God's truth from a man speaking from God's Word. I prayed to receive Christ while visiting this special congregation in Florida. When I returned home from my visit, it didn't dawn on me that I needed a local body to help me grow in my new-found faith. I became what D. Stuart Briscoe describes as "a "self-confessed believer" but not a belonger.[21] I didn't see the value, the blessing, the beauty of belonging to a local body of believers. I didn't take the time to consider the church.

I suffered for years as a very immature Christian. I was doubting and inconsistent due to a lack of teaching from His Word, celebrating His presence, prayer, and sweet fellowship. I needed church. Please don't

---

[21]   D. Stuart Briscoe, "Recommendation," quoted in Philip Yancey, *Church: Why Bother? My Personal Pilgrimage* (Grand Rapids, MI: Zondervan, 2001), 114.

think I'm ignorant of the church's struggles and failures, I know the church consists of people who make serious, hurtful mistakes (a tactful term), as we fall short of the glory of God. But God established the church. He entrusted His Bride with the task of embodying His presence in the world. C. S. Lewis wrote that God "seems to do nothing of Himself which He can possibly delegate to His creatures. He commands us to do slowly and blunderingly what He could do perfectly and in the twinkling of an eye."[22] God fellowships with humans and takes the "risk" of delegating to the weak much like a parent does when raising a child. God has a purpose for His Body, and He holds us responsible for our witness of His Life.

I'm concerned today about the statistics regarding those raised in the church and leaving it during their college years. I'm concerned about people wanting church on their own terms, at their convenience. I'm concerned that we have a generation of young adults who could beautifully represent His body but don't see the value of filling His house or proclaiming His truth. We tend to think we can represent Him while ignoring His love for His Bride, the church.

My children were raised differently from me. They were raised in church. At this point in time, they do not all participate wholeheartedly as His Body. I pray for myself (I can get weary of rolling dutifully out of bed each Sunday), for my family, for believers to honor His Body like never before, enjoying the freedom that we have, at this point in time, to gather together and boldly proclaim "He is worthy." I am thankful for the church. She has overwhelmingly represented the love of Christ to me. I hope that I am faithful to Him through honoring His Bride. I hope that I can pass on to others the great value of being His church as a visible, local assembly.

Week 39, Day 3

Read It All: Acts 10-18
Read a Bit: Acts 10-18

Dignity

---

[22]   C. S. Lewis, *The World's Last Night and Other Essays* (New York, NY: Harper Collins, 1960), 9.

Acts 17:28 — . . . for in Him we live and move and exist . . . .

You need to know that I'm a redhead, or ginger, as my son calls me. As I age, I'm less of a ginger due to fading, but the ginger label still sticks, which may explain what I'm about to confide.

I was listening to the radio last week and thought I heard people talking about those suffering "ginger identity crisis." My mind took off. I was thrilled that my subculture was being acknowledged. I guess I would say it has been rough at times growing up a ginger. I thought of the teasings, the comparisons to Orphan Annie, the inability to get a deep tan, and of course those wondering if I had a hot temper. I also had a physical education teacher who said redheads went bald instead of grey! (I hated physical education.) I started thinking of fellow sufferers, but as I was gaining a militant mindset, I suddenly realized the radio person wasn't talking about ginger identity at all, but gender identity! They weren't recognizing how misunderstood I am. How frustrating! I thought I had a bonafide label with a cause.

I have realized that everyone has some struggle with identity. There are those with nose identity crises, belly bounce issues, and unibrow disdain. No matter what the struggle is, I don't think labeling helps. Why focus on the struggle or what we or others just don't get or like about ourselves? How about focusing more on our character, how we can encourage others, and take the focus off self? Without the basics in life, knowing we are created by an amazing, good Designer Who loves us, we lose perspective. God created us for Himself and He supplies an eternal, wonderful identity when we seek His way and His truth. Remember, *"for in Him we live and move and exist, as even some of your own poets have said, 'For we also are His children'"* (Acts 17:28).

Week 39, Day 4

Read It All: Acts 19-24
Read a Bit: Acts 19; 24

Unity

Acts 20:28 — Be on guard for yourselves and for all the flock, among which the Holy Spirit has made you overseers, to shepherd the church of God which He purchased with His own blood.

I continue to present what I hope are very clear points regarding being His Bride, the church. I value the church as where I have been discipled, strengthened in the faith.

If you are a believer, then you are a member of the church universal (brothers and sisters who follow Christ throughout the world).

If you are a believer, then Scripture gives you the command to fellowship with other believers by assembling together in a local body (Hebrews 10:25).

If you are a believer, then Scripture reminds you that the church is key in overpowering Hades (Matthew 16:18).

If you are a believer, then the church serves to guide you in truth and helps discipline you when you need it (Matthew 18:17). This is good! We believers need accountability!

If you are a believer, then you'll appreciate knowing that helping the church increase provides a great witness to the world (Acts 9:31).

If you are a believer, then the church is your greatest support for prayer, teaching, fellowship, and comfort (Acts 12:5, 14:27, 15:4; 2 Corinthians 8:1).

If you are a believer, you are needed to support the church to provide the organization needed to send missionaries throughout the world (Acts 11:22).

If you are a believer, you are to seek to build up the church (1 Corinthians 14:12).

If you are a believer, then you should value what Christ purchased with His own blood—His Bride, the Church (Acts 20:28).

If you are a believer, then you are the church, and attending a local gathering makes that known to far more than you realize (Hebrews 12:22-24).

Christ Jesus, when He walked this earth, poured His truth into His disciples. His plan was that His followers would bless others with His Word. Blessing others would be a result of representing the Savior, and to represent the Savior, you must know the Savior. The church became central for learning about the Savior. Christ established a body of believers who would build one another up to have the mind of Christ. This community should be like a family that lovingly encourages, confronts, celebrates, and enjoys each member.

Week 39, Day 5

Read It All: Acts 25-28
Read a Bit: Acts 25-28

Priority

Acts 26:6-8 — *And now I am standing trial for the hope of the promise made by God to our fathers; the promise to which our twelve tribes hope to attain, as they earnestly serve God night and day. And for this hope, O King, I am being accused by Jews. Why is it considered incredible among you people if God does raise the dead?*

Springtime can be shocking. My yard was a mess of brown lawn and dried-up, dead debris. Then it suddenly changed. The green seemed to come out of nowhere. I didn't have grass, but from a distance, the weeds had appeared as a dense green lawn. The gardenia I thought dead from the frost had green growth at its base. My lantana suddenly had lush green fullness. Some bulbs had sprouted green, with vivid reds and pinks peaking from the new growth. The brown willow tree shot up with long wispy greenness seemingly overnight. These were shocking signs of sudden life.

I know this life isn't sprouting from the dead but rather the dormant. I have my share of dead plants to pile as compost. But the drastic difference a week in spring makes on my yard grabs my attention and reminds me that it is time to celebrate His resurrection, a true death-to-life encounter.

The priority of the church is to share the message of the resurrection. I remember first hearing of Jesus' resurrection when I attended a neighbor's vacation Bible school. There was a flannel board with Jesus, a cross, and a big rock tomb. Flannel Jesus went on the cross, into the tomb and came out of the tomb without ever changing expression. Nevertheless, His resurrection was powerful news to me.

I think some part of an Easter celebration service should be spent outside. Sunrise services or gathering in a garden gives a hint to the wonder of the day when Christ Jesus came out of the grave. Scripture tells us there were MANY witnesses to Resurrected Lord Jesus. There must have been, as He walked, talked, ate, and drank on this earth for over 40 days (1 Corinthians 15:3-8; Acts 1:9-10) after His victory over death.

According to Scripture, the resurrection is a reality. Believers are resurrected to meet our Maker, and we need to be ready. Those in Christ are promised a resurrection to a good life as forgiven and freed children of God. All my hope is in Jesus.

REST TIME

Week 40, Days 1-5

Matthew 11:29 — *Take My yoke upon you and learn from Me, for I am gentle and humble in heart, and you will find rest for your souls.*

The New Testament Gospels and the Book of Acts provide the history on the Lord Jesus Christ completely fulfilling God's Word regarding the Seed of the woman through Christ's birth, life, death, resurrection, and ascension to the Father. Matthew, Mark, Luke, and John report the evidence, their eyewitness accounts, so that the reader may have Life in Christ. It is a joy to meditate on these texts considering their Old Testament correlations and the hope we have in Messiah.

Journal any thoughts you wish to record at this point in your reading.

"And to Your Seed", that is, Christ

Galatians 3:16

NEW TESTAMENT LETTERS

In this day of electronic communications, I still enjoy a handwritten letter, maybe even more than ever because of its uniqueness. Mom taught me the beauty of the thank-you note. Gorgeous notecards and file folders delight me; the written word affirms.

This is why I really enjoy reading the biblical epistles. They are letters. Letters loaded with loving concern for their readers. These books were opened up to me by Dr. Baylis, my Bible group teacher, when he taught a class on the literary function and structure of letters prior to expounding on their content. Under his instruction, I learned to diagram a letter.

Biblical letters are typically written by an author impassioned to express truth that will help the reader overcome a problem or realign their thinking to avoid problems. They are also written to express feelings for the reader. When I read the New Testament letters, I ask myself these questions: who is the author, who is the reader, what is the motivation driving the writing (is there a problem being addressed), what changes should be the result of reading the letter, and who should the reader share this letter with?

The epistles have become personal gifts of truth to me. I appreciate the intensity and accept the authority of the authors. I marvel at God's concern for the reader expressed in the messages. I am thankful for the warnings and for the author's comprehension of people's natures, of me. Just as receiving a personal note brightens my day, reading the epistles encourages my faith and breathes new life into my step.

I remember visiting with a new believer who was reading Galatians and longing to understand the message more fully. She needed the Old Testament background to the letter in order to better comprehend its meaning. I admired her diligence in seeking to learn the author's intent for writing. I enjoyed a moment of reading this precious letter with her and seeing her realize it was meant for her.

Therefore, beloved, since you look for these things, be diligent to be found by Him in peace, spotless and blameless, and regard the patience of our Lord as salvation; just as also our beloved brother Paul, according to the wisdom given him, wrote to you, as also in all his letters, speaking in them of these things, in which are some things hard to understand, which the untaught and unstable distort, as they do also the rest of the Scriptures, to their own destruction. You therefore, beloved, knowing this beforehand, be on your guard so that you are not carried away by the error of unprincipled men and fall from your own steadfastness, but grow in the grace and knowledge of our Lord and Savior Jesus Christ. To Him be the glory, both now and to the day of eternity. Amen. 2 Peter 3:14-18

ROMANS

Paul wrote the Book of Romans from Corinth near the end of his third missionary journey, and Phoebe, a church woman he trusted, delivered this letter to the church. Paul would later visit Rome and be imprisoned there twice before his public martyrdom in Rome. The letter addresses the conflict in the local church over obtaining righteousness before God. Romans is Paul's longest epistle and supplies exhaustive teaching on redemption. This book was at the heart of the Protestant Reformation.

Week 41, Day 1

Read It All: Romans 1
Read a Bit: Romans 1

The Revelation in Summary

Romans 1:16-17 — *For I am not ashamed of the gospel, for it is the power of God for salvation to everyone who believes, to the Jew first and also to the Greek. For in it the righteousness of God is revealed from faith to faith; as it is written, "But the righteous man shall live by faith."*

From the moment one begins to read Romans to the ending verse, Paul's methodical presentation of the Gospel message is clear. Humanity is without excuse in their rejection of God, but God in His kindness provides Life to those who trust in His promised Seed. All believers should be continually praying and seeking how to best share and live in the truth of the Gospel. So much of Scripture conveys the importance of remembering the Gospel message of gracious God giving any who would call on His name His righteousness through belief in His Son. Take refuge in the Son!

The apostle Paul was not ashamed of the Gospel or of his own need for it. Paul emphasized the importance of comprehending the power of the Gospel, demonstrated in Christ's resurrection. Paul had a special message to the Gentiles, who had been grafted into the Seed-line of Abraham. Paul had a poignant message to the Jews. His heart's desire was for them to be saved, to be included in God's remnant forever.

After fully explaining the Gospel message for all, Paul explains how to walk in Gospel truth so that others may see the believer's transformed life and accept the love of God. Paul encourages self-denial on behalf of others and exhorts the dedicated service that strengthens the weak in faith.

Paul tells the reader that our response to the Gospel is a matter of life and death, a matter of joy or sorrow. Paul preached so that mankind could escape the deserved wrath of God and live in the rescuing power of the Gospel of Jesus Christ. Enjoy being rescued!

Week 41, Day 2

Read It All: Romans 2-5
Read a Bit: Romans 2-5

Integrity

Romans 5:10 — *For if while we were enemies we were reconciled to God by the death of His Son, much more, now that we are reconciled, shall we be saved by His life.*

When is old enough to know better going to kick in? Or when is spiritual enough to be better going to kick in? Maturity in the faith is recognizing our sin, hating it, and confessing it with the assurance of forgiveness more quickly than formerly. Maturity is becoming astonishingly free at welcoming criticism, particularly regarding sin in my life, and being grateful for the one pointing it out. I appreciate what Elyse Fitzpatrick writes about her heart's response to an accusation of wrong on her part:[23]

> Because the gospel tells me that I am more sinful and flawed than I ever dared believe, I'm no longer entrapped in trying to prop up my former flawed identity. . . . I don't have to pretend to be something other than what I am. I don't have a reputation to protect. I can freely admit my failure without needing to cover up, be defensive, or beat myself up. . . . Rather than trying to find a way to protect or justify myself, I am totally free to be who I really am, a very great sinner. Rather than raking myself over the coals, wondering, How could I be such an idiot

---

[23]   Elyse Fitzpatrick, *Comforts from Romans: Celebrating the Gospel One Day at a Time* (Wheaton, IL: Crossway, 2013), 79-80.

and sin like this? I am now free to say, Of course I sinned like this. It's just God's grace that I'm not like this every day! I am, after all, a very great sinner. But that's not all. Not only am I a very great sinner, but I've got a very great Savior.

Personally, as a great sinner with nothing to recommend me, I have experienced great love and honor through the years. My parents always treated me as valued, and they of all people know how flawed I am. I am thankful for a husband and children who have made me feel more loved than I could ever really comprehend. We can live together, as great sinners, and forgive and enjoy one another. Integrity comes from the Lord Himself, upright in all. Through the study of His Word, I've come to know God, Who calls me His beloved, not because of anything I do, but because of His Son's perfection and gift of righteousness to me. My foolishness serves to remind me to rely on my Savior completely and to be grateful for the Creator of the Heavens and Earth, Who supplies an abundance of grace and the free gift of righteousness to those who recognize their great need of Him.

Week 41, Day 3

Read It All: Romans 6-8
Read a Bit: Romans 6-8

Dignity

Romans 6:4 — *Therefore we have been buried with Him through baptism into death, so that as Christ was raised from the dead through the glory of the Father, so we too might walk in newness of life.*

British preacher Charles Spurgeon said, "To follow afar off and live at a distance from Christ, even if it does not make your soul perish, yet it will wither up your joys and make you feel an unhappy man, an unhappy woman."[24]

---

[24] C. H. Spurgeon, "Peter After His Restoration" (sermon, Metropolitan Tabernacle, Newington, NH, July 26, 1888).

Once the Scripture reader understands that they are right with God through Christ by the gift of His righteousness and not by "performing rightly," they may ask about the many imperatives about "right living" in the New Testament. If we are right with God and already have eternal life, why is persevering in His truth so important? The answer is that God wants us to live—really live. This is conforming to His image. This is glorious purpose. Life is Christ! Enjoy Life now!

For he who finds me finds life and obtains favor from the Lord. Proverbs 8:35

In the way of righteousness is life, and in its pathway there is no death. Proverbs 12:28

. . . for bodily discipline is only of little profit, but godliness is profitable for all things, since it holds promise for the present life and also for the life to come. 1 Timothy 4:8

Our Father knows what ultimately brings us the greatest joy. He provides guidance through His Word on how to live and live abundantly. His children delight in the dignity that representing their Father brings. Learn His Words, walk humbly in His truth, set your feet in His footsteps, and determine to do what may seem hard at times with the assurance that His way is best. Grow up in your faith. Maturity has great blessings. Experience LIFE.

Week 41, Day 4

Read It All: Romans 9-11
Read a Bit: Romans 9-11

Unity

Romans 9:1-8 — *I am telling the truth in Christ, I am not lying, my conscience testifies with me in the Holy Spirit, that I have great sorrow and unceasing grief in my heart. For I could wish that I myself were accursed, separated from Christ for the sake of my brethren, my kinsmen according to the flesh, who are Israelites, to whom belongs the adoption as sons, and the glory and the covenants and the giving of the Law and the temple service and the promises, whose are the fathers, and from whom is the Christ according to the flesh, who is over all, God blessed forever. Amen. But it is not as though the word of God has failed. For they are not all Israel who are descended from Israel; nor are they all children because they are Abraham's descendants, but: "through Isaac your descendants will be named." That is, it is not the children of the flesh who are children of God, but the children of the promise are regarded as descendants.*

Paul grieved the rejection of Jesus by His countrymen, the Jews. He longed for them to be united in Christ, joint heirs of God's Promise and children of God. But some were not. The Gospels describe the Jewish religious leaders as condescending to the forerunners of Christ. They did not value the revelation of God regarding the Promised One.

I can be condescending too. At this time, I am not willing to take a family vote to determine if they agree. I have heard a comedian say that all his mother ever truly wanted was to have the last word. I have learned that if you say something condescending, you get the last word because you close a conversation. I do know that I withdraw when "condescended upon." I do not want to be that woman who gets the last word but consistently shuts down communication.

"Condescending" – An adjective, showing or implying a usually patronizing descent from dignity or superiority. The Latin prefix con- means "with," and the Latin word for "descend" means "down," so the word "condescending" probably developed to describe someone who looked down on others. Synonyms include patronizing, disdainful, arrogant, snotty . . . .

Sadly, that's how many have viewed religious leaders through the ages. Some mistake quiet and reserved for condescending, but it's more obvious when you are really the subject of condescension.

Condescending behavior itself is, not surprisingly, looked down upon. You know if you are being condescending, as it typically makes others feel bad or stupid. Condescension emphasizes what the other doesn't know or have. It is rude to be condescending and, in my experience, condescension produces an awkward moment for all involved in the communication. My family points out awkward moments by saying so: "You just really made that awkward." They are a direct bunch. Pointing out that I just made it awkward is awkward for me. (Just saying.) I'll work on this too.

Sometimes condescension comes very naturally for me, for the self-righteous. It is hard for those so much more brilliant and beautiful than everyone else, in that moment, to not condescend. See the heart issue?

Technology provides a temptation to be condescending instead of helpful. When people do not know a simple trick of the trade, the one in the know can be tempted to feel superior. It takes great patience and humility to kindly remind me again how to quickly stop my audio Bible when it goes off in church. (Just saying—again.)

God knows all, and yet when He comes down (condescends), He lifts up. I'm thankful that the most powerful, beautiful, brilliant One patiently hears my cries for help and delights in raising me up. Otherwise, I would be crushed.

Week 41, Day 5

Read It All: Romans 12-16
Read a Bit: Romans 12-16

Priority

Romans 12:9 — *Let love be without hypocrisy. Abhor what is evil; cling to what is good.*

The believer's priority in sharing the Gospel is doing so in love.

> *Never pay back evil for evil to anyone. Respect what is right in the sight of all men.* Romans 12:17

> *Do not be overcome by evil, but overcome evil with good.* Romans 12:21

It seems dark. Devastated homes breeding devastated lives. A bride remembering being a child repeatedly raped by Mom's boyfriends and now resisting a Good Father she cannot comprehend. A failing marriage, panicked parents who cannot say anything nice and are blaming everyone, still not teachable . . . seems hopeless. Children witnessing it all. An abusive husband manipulating the mother of his children, using them as ammunition in his continued war to control. Gossip ruining friendships. The bottle that shatters homes, deceiving many into thinking it is filled with joy. Anxiety over petty things. Leadership with secrets . . . no way to revive character. Unopened Bibles and low attendance in study. Shock when someone bows to pray. Slavery today while the Emancipator is ignored. Children with no consistent place to lay their heads and no consistent person to show them value.

It seems overwhelmingly dark. God is good but there is evil, and He allows humankind to rebel against God-ordained responsibilities . . . repeatedly. God is good and the evil is us. We need the Redeemer every moment of our lives.

Persevere to do right; we are not home yet. Your acts of right make a tremendous difference in this wrong world. He is the Lifter of our heads, and He often does so through His Body of believers. Be an instrument of His Light, as darkness is readily consumed by even small flickers as they take flame.

> *And thus I aspired to preach the gospel, not where Christ was already named, so that I would not build on another man's foundation; but as it is written, "They who had no news of Him shall see, and they who have not heard shall understand."* Romans 15:20-21

I CORINTHIANS

Corinth was a city in Greece established before 1200 BC. It was a Roman colony and the capital of the province, with a commercial center that provided a means of physical wealth to the community. The region was also represented by many pagan religions that incorporated prostitution in worship. The Temple of Aphrodite could be seen on a high mountain south of the city.

Paul had preached the gospel and planted a church in Corinth after traveling to Athens. He met Priscilla and Aquila in Corinth, and they would be his traveling companions for many miles. Paul ministered in Corinth for about 18 months before leaving for Ephesus with them. Paul heard about immorality in the Corinthian church while he was in Ephesus, so he wrote to the church to address their problems.

Week 42, Day 1

Read It All: 1 Corinthians 1-3
Read a Bit: 1 Corinthians 1-3

The Revelation in Summary

1 Corinthians 1:10 — *Now I exhort you, brethren, by the name of our Lord Jesus Christ, that you all agree and that there be no divisions among you, but that you be made complete in the same mind and in the same judgment.*

One way to summarize the letter to the Corinthians is to simply list the problems that Paul addressed in his writing. He longed for the church to see every part of life through the Gospel in application. The problems in the church were many:

- Favoritism of leaders based on gifts (1:10-17)
- Divisions in the church based on an errant understanding of the gifts of speech and knowledge (1:10-4:21)
- Boasting in human wisdom rather than His Revelation (1:20-31)
- Disregarding Paul's apostolic gift (2:1-5)
- Immorality in the church (5:1-13)
- Taking a brother in Christ to court (6:1-11)
- Immoral use of the physical body (6:12-20)

- Misunderstanding the value of marriage (7:1-40)
- Eating meat sacrificed to idols (Chapters 8-10)
- Chaos instead of church order (Chapter 11)
- Ignoring authorities and cultural values, honoring the rich and ignoring the poor; elevating members based on gifts (Chapters 11-14)
- Denying the resurrection of Christ (Chapter 15)

The teachings in 1 Corinthians are crucial to strengthening our church today. Pick a problem to study, and see God's provision of hope and restoration in the trying situations in Corinth. See also God's desire for the church to be unified as His healthy Body. The church is community, and although community can be a bit messy, God challenges His children to address their problems and serve as one for the advancement of His gift of Life.

Week 42, Day 2

Read It All: 1 Corinthians 4-7
Read a Bit: 1 Corinthians 4-7

Integrity

1 Corinthians 7:10-11 — *But to the married I give instructions, not I, but the Lord, that the wife should not leave her husband (but if she does leave, she must remain unmarried, or else be reconciled to her husband), and that the husband should not divorce his wife.*

My daughter's wedding reminded me of many Biblical teachings on marriage. I know that the success of her marriage is an issue of integrity. Will they both value the integrity of God and one another in Him?

The wedding created an opportunity for lots of women to tell me their best marriage tips. I think the women assumed that I would share their tips with my daughter to provide an amazing foundation for this big step in life. The truth is that she had marriage advice ad nauseam and I didn't have the nerve to give her more. If I hadn't made the most of those teachable moments in the past, then c'est la vie. If I had brought up marriage tips right before her big day, it probably would have looked like I was second guessing the wedding. I wasn't. I thought the happy couple could have given me and Scott a little advice. I was so very happy for them and the godly foundation they had going into their wedding. In the pre-marital bliss frenzy, the better conversations are how much ice cream we prefer on hot brownies. Timing is everything.

That said, I did make a record of some of the advice I heard. You may wish to share these tips with your daughter or another while you have time, but these tips are helpful for all relationships, as they center on communication. I greatly respect the ladies who contributed these thoughts; they are passionate women who want the best for all marriages and who have modeled a high view of marriage through hard times. They believe His Word and apply it in their homes. So here is what they offered:

- Listen and talk about everything. There is no intimacy without knowing one another's thoughts, values, fears, and joys. We cannot read one another's minds. Honestly admit your strengths and weaknesses. Oftentimes, a simple confession of a "little secret" frees you to grow up. This is accountability. A special note here: Great physical intimacy takes talking about the specifics.
- Communicate without talking too; actions do speak loudly. Do the little things to demonstrate love. Be there. Tease a little without words. Actively listen, especially when you are bored. Love is an act of the will, not simply an emotion. Choose love.
- Talk about God's best (this means challenge one another to know and value His Word). Two people with the same beliefs and values will walk really closely together. It is key that a couple encourages one another about the goodness of God, the reality of sin, the means of forgiveness, their purpose in life, and their hope for the future.
- Pray together, worship together, grow more like Him together, and purpose to know God even better than you know one another.

Let no unwholesome word proceed from your mouth, but only such a word as is good for edification according to the need of the moment, so that it will give grace to those who hear. Ephesians 4:29

. . . glorify God in your body. 1 Corinthians 6:20

Week 42, Day 3

Read It All: 1 Corinthians 8-10
Read a Bit: 1 Corinthians 8-10

Dignity

1 Corinthians 8:8 — *But food will not commend us to God; we are neither the worse if we do not eat, nor the better if we do eat.*

One year, my husband gave me a Fitbit for my birthday. I am borderline ungrateful. I know the benefit of increased accountability regarding my "fitness" and the importance of being more intentional about good health. I know this was a loving gesture of help, as I do struggle with making regular exercise and good eating a priority, and I hear that a Fitbit helps. He was also thinking about the fun I'll have joining a lot of family and friends who are enjoying their Fitbit. But I really dread having one more thing that I need to charge and/or check and/or feed information to on a daily basis. I like a little more sparkle on my wrist. The Fitbit overwhelms and underwhelms me.

The Fitbit also reminds me that good health is a discipline for me, and I would rather it just come naturally. I don't want another reminder of what masters me at times—eating sweets and inactivity. My first week with the Fitbit was revealing. The bulk of my eating is from 7 p.m. to midnight. To my surprise and horror, the Fitbit recorded that I was asleep for 11 hours and 49 minutes one night and that I average around 9.8 hours of sleep each night. My blood pressure is usually pretty low; apparently I am nodding off whenever I sit down. I feel older and more worn out than ever, knowing that I appear to be sleeping through most of my life.

I do love to get in a long walk as often as possible, but now with my Fitbit, I am obsessing over 10,000 steps per day. I just have to have that little celebratory ding and buzz on my wrist affirming I've sufficiently moved before the day ends. I discovered that if I brush my teeth with an electric toothbrush, my Fitbit will add about 100 steps.

Like many things in life, I need to learn how to enjoy the blessings without obsessing over the blessings. I need to be patient with myself regarding growth in the important disciplines and to realize what a privilege it is to represent God through being disciplined in any area of life.

There is a fine line between discipline and fanaticism, and I'm hopeful I can find His balance. If you ever want to go for a walk, just give me a call.

> *All things are lawful for me, but not all things are profitable. All things are lawful for me, but I will not be mastered by anything.* 1 Corinthians 6:12

> *Therefore I run in such a way, as not without aim; I box in such a way, as not beating the air; but I discipline my body and make it my slave, so that, after I have preached to others, I myself will not be disqualified.* 1 Corinthians 9:26-27

Week 42, Day 4

Read It All: 1 Corinthians 11-14
Read a Bit: 1 Corinthians 11-14

Unity

1 Corinthians 13:1 — *If I speak with the tongues of men and of angels, but do not have love, I have become a noisy gong or a clanging cymbal.*

I was writing a newsletter for the last quarter of the year and decided to focus the articles on reconciliation. I asked a few of the ladies in my classes if they had a story for the newsletter. One didn't say anything to me right away, but after about a week, she timidly came by my office to ask if I still needed a testimony. I did.

Pam's dad had abandoned her family when she was a little girl. Her dad simply left one day when she was at school. She was confused, but her mom was not open to discussing the loss with Pam.

When Pam was older, she purposed to locate her dad. He had remarried, and his wife didn't want him to have anything to do with his former family, with his children. Pam was repeatedly rejected when she would contact her dad. Her family was confused by her desire to have him in her life.

Years later, after Pam had raised children of her own and was living in Florida, she got a call from her dad in Georgia. He needed her help. He said his wife wasn't doing well and asked if Pam would come and see him on the weekend. Pam said yes. "Coincidently," Father's Day was that weekend.

When Pam arrived at his home, a home she had never been allowed to enter, she saw immediately that her dad and his wife were struggling with memory issues and taking care of themselves. She packed them both up, brought them home, and had them live with her . . . for years. In the midst of their years together, under Pam's roof, her dad apologized to her. Pam had forgiven him a long time before his apology.

Eventually, she couldn't take care of them, so they were lovingly moved to an assisted living facility near Pam's home. Her father passed away knowing the love of Jesus through his daughter. As far as I know, Pam still visits his wife, her step-mom, regularly and enjoys reminding her that she is loved.

> *Love . . . does not take into account a wrong suffered, . . .*
> 1 Corinthians 13:5

Week 42, Day 5

Read It All: 1 Corinthians 15-16
Read a Bit: 1 Corinthians 15-16

Priority

1 Corinthians 15:1 — *Now I make known to you, brethren, the gospel which I preached to you, which also you received, in which also you stand, by which also you are saved . . . .*

While many others are thinking of bunnies (chocolate or furry), bonnets, springtime, and eggs at Easter, I, along with a remnant, think of the Gospel and the power of the resurrection. This Good News is why celebrating Easter is so precious to me. Remembering His promises and provision for life is essential to solidifying our walk of faith. In the Old Testament Law, truth was validated by two witnesses. There are four Gospel witnesses to the life of the Lord Jesus Christ and literally hundreds of witnesses to the resurrected Christ. I love God's overwhelming mercy in helping humanity recognize His deliverance.

I celebrate the resurrection any time of the year by reviewing Paul's words in 1 Corinthians 15. The believer is destined to be raised imperishable with Him, as He is the Resurrection and the Life. This news is life-changing. Happy Resurrection Day every day!

2 CORINTHIANS

The authority of the apostle had to be established for the spread of the Gospel. An unreliable source would not be taken seriously for long. The witness must be believable as sent by God! Paul affirms his credentials in 2 Corinthians as the church continues to doubt the apostolic Word of Life. People tend to belittle those who suffer, and Paul was known for his suffering, as he was persecuted, even imprisoned, during his many travels. Paul provides teaching on why suffering for the gospel authenticates rather than diminishes the message. He also points out that sacrificial giving by many believers to other churches in need also authenticates the message. This leads to his written guidance on giving and suffering so that others, throughout the ages, may receive God's comfort by reading Paul's words.

I love the eternal perspective of the book. I tend to get caught up in temporal things and pettiness. This book redirects me to His perspective on this realm in relation to the future Kingdom. Seeing the difference between the temporal and the eternal is heart changing.

Week 43, Day 1

Read It All: 2 Corinthians 1-2
Read a Bit: 2 Corinthians 1-2

The Revelation in Summary

2 Corinthians 2:4 — *For out of much affliction and anguish of heart I wrote to you with many tears; not so that you would be made sorrowful, but that you might know the love which I have especially for you.*

This letter provides a deep look into the heart of Paul and his discipling of the Corinthian believers. Paul is confessing that their relationship has been tearful for him, a hard one because of divisions and outright rebellion against his authority. He remains a part of their lives as he longs for them to understand the love God has given him for them. He longs for them to experience the comfort that comes from comforting and encouraging others. God has a plan for His children, and Paul does not want the Corinthians to miss the blessing of living for God.

Christ's cross is really a foreign concept to the Corinthian church. They judge leaders by appearance, possessions, and strengths, while the cross calls us to value humility and suffering. They forget the needs of others; the cross calls us to give our lives for others. They refuse to be sorrowful; the cross draws us into the horrific sorrow of sin. They commend the strong; the cross is exhorted as we confess our weakness. They dread discipline; the cross pictures the discipline of Christ to do the Father's will.

Paul explains that believers are known for their ability to reconcile. They are called to be ambassadors of reconciliation to the world. They value sorrow especially when godly sorrow brings repentance and life change. They are also known for their generosity, graciously giving to others as they have received so much themselves. They are commended not for beauty or strength, but for their identity in Christ. Paul prays for the church to be unified. Like a mother longs for her children to get along and be an encouraging help to one another, Paul preaches unity and like-mindedness to the Corinthians. We see Paul's dedication to helping the church grow to resemble their Savior. We see that Paul's authenticity as an apostle is not in his accolades but in recognizing his own weaknesses and trusting the Lord Jesus Christ's strength to deliver him and make him willing to suffer so that others might have Life.

Week 43, Day 2

Read It All: 2 Corinthians 3
Read a Bit: 2 Corinthians 3

Integrity

2 Corinthians 3:18 — *But we all, with unveiled face, beholding as in a mirror the glory of the Lord, are being transformed into the same image from glory to glory, just as from the Lord, the Spirit.*

Paul says that the believer's commendation is that they are a letter of Christ, cared for by the apostles and written not with ink but with the Spirit of the living God, not on tablets of stone, but on tablets of human hearts. Wow! I have worked so hard for so many hours to commend myself to others by what I perceive as good that I have enslaved myself to always needing to better myself. According to Paul's teaching, I am adequate because my adequacy is from God, based on a New Covenant that gives Life. This is liberating to me!

This teaching impacts all my relationships. I know that many times I've been excited to get together with family and friends only to be bitterly disappointed when I felt discouraged because I couldn't make everyone happy. My self-image was based on whether or not I was sufficient for another. My confidence was in me, so being with others made me really aware of my insufficiencies.

People really don't have the power to steal our confidence or joy, we just tend to readily give it away with wrong thinking. We accept the cultural norm as a right definition of success or beauty. We base what we like or don't like about ourselves on the cultural norm. In the western world, norms are highly influenced by all types of media. Based on media, the cultural norm of commendability is attainable through education, wealth or a generous relative, athleticism, an air brush, some Botox, and intense food avoidance (no enjoying the holiday cookies). Look around: few fit how our culture defines success and beauty, but we beat up others and ourselves with these wrong concepts. We compare ourselves to others, and when we get together we say things like, "Looks like life has been good to you" (referring to materialistic gain), "I look so fat" (in comparison to the slimmer person), or "My, you look mature" (acting shocked by someone's aging). Comparing appearance, professions, kids, or presents does not lead to happy gatherings. Paul says our commendation is that our Creator sees us as valuable and gives us His Spirit.

This is so important that I will list some other Scriptures that fuel Paul's lesson to the Corinthians:

> *God created man in His own image, in the image of God He created him; male and female He created them.* Genesis 1:27

> *I will give thanks to You, for I am fearfully and wonderfully made; wonderful are Your works, and my soul knows it very well.* Psalm 139:14

> *Your adornment must not be merely external—braiding the hair, and wearing gold jewelry, or putting on dresses; but let it be the hidden person of the heart, with the imperishable quality of a gentle and quiet spirit, which is precious in the sight of God.* 1 Peter 3:3-4

I talked to my favorite family and marriage therapist, my daughter, about what hurts our self-image. She said that our self-image is based on what we are saying (and thinking) about ourselves and oftentimes on what we hear others say about us or what we perceive others think of us. We need to think about our thinking. Are our thoughts the messages that we want to keep telling ourselves? Are they keeping us from seeing the beauty in ourselves? Negative talk does nothing to build up anyone. It can rid us of any chance of seeing beauty in ourselves, and each and every one of us is beautiful in Him.

Being commendable in Christ is not saying it is okay to ignore health issues that we need to address. Women and men of all shapes and sizes should take care of their bodies, as they are a gift from the Lord. But we don't need to be degrading to ourselves in order to make changes. I call this self-bullying. I hope to avoid false humility, negative comments, and discouraging digs to myself and others as I enjoy my friends and family. You should too. Let's remind others of the truth that we are created in His image and precious in His sight. And let's give ourselves the greatest present possible, the reality that believing in His Son's sacrificial death and life covers our sin and that giving us new Life means we are perfected in the eyes of God. We all have a beauty that originates in our Creator. We can commend ourselves as adequate in Him.

Week 43, Day 3

Read It All: 2 Corinthians 4-7
Read a Bit: 2 Corinthians 4-7

Dignity

2 Corinthians 5:17-21 — *Therefore if anyone is in Christ, he is a new creature; the old things passed away; behold, new things have come. Now all these things are from God, who reconciled us to Himself through Christ and gave us the ministry of reconciliation, namely, that God was in Christ reconciling the world to Himself, not counting their trespasses against them, and He has committed to us the word of reconciliation. Therefore, we are ambassadors for Christ, as though God were making an appeal through us; we beg you on behalf of Christ, be reconciled to God. He made Him who knew no sin to be sin on our behalf, so that we might become the righteousness of God in Him.*

I like the idea of being an ambassador. I picture ambassadors as traveling to exotic places, having an extensive wardrobe that represents diverse cultures, eating foods I cannot pronounce made by chefs wearing puffy white hats, and being chauffeured. I really like the idea of being an ambassador. I tell lots of fellow believers that we are ambassadors.

In reality, my ambassador experience has more resembled me with hair askew, and makeup running from teary eyes, as I struggle to convey God's reconciling love for the broken and offended people I meet. I look like a wild woman trying to rescue a cat from a tree or two dogs from biting one another. I keep asking myself, why can't believers get along with one another? Why is the ministry of reconciliation so hard? I must have the wrong passport for this ambassador thing.

So I go back to His Word and look for guidance on being an ambassador. To bear the image of God beautifully is to realize how He has blessed me and, from that wealth of sacrificial mercy, to bless another. A simpler phrasing of this thought is, "I'm blessed to bless," just as Abraham was promised great blessing so that he, and ultimately the people of God through him, would bless all nations (Genesis 12). This is the way of God and thus a very good way.

This is also a freeing way. Rather than passing judgment on others, we are ambassadors of His grace. Christianity, NOT being a religion of works, is the only belief system that has this glorious message of grace. God is the great Covenant Blesser. Out of the forgiveness and mercy He has shown, Christians have the privilege of telling all others that they can be right with God by believing in His perfection and goodness through the atoning life of the Lord Jesus Christ. The good news is that Jesus saves us from condemnation not because of our "good acts" but because of His lovingkindness. He delights in being sacrificially merciful. It is freeing to explain why every person may have hope in Him as Redeemer in contrast to trying to get everyone to behave like they "should." This freedom motivates the recipients of His grace to love to reconcile in Him.

The Gospel message, if celebrated in the home, makes the home a haven. Rather than policing our families, the message frees us to share our weaknesses and to rejoice in God's provision of dignity to our family versus stinging performance reviews. The Gospel message gives us hope for one another. The Gospel message eradicates expectations of holiness for one another apart from Him. The Gospel message resurrects love.

The believer is called to be an ambassador of God's grace, to be a blessing to all the nations by proclaiming the way of salvation. We do this by pointing to Him, not ourselves.

Week 43, Day 4

Read It All: 2 Corinthians 8-9
Read a Bit: 2 Corinthians 8-9

Unity

2 Corinthians 9:15 — *Thanks be to God for His indescribable gift!*

I know the power of unity in the area of giving. Some of my most favorite memories are of being a part of something bigger than little me; being a part of a giving, sending, caring church who knows the generous grace of God and revels in it by being generous with others.

I have seen people united to serve by sending thousands of gift boxes overseas to orphanages, mission homes, military members, and the homeless. I know of hundreds of bikes sent to missionaries in areas with few cars and mainly bike trails. Wells and church buildings have been built throughout the world. Missionaries have been sent to faraway continents and in areas that can't be announced in Wednesday night service because the area is closed to Christians. Monies and clothing has been donated to local orphanages, crisis pregnancy centers, human trafficking victim homes, prayer groups, and food pantries. I've seen people joined in service to schools, delinquent programs, assisted living facilities, and children's home kitchens. United, we can be a generous example of our Savior throughout the world, particularly to our neighbors, and it is a joy to help so many in so many ways.

Generosity unifies. When people join together and give, the practical help of supplying another's need purifies our own list of wants. The helping redirects our focus from the temporal to the eternal and births a gratefulness for all we have in Christ.

Suffering a loss, by giving away what you rightfully have, can be the greatest joy as we realize the value of others. Sharing isn't just for young preschoolers, it is for His children of all ages. Generosity is the direct outcome of a thankful heart that comprehends His indescribable gift to them.

For I testify that according to their ability, and beyond their ability, they gave of their own accord, begging us with much urging for the favor of participation in the support of the saints, ... 2 Corinthians 8:3-4

Week 43, Day 5

Read It All: 2 Corinthians 10-13
Read a Bit: 2 Corinthians 10-13

Priority

2 Corinthians 12:9 — *And He has said to me, "My grace is sufficient for you, for power is perfected in weakness." Most gladly, therefore, I will rather boast about my weaknesses, so that the power of Christ may dwell in me.*

My first realization that some people actually spent time in prayer came during a visit to my Grandma Burns' home when I was a young girl. I got up early one morning and couldn't find Granny, so I went to her room to see if she was asleep. She was kneeling by her bedside, and I panicked thinking she was ill and had fallen over. I rushed to her and grabbed her shoulders only to be rebuked by a fully healthy and startled Granny. I got my first lesson on prayer. I also learned something I have never forgotten. My Grandma loved me so much that she prayed for me every day. I was overwhelmed.

Years later, when my son was about to enter kindergarten, I realized that I was a lonely mess and feared my son being outside my sheltering presence. I remembered Grandma Burns praying for me and purposed to pray regularly for my son's school. I had heard about a prayer group organized around schools. The group was international and had training materials. I got a manual and set up a prayer group in my home. This was the beginning of a new season in my walk of faith, and it was good.

The ladies who came to pray with me not only held me accountable to pray, but they taught me about life beyond my little world. They shared their hearts. They loved me and they loved my children. I in turn fell in love with their families. Praying for one another makes you aware of an enemy in a way that knits you together against that enemy. Praying for one another nullifies the tendency to compare, as you purpose for each home to have victories in the battles. My best friends came out of this group.

There were answered prayers and prayers we still labor over even though our children are long out of kindergarten. There were tears and much laughter. We benefitted from shared information like test dates, teacher appreciation, science fair timelines and ideas, and shot record requirements. It helps to do life with others. Prayer united us as we shared our weaknesses and encouraged one another of the power of Christ that dwells in each one of us. Prayer gave me sisters.

I thank God for directing His children to pray.

> *Finally, brethren, rejoice, be made complete, be comforted, be like-minded, live in peace; and the God of love and peace will be with you. Greet one another with a holy kiss. All the saints greet you. The grace of the Lord Jesus Christ, and the love of God, and the fellowship of the Holy Spirit, be with you all.* 2 Corinthians 13:11-14

GALATIANS, EPHESIANS, PHILIPPIANS, COLOSSIANS

These letters highlight essential truths that have been foundational for the perseverance of the church through the centuries. The Book of Galatians exhorts believers to stand firm in their freedom in Christ. When enemies of the Gospel would question justification by faith, church leaders would turn to Galatians and have Paul's defense in hand to strengthen their response to opposition. Paul wrote Ephesians, Philippians, and Colossians (as well as Philemon) when he was in prison in Rome. These books, when applied, reveal how the believer, sealed in God's Spirit, is to walk in a manner worthy of the Savior. The books clarify Who God is, who the enemy is, and who the believer is in Christ. There is a richness to these epistles that assures His followers of their nobility in the King. I thoroughly enjoy time in these dear letters.

Week 44, Day 1

Read It All: Galatians 1-6
Read a Bit: Galatians 1-2, 5

The Revelation in Summary

Galatians 1:6-9 — *I am amazed that you are so quickly deserting Him who called you by the grace of Christ, for a different gospel; which is really not another; only there are some who are disturbing you and want to distort the gospel of Christ. But even if we, or an angel from heaven, should preach to you a gospel contrary to what we have preached to you, he is to be accursed! As we have said before, so I say again now, if any man is preaching to you a gospel contrary to what you received, he is to be accursed!*

Paul saves his strongest language for the Galatians that are allowing false teaching to enslave them back under the law. He seems to be yelling as he preaches. He cries out for those preaching this contrary gospel to be accursed. He recounts opposing the church leadership that has adopted legalistic requirements for new believers and considers them condemned when they err by imposing the law on believers, as if that will save. He calls the Galatians foolish for letting false teachers bewitch them. He quotes the Old Testament to establish the validity of his teaching in every age. He verbally fights for God's children to have God's full emancipation.

Therefore, be sure that it is those who are of faith who are sons of Abraham. The Scripture, foreseeing that God would justify the Gentiles by faith, preached the gospel beforehand to Abraham, saying, "All the nations will be blessed in you." So then those who are of faith are blessed with Abraham, the believer. Galatians 3:7-9

The letter to the Galatians is Paul's reminder that justification is by faith not by the works of the law. The free in Christ have a really hard time consistently believing that they have been forgiven by God and do not need another sacrifice to lay to rest their old Adamic self. We forget that in God's courtroom, those in Christ have had their old nature declared judicially dead by the Great Judge. God sees His child with His new character and completely free from sin. The Book of Galatians is our pass out of the courtroom and into a life of walking in His Spirit. Free indeed.

Week 44, Day 2

Read It All: Ephesians 1-2
Read a Bit: Ephesians 1-2

The Revelation in Summary

Ephesians 1:3-4 — *Blessed be the God and Father of our Lord Jesus Christ, who has blessed us with every spiritual blessing in the heavenly places in Christ, just as He chose us in Him before the foundation of the world, that we would be holy and blameless before Him.*

> *Wait on the Lord; Be of good courage, and He shall strengthen your heart, wait, I say on the Lord!* Psalm 27:14

Are you a lady-in-waiting or a man-betrothed? Are you constantly finding yourself in the midst of life, relationships, ministry, commitments, and all else that is happening, moving and yet waiting on the Lord for His answer or for peace or guidance? As long as we walk in faith, we live in an unseen realm, waiting for Him and for ourselves and those we love to become more aware of His goodness.

As we wait on the Lord, it is important to maintain a good perspective. This is like looking toward the horizon when we travel so that we do not lose balance. This is essential in overcoming the frustration, angst, anxiety, and worry that typically accompany waiting. We are an impatient people at times. It is critical that we view life through a Gospel lens, valuing the Scriptures and trusting that they will ground our faith. Life's chaos can blind us. Ephesians helps clean our lens. So I read Ephesians and find these foundational truths (and so much more) for my journey:

- God's assuring plan (Ephesians 1:3-14)
- God's gift of His Spirit (Ephesians 1:13-15)
- Prayers for the believer (Ephesians 1:16-23; 3:14-21)
- The definition of life (Ephesians 2)
- God's plan for His Body (Ephesians 3)
- How to walk in the Spirit, building unity (Ephesians 4)
- How to be purified (Ephesians 4:25-5:21)
- How to love, imitating God in my relationships (Ephesians 5:1-6:9)
- How to be strong in Him (Ephesians 6:10-20)
- How to pray (Ephesians 6:18-20)

As I wait, I appreciate good counsel. I also value truth that applies to everything that comes across my path. Ephesians is an encouraging resting place for the weary traveler.

Week 44, Day 3

Read It All: Ephesians 3-6
Read a Bit: Ephesians 3-6

Integrity

Ephesians 3:8-10 — *To me, the very least of all saints, this grace was given, to preach to the Gentiles the unfathomable riches of Christ, and to bring to light what is the administration of the mystery which for ages has been hidden in God who created all things; so that the manifold wisdom of God might now be made known through the church to the rulers and the authorities in the heavenly places.*

The church, Jews and Gentiles as one in Christ, is part of the mystery revealed in the New Testament. The church is the core for the spread of the Gospel. The church is the Body of Christ. The church is the fellowship of believers. The church is the community of His beloved working in His sanctification process. The church is the Bride for whom His servants risk their lives. The church demonstrates His order and care. The church provides for continual prayer and thanksgiving. The church is precious to our Lord and Savior. The church represents the integrity of God to the world. There is great responsibility in being His Bride.

God intends for His children to move together in community, as His Body, so that the world may see the glory of life in Christ. Western culture exalts individualism. But to read the Bible and apply the teachings is to see the value of community, church. We cannot accomplish the will of God (praying continually, giving thanks in everything, and always rejoicing) unless we are part of His Body. We pray without ceasing as a church. We give thanks in everything through the church. We rejoice always as His church. We learn humble reliance on one another and the importance of reproving one another with love in church. We become His family in church. We minister to each other and to others as His church.

It is said that the church in America is on the decline. This is based on things that are measurable: attendance, membership, offerings, baptisms. There are more church buildings but fewer church members, and members are not regularly attending church. There are too many other things to do during the week and especially on the weekends! Many are more faithful to hobbies, parachurch groups, rest, recreation, and sports than to His Body in community. God created the church for the spread of the Gospel and for the maturing of the Saints. Pray for the protection of all our local church bodies. His people are to unite as His church, this mysterious entity awaiting His promised return. This is His representation on earth. If you are a believer, then you are a part of His church. Walk in His integrity and build His Body so that many will be blessed.

Week 44, Day 4

Read It All: Philippians 1-4
Read a Bit: Philippians 1-4

The Revelation in Summary

Philippians 1:21 — *For to me, to live is Christ and to die is gain.*

Philippians 4:11 — *Not that I speak from want, for I have learned to be content in whatever circumstances I am.*

The letter to the Philippians boldly addresses what many consider their main goal in life: happiness, joy. Imprisoned Paul knows the way of, even in the meanest circumstances, having joy. He doesn't hesitate to let his friends know that he has some physical needs, particularly a cloak to withstand the cold, but his main message is that even prison can be a blessing if it serves to spread the Gospel. God has so greatly blessed Paul that he finds happiness in living for God. Even in hardship, there can be contentment as one identifies with the suffering servant, the Lord Jesus Christ. Paul says that to live is Christ.

Some questioned Paul's authority as an apostle because he was imprisoned. Paul explains that believers shouldn't think that their salvation equates to comfort in living. God has a purpose in our suffering at times, and our response to our circumstances impacts the spread of the Gospel. We have the capacity to encourage or discourage one another in the midst of trials. What we really believe about God is communicated when we suffer.

My friend Heidi is a committed University of Florida alumni and fan. Her son Winton is in the UF band, and his mom visits Gainesville frequently. One of her favorite things to do in while there is the Ladies Football Clinic, or "Huddle." The Huddle is fun as you get to meet the Gator football team coaches and they teach attendees some fundamentals and run some drills. Heidi overcame her fear of catching a football at the clinic and I overcame my fear of getting my head stuck in a football helmet. I attended the Huddle several times, and I have learned some vital secrets to great team play.

Topping the list of secrets shared is that communication makes or breaks a team. A team needs to know one another well enough to ask the hard questions, challenge one another at just the right moment, and engage all in the overall vision for the team. They need to do this without deflating one another. The Defensive coach told us that at every practice the coaches identify the team player that is the "Juicer." The Juicer is the one who gets the big picture and unites the team in pursuing victory. The Juicer is known for his enthusiasm, hard work, preparation, humility, and ability to triumphantly overcome setbacks. The Juicer is the influencer. He reminds his teammates of their dignity. At the end of the practice, the Juicer is given a bottle of juice to celebrate his positive effect on the team. Many seek to be the Juicer.

In contrast, a team also tends to have Energy Vampires. You get the picture—the one who sucks the life right out of others. The Energy Vampire dwells on the negative: what is impossible, the past, distrust, disunity, particular failures, their own priorities. When someone is joyful, the Energy Vampire points out why they shouldn't be.

In our team play, as the church of Christ, it is important to be realistic, set right priorities, and speak the truth in love. Our fear of God should drive us to exercise what is needed in the moment. Our priorities help us have that long-term perspective that makes us a blessing to others now. The Lord God formed man of the dust from the ground and breathed into his nostrils the breath of life. It is His divine power that has granted us everything pertaining to life and godliness through the knowledge of Jesus. In Timothy 4:8 we learn that bodily discipline is only of little profit, but godliness is profitable for all things because it holds promise for the present life and also for the life to come.

May His church be such an encouragement within that our victory engages those outside so that many seek safety in His huddle.

> *Finally, brethren, whatever is true, whatever is honorable, whatever is right, whatever is pure, whatever is lovely, whatever is of good repute, if there is any excellence and if anything worthy of praise, dwell on these things.* Philippians 4:8

Week 44, Day 5

Read It All: Colossians 1-4
Read a Bit: Colossians 1-4

The Revelation in Summary

Colossians 1:13-15 — *For He rescued us from the domain of darkness, and transferred us to the kingdom of His beloved Son, in whom we have redemption, the forgiveness of sins. He is the image of the invisible God, the firstborn of all creation.*

Colossians is a beautiful presentation of the supremacy of the Lord Jesus Christ as completely God and our powerful Redeemer. The book assures the reader that God loves the hopeless and makes a way for all to completely identify with Him. If you wonder how God views His children, study Colossians. God affirms that the believer's identity is secure, holy, blameless, and beyond reproach in Christ.

When you read through Colossians, you will discover that Paul tells you about Christ, affirms that the believer is identified with Christ, encourages the believer to walk in Christ as fully identified with Him, and then repeats this teaching. It is as if he knows that he has to keep reminding us of our identity in Christ before he gives direction for walking in Christ. Paul knows that if we are deceived about Christ, then we will stumble in our attempts to walk in Christ. Identity matters. We are what we believe. So Paul writes some of the most affirming passages in the New Testament on the believer in Christ and how this affects our walk of faith.

One of the Bible students in the groups I've taught for years continually smiles. She has one of the most consistently radiant countenances I have ever witnessed. I think she understands what it means to be in Christ. I have asked her to share her testimony on a number of occasions. It is hard to imagine that this pretty mom of two cute girls once struggled with addiction and served prison time. She shares the meaning behind her tattoos. Sometimes her family members will bring up her past, as they were greatly impacted by her former lifestyle. They suffered from her sin. When reminded of her old identity, this young mom graciously responds based on her new identity, which acknowledges the importance of and need for forgiveness while also resting confidently in her full deliverance from sin, confident in her new identity. She appreciates the repeat message of Colossians.

So, as those who have been chosen of God, holy and beloved, put on
a heart of compassion, kindness, humility, gentleness and patience;
bearing with one another . . . . Colossians 3:11-13

1 & 2 THESSALONIANS

Life can be hard, and sometimes it seems that our efforts to represent God are just causing a lot of pain to ourselves and, even worse, to those we love, as we watch others who do not represent Him seem to nevertheless gain comfort and success in this earthly realm. The believer may wonder if serving God is worth everything. The letters to the Thessalonians encourage believers to endure in holiness because Christ will return one day, regardless of those who say Christ has already come or isn't coming at all. Paul explains numerous details regarding the End Times to exhort Christ's followers to endure until He returns. Believers will want to be ready for Christ's return, as His second coming will not be anything like the first. He won't be arriving as a babe in the second coming, but as Judge. Deliverance is in being His when the wrath of God is finally poured out in holy judgment.

Week 45, Day 1

Read It All: 1 Thessalonians 1
Read a Bit: 1 Thessalonians 1

The Revelation in Summary

1 Thessalonians 1:9-10 — *For they themselves report about us what kind of a reception we had with you, and how you turned to God from idols to serve a living and true God, and to wait for His Son from heaven, whom He raised from the dead, that is Jesus, who rescues us from the wrath to come.*

Paul was only in Thessalonica a short time before he had to leave because of the persecution he was suffering. The new believers there felt like they had little support as they faced opposition for their new beliefs. Paul encourages them by reminding them of his sacrificial ministry to them and the provision of Timothy to lead them in the midst of many afflictions. Paul rejoices in the report he has from Timothy of their faithful, earnest stand in the Gospel even though they are suffering. As Paul reflects on their faithfulness, and he teaches them more about God's future return than he has written before, purposing to give them great hope that will help them endure through their trials.

Having a future hope is a great comfort. We can endure the rough times more earnestly when we realize that we are part of a grand design that ultimately leads to a glorious home with our merciful Savior. We can also endure troubling times with compassion for our enemies when we have a glimpse of what awaits those who do not take refuge in Christ. Paul paints a detailed picture of the destruction that awaits the nonbeliever who is destined for God's wrath. This should motivate us all the more to be messengers of His Life.

When our kids were young, Scott and I would include them in planning family times. We always wanted them to have something to look forward to, especially when the days seemed drab. This planning included regular weekly family game nights and then events that were further out, a beach day or a week of family vacation. These little insights into the future comforted us in the sometimes present monotony of life. They also taught us about the nature of hope, looking forward to and trusting in the future promised by someone who is faithful to do as they say. Thankfully, we didn't have to cancel too many of the future plans, as the planning and details were part of helping our children see by the example we set that they could rely on God to deliver us into His Kingdom as He said He would. At times, our planning did reveal that we are not in control of life, particularly the future. But this made for conversations about Sovereign God.

Future plans are as important to my adult children as they were to them as young children. Something to look forward to makes present hardships more bearable. God is merciful in giving His children a glimpse into His future restoration of mankind. His revelation lifts my head as I groan in eager anticipation of His promised kingdom and renewed humanity.

Week 45, Day 2

Read It All: 1 Thessalonians 2-3
Read a Bit: 1 Thessalonians 2-3

Integrity

1 Thessalonians 2:7 — *But we proved to be gentle among you, as a nursing mother tenderly cares for her own children.*

I nursed my children and can still remember the feeling of them snuggled close and feeding. I was protective of them, amazed by their beauty, blessed to be a source of nourishment for them, and overwhelmed with the joy of mothering. The nursing forced me to slow down, hold my babies, and marvel at His creative genius. Oftentimes, my babies would fall asleep in my arms. I would tenderly cradle their heads, making sure their necks were not at odd angles. My babies grew up quickly, and I miss the snuggles.

I long for my children to be influenced by people of integrity, people who will model and tell them the truth in love. There are too many deceivers in this world, especially people in leadership that represent self-centered living and belittle others. One case in point: When my son was little, after coming home from school one day, he turned on the TV just in time to hear a breaking news report about the President of the United States having oral sex with his intern. My son asked what oral sex was and if this would hurt the President's wife. Reports of people abusing power seemed to be everywhere as I was raising my children. I was grieving the poor influences on my children's lives so much during that time that I actually wrote a poem (even though I'm not typically even a reader of poetry). Sometimes there is just no other way to deal with frustration than to rhyme. I identify with the Psalmists.

> A Child with a View
> My eight year old asked me
> about the President's lies today.
> I stood there stirring our dinner,
> trying to choose the best words to say.
>
> I hated to think that my son's first impressions,
> of the man he knew our nation had elected to serve,
> included the words sex, adultery and forced confessions
> instead of honesty, self-denial, integrity, and protective reserve.
>
> I resented that two sacred unions,
> that of nation to leader and woman to man,
> had been mocked and defiled by our leader and an uncaring nation
> and so belittled to my little man.

I had to explain the beauty in loving another,
physically and relationally all your life,
denying that which is deceitful
to be one with your husband or wife.

I voiced my concerns regarding character
and the need to appoint leaders who are strong without and within.
I cried for our people, our country,
expecting and accepting less and less from our fellow men.

I long for my son to rise above us,
to know and teach values that free,
and for a future President who'll set an example
worthy of all children to see.

Week 45, Day 3

Read It All: 1 Thessalonians 4-5
Read a Bit: 1 Thessalonians 4-5

Dignity

1 Thessalonians 5:14 — *We urge you, brethren, admonish the unruly, encourage the fainthearted, help the weak, be patient with everyone.*

The story I'm about to tell seems to strangely encourage people when I am willing to share it, so I am being very vulnerable here as I convey one of my most embarrassing moments, solely with the hope of making your day. This does tie in with Thessalonians in that while we wait for the Lord, we may need to patiently work on helping one another figure out life.

When my children were in elementary school, I longed to be one of the best homeroom moms, PTA participants, and child surrogate parents ever. Part of this was because I saw a need, part was because I do wish to be a Christian who draws others to the Lord Jesus Christ, and part was because I like feeling that I am a tremendous help to the many needing my magnanimous assistance (my ego).

If you know elementary schools, you know that the annual book fair is a prime time for volunteerism. The school librarian is usually the one with the added responsibility of setting up and managing the book fair.

I had become good friends with the librarian so I committed numerous hours to the fair. One of my primary goals was to guide young minds to the best reading materials. No *Goosebumps* under my watch (apologies to those of you who find them "frighteningly fun").

The busiest time for the book fair was family night. This is when parents find out how many books the librarian and their students have put on their book fair wish list. Elementary schools provide lessons in marketing at a very early age. I was set to volunteer and to be a great blessing to many that night. I arrived at the library to find a very excited librarian with a huge Clifford, the Big Red Dog, costume in her hands. For some reason, she had envisioned me as Clifford for the night. I thought, surely, that couldn't be too difficult.

The crowd was growing, so I was rushed back to a storage closet and told to suit up. I'm pretty compliant and so responded quickly, but this was no easy task. I was struggling with the zipper of a Big Red Dog costume that was overflowing the closet and that seemed like a shedding, hot blanket. Just getting out of the storage area was not easy.

I should have known immediately that something was wrong. From what I could see out of the eye holes, children were running from me rather than to me. Parents seemed to look away in embarrassment. I kept trying to advance to groups of people and was having a hard time not tripping. The heat was rising, and I was feeling rejected.

Then, thankfully, a young boy stood boldly in front of me and asked his parents, who were quivering behind him, if that was Clifford's tail on his front or something else. It dawned on me that I was backwards in the bottom half of the costume and that I might be giving a very wrong anatomy lesson to some young and old minds! I rushed to the storage room, dropped the costume, and waited to make a timely exit so that no one would realize who the perverse Clifford was. I was mortified!

I don't think the librarian ever learned of my poor representation of Clifford; at least we never talked about it. I appreciate people who will give you the benefit of the doubt, and understand that some days, just getting dressed can be a struggle for dignity.

Week 45, Day 4

Read It All: 2 Thessalonians 1
Read a Bit: 2 Thessalonians 1

Unity

2 Thessalonians 1:11-12 — *To this end also we pray for you always, that our God will count you worthy of your calling, and fulfill every desire for goodness and the work of faith with power so that the name of our Lord Jesus will be glorified in you and you in Him, according to the grace of our God and the Lord Jesus Christ.*

2 Thessalonians continues the reminders that believers have received His great gift of salvation and will escape the impending wrath of God. Suffering presently for the truth will be worth it all at the return of the Lord Jesus Christ. 2 Thessalonians explains that as we await His return, we purpose to pray, work heartily, stay away from those who contradict the Gospel, and glorify our Savior so that the faithless might be rescued. We are to be discerning and lovingly helpful.

Tara at our church believed that while she awaits Jesus' return she could be a blessing to foster girls. She talked with workers at children's homes and to foster families and discovered that many of the foster girls were middle and high school age, and like most girls that age, would like the opportunity to pick out their own clothing, to shop. But foster girls typically wear what has been handed down to them from others in the system.

This bothered Tara, so she started a ministry. She asked church members to donate new or gently used clothing, shoes, and jewelry or new underwear. She enlisted some friends to help her set up a "boutique" in some meeting rooms at church, complete with zebra-print curtains in the "dressing rooms." The donations were organized beautifully on racks, in pretty containers, and on jewelry displays. Ladies brought in snacks and bought new, pretty Bibles. Tara prepared a devotional and invited all the foster care leaders she had in her contacts to bring their foster girls.

The boutique was a huge success. One group of girls would shop while in another area of the church, a different group was given a devotional and a new Bible; then they changed activities. The donations were plentiful and useful. Volunteers waited on the girls, helping them get sizes they needed and taking them snacks. One girl got her first pair of tennis shoes, which meant she was excited about physical education at school, something she had always avoided because of her shoes.

Tara and her group began setting up the boutique once a month for foster care groups throughout the state. It took a lot of hours to set up and break down the boutique monthly, so the leaders prayed for a permanent location. Another believer heard about the need and donated a house. The boutique continues to this day and is always ready for appointments by those with a need. The ministry instills a moment of dignity to attendees and unifies a group of believers in lovingly helping many who feel unloved. The ministry devotional time is preparing many for The Day of the Lord by helping the attendees to be covered in more than merely boutique clothing; they will wear His righteousness from receiving His message of grace at Loft 181.

Week 45, Day 5

Read It All: 2 Thessalonians 2-3
Read a Bit: 2 Thessalonians 2-3

Priority

2 Thessalonians 3:12-14 — *Now such persons we command and exhort in the Lord Jesus Christ to work in quiet fashion and eat their own bread, but as for you, brethren, do not grow weary of doing good.*

In the Western culture, we often think of work as a curse. We long for many more hours of vacation. We forget that sometimes we need a vacation from vacation. I've seen families without a means of work, and I know what an answer to prayer it is for someone in the family to have the dignity of good work. A God-given vocation that blesses others edifies the worker.

The work God gives to all His children is to enjoy Him and to represent Him to the world. God provides purpose in this world. He gives us worthwhile work to prioritize; good work of telling others how they might have Life. Israel's work was to build a tabernacle that would house the presence of God and lead the nations in true worship. Believers in Christ are to take care of His temple in themselves and serve so that others will receive His merciful presence through His people.

I remember a 6 a.m. morning when my son had already gone to his internship, and I kneeled to thank God for his work. He had spent months applying for jobs and being discouraged. As I thought about his schedule that day, I realized he had had a lot of early days traveling to various offices and several late days trying to get everything done at those offices to avoid more travel hours. I got a little weary and overwhelmed just thinking about his work, but I was so glad for him to have responsibilities that fulfilled so many basic needs in life, including the desire to contribute to his community and provide for himself and others. He is thankful for work. Counting schooling, it had been many years of struggle to find this job.

The apostle Paul instructs regarding work, *"But we urge you, brethren, to excel still more, and to make it your ambition to lead a quiet life and attend to your own business and work with your hands, just as we commanded you, so that you will behave properly toward outsiders and not be in any need"* (1 Thessalonians 4:10-12).

We need urging to work, as work can go hand-in-hand with weariness. Spent energy means a need for renewed strength. As Israel built the tabernacle, their leaders would remind them of God and the value of the work. Remembering their God would encourage the Israelites to overcome weariness and finish the tabernacle, which pictured God's way for people to be restored to their Maker, to have rest in Him. Worship refreshes the worker.

> *Come to Me, all who are weary and heavy-laden, and I will give you rest. Take My yoke upon you and learn from Me, for I am gentle and humble in heart, and you will find rest for your souls.* Matthew 11:28-29

> *Let us not lose heart in doing good, for in due time we will reap if we do not grow weary. So then, while we have opportunity, let us do good to all people, and especially to those who are of the household of the faith.* Galatians 6:9-10

I pray that the worker is honored with a place of rest when wearied. God has provided a tabernacle in the wilderness.

1 & 2 TIMOTHY, TITUS, PHILEMON

These letters are addressed to leaders in the early churches. Timothy had been appointed to care for the church at Ephesus, and Titus was in Crete. The letters to Timothy and Titus provide practical instructions for church leadership that continue to be relevant today. Philemon deals with the equality of men, women, slaves, and free in Christ, and Paul's concern for reconciling a former slave to his owner.

Paul's love for these leaders and his authority in the early church are expressed in these writings. The reader gains an appreciation for how Christ's teaching and the Spirit's leading influence the believer to live sacrificially for the benefit of others. This oftentimes involves going against cultural norms. The church was to have order in leadership that was not based on political gain or power, but the love of brethren. Slaves were to be considered equals with their masters as joint heirs with Jesus. Fathers were not to rule over their households, but to be loving protectors, compassionate to their families. Widows were to be cared for and monies shared. Many of the teachings are revolutionary thoughts still today!

Week 46, Day 1

Read It All: 1 Timothy 1-3
Read a Bit: 1 Timothy 1-3

The Revelation in Summary

1 Timothy 3:14-15 — *I am writing these things to you, hoping to come to you before long; but in case I am delayed, I write so that you will know how one ought to conduct himself in the household of God, which is the church of the living God, the pillar and support of the truth.*

The church has been established during this period of delay, between the first and second comings of Christ, to proclaim the Gospel and maintain the integrity of the Gospel message. In every age there are those within the church who teach obedience to the law as the way of righteousness. Timothy is given the task of persevering against such leaders and consistently leading others to life in Christ through His imputed righteousness. To do so, Timothy must fight against the self-elevation of those who think they are superior to others in the church based on their obedience under the law. Timothy must purpose to encourage humility in the church and to assign leadership based on their contrite reliance on God for guidance to lead. At the heart of leading the church is the consistent public reading of the Scriptures to instruct the listeners on truth so they will recognize and reject the strange teachings based on prideful human reasoning.

1 Timothy shows Paul's mentoring relationship to Timothy and Paul's great confidence in Timothy's ability to lead. Paul commissions Timothy at both the start and end of the letter, as it is very important that the church understand young Timothy's authority to lead them. The letter is practical in providing direction to Timothy as he confronts false teaching, and as he organizes the people to administer the rescuing power of the Gospel. The letter includes poetic exclamations that honor Christ, becuse so many of the church issues are errant theology taking them away from the worship of Jesus. Timothy is to set the example of worshipping the Risen Savior, pointing to Christ as the believer's sole means of salvation.

Week 46, Day 2

Read It All: 1 Timothy 4-6
Read a Bit: 1 Timothy 4-6

Integrity

1 Timothy 4:11-12, 18 — *Prescribe and teach these things. Let no one look down on your youthfulness, but rather in speech, conduct, love, faith and purity, show yourself an example of those who believe . . . fight the good fight.*

As I think about Timothy and the high calling he had to shepherd a group of people that were struggling with applying the Gospel to their diverse gathering, I also think about my pastor. I have watched Ken Whitten pastor the church I attend for over thirty years, and I continue to thank God for him. Though a young husband and father of four when he took the head pastoral position at our church, he quickly gained respect for his humility, gentle humor, hard work, tender heart for the lost, and his spiritual maturity. Pastor Ken was hired at a crucial time for our church, as the members were grieving the loss of a pastor that had supposedly left for mission work, but in reality had been unfaithful to his wife. Our congregation had some trust issues.

I have watched Pastor Ken shepherd our church for over thirty years and I continue to thank God for him. Though a young husband and father of four when he took the head pastoral position at our church, he quickly gained respect for his humility, gentle humor, hard work, tender heart for the lost, and his spiritual maturity. Pastor Ken was hired at a crucial time for our church as the members were grieving the loss of a pastor that had left supposedly for mission work, but in reality had been unfaithful to his wife. Years later, this pastor did return to the church to publicly confess and ask for forgiveness. But in the interim, our congregation had some trust issues.

Pastor Ken faithfully teaches from the Word. He repeatedly shares the Gospel because he sincerely doesn't want anyone to die without being reconciled to God. Pastor Ken, and his wife, have served through years of dynamic growth while also parenting four children that have become ministry leaders who also bless many. In addition to sharing his passion for evangelism and missions, Pastor Ken has set the example of reaching the hurting and helpless. He has partnered with area leaders to revive churches that were in severe decline and to establish inner city outreaches. Our church volunteers are welcomed in the community as Pastor Ken has helped us gain the respect of believers and unbelievers throughout the city as he has tirelessly serving and sending servants to help where needed, particularly supporting two nearby school districts. Pastor Ken encouraged our members to engage in the community, to serve. I think Pastor Ken has sat at the feet of our Savior and understands our Savior's teaching on serving.

I do not need lengthy teaching on what a godly pastor is like as I do have a faithful example in Pastor Ken. I know this is a rare blessing as leaders of any church can easily be pulled away by arrogance, impurity, covetousness, or weariness. Shepherding is hard work. We need the influence of godly men bent on helping others.

You may think I've written a bit too magnanimously regarding Pastor Ken as I don't record his weaknesses. Please do not take my thankfulness and praise of Pastor Ken as saying he is perfect. I have been in church meetings where he has apologized for sin that has affected our church. I have witnessed his shortcomings in leadership at times and his insecurities. So, I appreciate his desire to grow and improve as a leader. I appreciate his humble confessions of needed heart change. I thank God that he relies on God's Word for direction and as a mirror for his heart.

Timothy and Pastor Ken have much in common. For one, they are both dearly loved. They also stand for God's truth even when it's hard. I believe, that if Pastor Ken read this summary, he would remind me that wisdom comes from the fear of the Lord and that He alone is worthy. Yes, God alone is worthy. And God has encouraged us to acknowledge the valuable impact good leaders have in God's Body. Pastor Ken has represented the heart of God to me in many ways. I am eternally grateful. God help us all to represent His grace and mercy well to many. This is a matter of Life and death.

Week 46, Day 3

Read It All: 2 Timothy 1-4
Read a Bit: 2 Timothy 1-4

Dignity

2 Timothy 3:16-17 — *All Scripture is inspired by God and profitable for teaching, for reproof, for correction, for training in righteousness; so that the man of God may be adequate, equipped for every good work.*

We instill God's dignity in others when we take time to teach others His Word, for it is profitable to teach and equip people for His work.

When my son Samuel was 6 years old, he told me that one little boy in the neighborhood had never heard about Jesus and didn't know a thing about the Bible. Samuel said, "I gave him my Bible and told him to have his mother read it to him so he'd know about Jesus and would be good to people." He said, "I didn't have anything for the other boys, so I just gave each one of them a dollar." I told my son, "It's wonderful to give a Bible to someone that needs one. That's fine, but next time, tell me before you give away lots of things. You can't buy friendship."

I thought I would try teaching an even deeper lesson from God's Word on discerning when to share truth or your things, so I said, "Do you know the Bible passage about casting pearls before swine?" Samuel said, "No, I sure don't." I asked, "Do you know what swine are?" Samuel answered, "Of course! That's what the sailor boys drink."

It helps to know what your child is thinking when you teach.

Week 46, Day 4

Read It All: Titus 1-3
Read a Bit: Titus 1-3

The Revelation in Summary

Titus 2:1-5 — *But as for you, speak the things which are fitting for sound doctrine. Older men are to be temperate, dignified, sensible, sound in faith, in love, in persever-ance. Older women likewise are to be reverent in their behavior, not malicious gossips nor enslaved to much wine, teaching what is good, so that they may encourage the young women to love their husbands, to love their children, to be sensible, pure, workers at home, kind, being subject to their own husbands, so that the word of God will not be dishonored.*

In his letter to Titus, Paul provides teaching for the instruction of the saints on the island of Crete[25] as they await the Lord's return. The instructions address the need for godly daily living, having a rightful attitude towards others, and how to overcome divisions caused by unsound teaching. The letter is straightforward in design: a reminder of the Gospel message, practical instructions for living out the Gospel daily, how to appoint good leaders and remove corrupt leaders from service, purifying the leaders' households to better their witness of God's grace, and loving as God would love. How is all of this possible? Titus was to convince the people that their walk of faith in His Spirit would help them engage the culture and reach the world with the Gospel.

Titus is the book frequently referred to as containing the instruc-tions for believers to mentor others in the church in the ways of God. There are numerous women's ministries named after Titus 2 because of Paul's instructions for older women to teach younger women in the church. Sometimes I get asked if I resent being a women's leader in a Southern Baptist church because my role is so "limited." After all, people assume, you can "only" teach women and children. This question reveals the asker's low view of women and children. I fully realize that a woman committed to fulfilling her God-ordained responsibilities and roles influences all she meets. Edifying women and freeing them to live

---

[25] Located off the coast of Greece, location of many strategic harbors.

for Him greatly impacts the world. Women in the church should have someone focused simply on women. Think of some of the Christian women who have influenced amazing compassionate works throughout the world: Florence Nightingale, Clara Barton, Amy Carmichael, Mother Theresa, Susan B. Anthony, Evangeline Cory Booth, Sojourner Truth, Lottie Moon and others.[26] Thank God for godly women.

The Pastor of Men's and Stewardship Ministries, Rob, at my church asked his men's class how many of them came to Christ as a result of a woman sharing the Gospel in word or deed with them. The bulk of his class raised their hands; only 2 of 75 did not. Thank God for godly women.

All are equal in the eyes of God. His children all have the same Holy Spirit within them. The men and women of my Baptist church are grateful for one another. We do have much we can learn about serving as brothers and sisters in Christ, but we acknowledge one another as precious in His sight and worthy of focused ministry.

Week 46, Day 5

Read It All: Philemon
Read a Bit: Philemon

The Revelation in Summary

Philemon 17 — *If then you regard me a partner, accept him as you would me.*

Paul makes an appeal in his letter to Philemon for Onesimus, a former runaway slave, to be accepted by Philemon as a brother in Christ. Paul is turning the culture upside down with his request—his strong request. When you read this short letter, you get a sense that Philemon has no choice but to accept Onesimus, as Paul reminds Philemon that Paul could command him to receive Onesimus because Paul was the agent of Philemon's freedom, but instead, Paul is requesting Philemon to hear

---

[26]   Laura Polk, "20 Women Who Shaped History" iBelieve.com, article accessed Sept. 14, 2018, https://www.ibelieve.com/slideshows/20-christian-women-who-shaped-history.html.

and accept the teaching of God on equality in Christ. Paul is challenging the social hierarchy of his day to realize that in Christ all are equal: men, women, slave, free, young, old, Jew, Gentile. God's love levels the social order.

Awhile back, I saw a Facebook post that made me very angry and hurt for friends of mine, who wrote these words:

> We decided to take our dog for her evening walk tonight and our time was interrupted by something hurtful. As we turned the corner to come home, a truck drove by and someone yelled, "DIRTY N******!!" I have never, to my knowledge been called a n****** before. I have been quick to tell my children that sticks and stones may break their bones, but words will never hurt them. That is a lie! My feelings are hurt and that's just the truth.

Prejudice is a preconceived opinion that is not based on reason or actual experience. I think this is why my friends' experience enrages and frustrates me so much. How can you confront with an expectation for change that which isn't "reasonable" in any shape or form? And such craziness is highly contagious. One of my favorite things about God's creation is the incredible diversity and wonder of it all. I marvel at the gorgeous array of flowers and their many colors. Why would an array of skin color be any less marvelous? Pigmentation has been used as an evil means of segregation.

My parents brought me up under the example that "all men are created equal," an American ideal that is Scriptural. My parents grew up on farms and believed a person's word and work ethic were what really mattered. My parents respected those who were hard working and honest. They modeled these truths by not distinguishing people based on appearance.

I so lived by my parents' teaching as my norm that in a North Carolina high school in the late 70s I didn't hesitate to say "yes" to dating a kind, courteous young man who was also "black." I got my own crash course in prejudice. My mom got called into the principal's office because the school wanted to be sure she knew what her daughter was up to. Mom gave the school administrators a crash course on stupidity.

My young relationship gave me an opportunity to experience preju-dice. I lost some friends, but it was due to a big difference in our value systems, and that was okay. I also discovered that there are many wonderful people who see and accept others for the right reasons. My school leadership voted me "Most Outstanding Senior Young Lady," and my boyfriend "Most Courteous." Hopefully, we represented getting beyond the petty and focusing on the goodness of a Mighty Creator Who created man and woman in His image, fearfully and wonderfully made.

> *There is neither Jew nor Greek, there is neither slave nor free man, there is neither male nor female; for you are all one in Christ Jesus.*
> Galatians 3:28

REST TIME

Week 47, Days 1-5

Romans 5:1 — *Therefore, having been justified by faith, we have peace with God through our Lord Jesus Christ . . . .*

These New Testament letters provide wisdom for His children to walk in His Spirit. Paul expounds on the Gospel message and the joy of knowing that he is holy and blameless in the eyes of God because God has imputed His righteousness to the believer through His Son, the Lord Jesus Christ. Paul's passion for sharing the Gospel motivates his teaching on all believers becoming ambassadors for Christ. Paul's letters provide the foundational truth necessary for God's people to become His Body, representing His merciful grace to mankind, through the ages. I'm blessed to be reminded of my identity in Christ and to be counted among the beloved of God.

Journal any thoughts you wish to record at this point in your reading.

NEW TESTAMENT LETTERS (CONTINUED)

The remaining New Testament letters are messages from early church leaders to encourage believers to have hope, faith, and love as they persevere to proclaim Christ when they are rejected or even persecuted. Hebrews is the only letter not titled with the author's name. Some scholars group Hebrews with the letters from Paul because it reads like one of Paul's letters. But, Paul typically identifies himself in his letters, and the author of Hebrews isn't indicated in the letter.

As I was going through the rest of these letters, I decided to play a word association game with my family because I was curious as to the deep, meaningful responses just hearing these wonderful letters' names would bring to my godly family. The following list is their responses. The book's name is listed first and their corresponding response second; my comments are in parentheses next to each association as I felt a need to comment on their responses:

James — "Works" (Just what you don't want to associate with James; he's exhorting faith!)

2 John — "1 John" (Really?)

Jude — "Revelation" (They know the order of books but not their content, argh!)

Jude — "Law" (I got a string of responses on Jude; I think they were teasing me now.)

Jude — "The Beatles" (See above.)

Hebrews — "Ahhhhh, Abraham, Faithful" (The Hall of Faith in Hebrews 11 is remembered)

Titus — "-ville" (I threw in a Pauline epistle, but no one got that, and the association was a city in Florida unrelated to the Book of Titus.)

3 John — "Trey, the baby of the bunch" (Gotta admit, this did make me smile.)

What my word association game taught me is that even people who have grown up in the church don't remember the messages of these short epistles. These books nourish a life of faith. We need to get back to the dining table and feast.

HEBREWS

Week 48, Day 1

Read It All: Hebrews 1-2
Read a Bit: Hebrews 1-2

The Revelation in Summary

Hebrews 1:1-3 — *God, after He spoke long ago to the fathers in the prophets in many portions and in many ways, in these last days has spoken to us in His Son, whom He appointed heir of all things, through whom also He made the world. And He is the radiance of His glory and the exact representation of His nature, and upholds all things by the word of His power.*

The author of Hebrews is not identified, nor is the audience except that they may be Hebrew believers, hence the name of the letter. The problem this letter addresses is believers leaving the faith because their suffering is causing them to rethink their identity in Christ and to be deluded into thinking the Old Covenant is better than the New Covenant. The author insists that the readers remember that Jesus is God. We can tell from reading the letter that the author assumes the recipients clearly know the Old Testament, particularly the Pentateuch. The author uses the history of Israel from Abraham to the wilderness wanderings to instruct the reader on why they should continue to trust in Christ as their Redeemer even when persecuted. The author presents Christ as supreme in contrast to the angels, Moses, God's Covenant, the priests (including Melchizedek), the sacrifices, and the tabernacle. This presentation should encourage the reader that Jesus is worthy of all and that they should remain faithful to Him even though they may suffer persecution.

The Book of Hebrews also addresses why the believers are not experiencing the promised Covenant rest promised to those under the New Covenant. They are still in a period of delay of the promises and should be anticipating Christ's return. A large reason for their current struggle is that they suffer because Jesus isn't with them and they long for His kingdom. The book includes numerous strong warnings about the consequences of turning from Life in Jesus, because He will return and establish His rule. These warnings are not to frighten the reader but to get their attention by reminding them of God's holiness and goodness in being their Savior. Near the end of the letter, there is a long list of those who walked by faith on this earth without seeing God's full provision of His righteousness in their lifetimes. These faithful ones give examples for the reader to follow.

Week 48, Day 2

Read It All: Hebrews 3-4
Read a Bit: Hebrews 3-4

Integrity

Hebrews 4:1 — *Therefore, let us fear if, while a promise remains of entering His rest, any one of you may seem to have come short of it.*

Rest is a frequently used Old Testament word associated with the integrity of God. God promised rest to those who would enter Covenant with Him. A good God, a God of integrity, would provide what He promised.

The rest described in the Old Testament is defined as rest from enemies, rest from having to fulfill the Law to be right with God, and rest from labor. In the Old Covenant Law, God commanded that the people rest every seventh day and that they give the land a rest every seventh year. God knows His creation needs rest. Rest is an essential in life.

Culture after culture has downplayed the need for rest as defined by God. We think we have rest from our enemies if we are not officially on a battlefield. We forget the battle we should be fighting with sin. We think we are fulfilling the law because we haven't done anything too awful in our own estimation, and we love time from our labors, but not to rest—only to wear ourselves out with entertainment and play. Rest is for the sick.

The Hebrews were longing for God's definition of rest. They were longing for time in His presence without having to prove anything to anyone.

I see God's goodness in mandating rest on this earth. I want to be more intentional about prioritizing rest in my own schedule primarily because I see the effects on all my relationships as I rush around overdoing, and living in exhaustion. Nonstop busyness breeds anxiety. We forget to recognize our limits physically and mentally. We forget to mind our own business and can become obsessed with controlling what is really another's responsibility. Pursuing excess and surrounded by clutter, we forget to enjoy what we already have. In summary, a lack of rest is enslaving.

Here are few Biblical principles regarding rest that have resonated with me:

It is good to intentionally cease from doing to remember what I have overcome, what God has accomplished, and that He is sovereign (in control).

Rest is a gift that helps us guard against being enslaved to crazy priorities, another's expectations, or our own flesh.

Being rested makes us better representatives of the Lord's mercy; it means we place some margin in our lives so that rather than attempting to do everything, we may remember to focus on what matters most. When our bodies are rested, we may find that we are more likely to remember others and extend His mercy in acts of kindness.

Rest enhances our worship.

The ultimate rest is in Christ Jesus. He has delivered us from having to continually work according to the law. This is the rest that we may enjoy every day of the year.

> *So there remains a Sabbath rest for the people of God. For the one who has entered His rest has himself also rested from his works, as God did from His. Therefore let us be diligent to enter that rest, so that no one will fall, through following the same example of disobedience.* Hebrews 4:9-11

Week 48, Day 3

Read It All: Hebrews 5-7
Read a Bit: Hebrews 5-7

Dignity

Hebrews 7:17 — *For it is attested of Him, "You are a priest forever according to the order of Melchizedek."*

In the Old Testament, there was great dignity, respectability, in being a prophet, a priest, or a King. In this section of Hebrews, the Lord Jesus Christ is identified as the fulfillment of all the Old Testament roles. He is the ultimate mediator for mankind.

Melchizedek is a mysterious character in Genesis. He comes out of Salem (an area later to be Jerusalem) and blesses the mighty Abraham. Melchizedek represents an order of Priest-Kings existing before Israel's patriarch.

Psalm 110 reveals that God's Anointed One would be associated with Melchizedek:

> *The Lord says to my Lord: "Sit at My right hand*
> *Until I make Your enemies a footstool for Your feet."*
> *The Lord will stretch forth Your strong scepter from Zion, saying,*
> *"Rule in the midst of Your enemies."*
> *Your people will volunteer freely in the day of Your power;*
> *In holy array, from the womb of the dawn,*
> *Your youth are to You as the dew.*
> *The Lord has sworn and will not change His mind,*
> *"You are a priest forever according to the order of Melchizedek."*
> *The Lord is at Your right hand;*
> *He will shatter kings in the day of His wrath.*
> *He will judge among the nations,*
> *He will fill them with corpses,*
> *He will shatter the chief men over a broad country.*
> *He will drink from the brook by the wayside;*
> *Therefore He will lift up His head.*

The author of Hebrews emphasizes Christ's priesthood as being of the same order as Melchizedek's, an eternal priesthood that mediates the blessing of God throughout the nations. Remember that to reject Jesus as Savior is to reject your only chance to be reconciled with God. He is our source of dignity.

Week 48, Day 4

Read It All: Hebrews 8-10
Read a Bit: Hebrews 8-10

Unity

Hebrews 10:23-25 — *Let us hold fast the confession of our hope without wavering, for He who promised is faithful; and let us consider how to stimulate one another to love and good deeds, not forsaking our own assembling together, as is the habit of some, but encouraging one another; and all the more as you see the day drawing near.*

Christ's sacrifice on the cross provided the one sufficient act of reconciling mankind to God. The Old Testament tabernacle in the wilderness was the visual reminder to the Israelites that God desired to be with them. He wanted His presence knit with theirs. The tabernacle also reminded the people of the holiness of God and their need for redemption. Because of Christ, the believer tabernacles with God continually as He resides in the believer, and the believer worships God with other believers in the local assembly of believers, the church.

The author of Hebrews makes a tremendous appeal to the reader regarding assembly with fellow believers. Christ's followers find purpose and worth in imitating His steadfastness to the Word of God. We need the assembly of believers so that in times of temptation and persecution, we can be encouraged that our walk of faith is worthwhile. Only fellowship with mature believers can help us in our struggles to uphold God's truth. The author of Hebrews is concerned that the readers are already being drawn to the easier lifestyle of the world and their former sinful compromises. Hebrews is no little chide to be regular in church attendance but rather a command to value the assembly of God's followers as a means of protecting ourselves from falling away from God.

To tabernacle with Christ is to be identified with His Body. In addition to continually being under the teaching of God's Word through fellowshipping in assembly with believers, the Lord Jesus commands two sacraments (oaths of fidelity) with Him: baptism and the Lord's Supper. Baptism is a one-time sacrament believers submit to following conversion. The Lord's Supper is a sacrament that is to be repeated in remembrance of Christ's atoning work for our salvation. The Jews celebrated Passover annually, but their memory of their Deliverer suffered at times. The more often we enjoy the opportunity to commemorate the Christ, the more often we formally reflect on Him and return to focusing on Him. When we find a church that teaches His Word faithfully, we find a place to regularly take the Lord's Supper. Through the taking of the bread and the cup, we publicly profess communion with our Lord and Savior. We announce to those around us that the Gospel message is life. To the glory of God, we honor Him by commemorating the Son. We need this reminder to fulfill a responsibility to our Savior and to reiterate our place in the Gospel message. Our worship is incomplete without assembling for the Lord's Supper.

We also need the opportunity to serve others as the church affords. The church needs believers. We can be the source of encouraging another in the faith. Serving blesses the server. I've seen with my own children that they are most excited when they are useful. They love being able to help another understand a concept at school, have a good laugh, heal a broken relationship, and supply a direct need. People feel powerless without some opportunity to encourage another. Some do this regularly outside the church, but the church gives the believer the opportunity to show kindness without the possibility of getting that kindness returned. The church gives the opportunity to serve in the name of Christ and, in doing so, to glorify God. The church connects the family of God, the brothers and sisters in Christ. We are called to care for our family in Christ. We need that care more than we realize. Value the church, because the believer is not an orphan; you have family and you have a home in almost every city in the world.

Week 48, Day 5

Read It All: Hebrews 11-13
Read a Bit: Hebrews 11-13

Priority

Hebrews 13:1-2 — *Let love of the brethren continue. Do not neglect to show hospitality to strangers, for by this some have entertained angels without knowing it.*

I think the author of Hebrews added this verse on hospitality because the persecuted believers had become fearful and were hesitant to welcome anyone into their homes for fear they would be persecuted by the visitors. In the early churches, mainly home gatherings, traveling Bible teachers were highly dependent on the hospitality of the believers, as the teachers traveled to make known the Gospel. Hospitality was a characteristic of the early church. People knew them by their love for one another.

I have traveled to the Middle East, and I experienced a hospitality that I did not know existed. American hospitality tends to be about how well you know someone and emphasizes safety in the home. Privacy is a concern. When I traveled to the Middle East, I had offers to visit the homes of complete strangers. A Palestinian Christian in the airport invited my entire group to his home. A teacher at the school I served in expressed wanting our group to come for dinner, but said she sadly couldn't have the honor, as her neighborhood would not be safe for us.

After my visit to the Holy Land, I realized that the American telling of the nativity with the inclusion of an innkeeper who rejects the holy family didn't ring true any longer. The innkeeper doesn't seem right in the list of main characters: Surprised Virgin, Surprised Fiancée, Surprised and Pregnant Relatives, Angry King, Seeking Magi, Slaughtered Babies, Stunning Angels, Shocked Shepherds, but Selfish Inn-Keeper. A little explanatory phrase, "no room for them in the inn," can be distorted into a national crisis in church productions. The Inn-keeper gets a lead role in our plays ever since Charlie Brown's Christmas. I don't think the innkeeper was really a part of the story. In the Holy Land, hospitality is an honor. Hospitality, not isolation, is part of the Middle Eastern identity. Most of the people live in small places with many family and friends, and they are community. There isn't an individualistic identity like we have in the West. There is not the Western world's right-to-privacy mentality. I met people who I thought would be highly suspect and judgmental of me, but who instead readily invited me to their homes to stay as long as needed . . . and, oh by the way, my entire group of 13 was welcome. The Armenian Christian at the airport told me how to get to his village and house. The father of one of the girls in my day school class asked me and two others to come to his home and, if that wasn't convenient, to dinner. Further surprising me, he seemed genuinely sad that we couldn't schedule a visit. Even tour guides were handing out invites. Surely, hospitality would cost as much as their daily wage. Shop owners brought our group free refreshments on platters when we entered their stores. The spice shop owner, a world-renowned traveler, offered dinner at his home and really pushed to have us reschedule to meet his friends and family. In the Middle East, the Arabic people see hospitality as part of their character, their dignity.

This hospitality is extended to strangers and even more so to family. They look out for family. What's mine is yours, and they take pride in helping one another pay for school, travel, and work. In Bethlehem, at Christ's birth, Joseph was traveling to the area of his family, descendants of David. It would have been a huge dishonor not to look after this man and his expectant wife. The homes in Bethlehem are constructed out of the rock, the stone of the land. Joseph's family were not carpenters, but constructors/builders—that's a better translation found in Arabic Bibles and obvious to all in an area of stone, not forests. The houses were mainly one room, slanted so that a low area was near the front door, and a stone manger would separate the lower area from the main room. The animals were brought into the house at night, into the lower area at the base of the room. The family all lived, and slept, in the large area on the other side of the stone manger. If the family had space and ability, they built another room above or uphill from the main room. This is the "inn," a space for guests (usually more family). Joseph and Mary would have been welcomed into the house by family. They would have stayed in the main area if others were already in the extra "inn" room, and a stone manger in the lower section would have been very handy, as nearly every house had such an area to protect livestock at night. All families had livestock to maintain the home and their sacrificial system.

An inhospitable innkeeper is an unlikely character for the culture. Our addition of this character to the Bible story would be an offense to the Middle Eastern mindset. I can imagine the house the Lord Jesus was probably born into, the chaos of animals and mankind in tight quarters, the hardness of chiseled stone, and the absence of my view of comfort. Even if a family couldn't fit you in the area of the house that they would prioritize for guests, I think hospitality would have been shown the Savior. What a good way to get out the Good News . . . God with us, right in the midst of it all. Hospitality is vital to the spread of the Gospel.

JAMES, 1 PETER, 2 PETER

These three letters confront poor theology on what it means to be a believer. James, believed to be the half-brother of Jesus, contrasts a faith that is tainted by partiality to the wealthy upstanding citizens and human reasoning. Such faith results in a theology of works. In contrast, when one's faith is linked to a belief in God's sanctifying work of mercy, not works, for growth in Christ, the resultant faith leads to endurance and merciful, sacrificial kindness. Good works are motivated by realizing you've received the mercy of God. The believer perceives that all are rich if they walk with God. He is sufficient in this life. There is nothing to favor apart from God.

According to Acts and Galatians, James was a leader in the early Jerusalem church. He was known as a peacemaker and to be faithful during really difficult times in Jerusalem. The Book of James is thought to be the earliest New Testament letter. His inclusion of so many Old Testament passages and characters indicates he was probably addressing many Jewish people who had believed in Jesus as Messiah. If the reader thinks they could do anything to work out their righteousness, they could misapply James' teaching, which sounds a bit like the Proverbs, one wise saying after another. But at its core, James' teaching echoes the Sermon on the Mount and convicts the humble reader that they have no means of righteousness apart from Christ. They cannot love like they should love and are dependent on Christ in them for any good. James challenges the believer to increase their devotion to God by loving more purely in words and actions, knowing that in Christ they have the capacity to do so.

1 & 2 Peter are written by Jesus' apostle Peter, who is in Rome, to Christians throughout Asia Minor who were suffering for the gospel. 1 Peter explains that the Gentile believers are like the Israelite remnant who had to wander for years before entering the promised land. Peter encourages believers to overcome the tribulations of this world by remembering the Kingdom to come. Peter calls believers to view suffering as a powerful resource for the proclamation of the Gospel. Like James, Peter provides persecuted believers instruction on living out their faith in a manner that witnesses of God's great mercy.

2 Peter reads a little like Peter's last will and testament as he prepares to be martyred in Rome. The teaching addresses the imminent crisis of false teachers in the midst of the believers. Peter tells believers how to combat the false teaching and to advance the Gospel in spite of great

opposition. Peter knows that no one can come to Christ without God's true revelation of Himself. False teachers must be refuted.

Week 49, Day 1

Read It All: James 1-3
Read a Bit: James 1-3

The Revelation in Summary

James 1:1-4 — *James, a bond-servant of God and of the Lord Jesus Christ, to the twelve tribes who are dispersed abroad: Greetings. Consider it all joy, my brethren, when you encounter various trials, knowing that the testing of your faith produces endurance. And let endurance have its perfect result, so that you may be perfect and complete, lacking in nothing.*

In summary, James contains instructions for the believers dispersed abroad to live in such a way that the mercy of God is represented to all, especially to those who are persecuting the Christians. James provides counsel on wise living in a world that hates believers. He convicts the believer of the importance of merciful living that exhorts Christ. He convicts the believer of our need for His righteousness.

According to James, God gives wisdom to His children in response to their asking Him for it. Christians are called to continually make wise judgments as they walk by faith in a world opposed to their Savior and His teachings. For example, believers are to discern whether their companions will value walking by faith or will discourage Gospel living. Christians are called to judge their own hearts, to search out sin, to recognize evil and flee from it, and to judge the acts of men and determine when fellow Christians should be disciplined so that restoration may occur. Christians are called to make judgments as to what is best for the people they lead. Christians are called to enforce the laws of the land, to watch over their children, and to cast out false teachers from their midst. Christians are called to judge the sexual sins of their brethren and to bring these sins into the light, encouraging repentance and cleansing.

God has a high calling for His children. We feel that high call when we read James. Believers are to represent their Lord and Savior, which requires making righteous judgments. Believers are to be conscious of their own prejudices and self-centered motives so that they may eliminate any attitudes that would lead to poor judgments. As a representative of God, believers are equipped to help one another determine what is right in God's eyes and to serve Him. Christians are called to serve others wherever they go with the right, good judgment that only comes from knowing God's Word.

> *But the wisdom from above is first pure, then peaceable, gentle, reasonable, full of mercy and good fruits, unwavering, without hypocrisy.* James 3:17

Week 49, Day 2

Read It All: James 3-5
Read a Bit: James 3-5

Integrity

James 4:10 — *Humble yourselves in the presence of the Lord, and He will exalt you.*

I cannot think of any other New Testament writer that gives such convicting counsel on our tongues. What we say reveals what we really believe about God and whether or not we represent His integrity. James sounds harsh in his assessment of quarrels and conflicts among believers, but this isn't harshness as much as it is a reality check for the church.

James knows the Old Testament Law. He knows that God is jealous for His name and His children. God commands that we do not take His name in vain and that we honor others with our words. There is a right, good jealousy. I am jealous for my family. I am jealous for truth as defined by Scripture. I am jealous, very jealous for my spouse. He is a part of me, like no other, and I am not willing to share what is intimate for us with anyone. God is jealous for those He loves. He reveals Himself to His children through the Bible so that there can be an intimate relationship between God and man, and He commands us to guard that intimacy with Him. The Bible contains story after story of God's children being unfaithful, committing heinous acts of adultery. God forgives and makes a way for His children to return to Him at any time. He is merciful. But what a joy to be the faithful spouse who has honored the marriage. What a joy to be jealous for those you love rather than to be careless of our intimates. God is worthy of our love, and His jealousy for us is a gift demonstrating that we are His.

Our words reveal our hearts. When you love someone, you guard their name. Since we were created to represent God by bearing His image, when we defame God, we contradict our own existence, His purpose for us. In our culture, little thought is given regarding the name of God. Rarely does a day go by without hearing someone flippantly say God's name. We do not seem to notice lyrics, speeches, or casual talk that insults God's name.

Vile speech is not the only way to misuse the name of the LORD. I am concerned that the church has an insidious means of defaming the Lord. With our "Christianese," we presume on Him in His name. We talk as if God continually, audibly guides us: "God answered my prayers with a 'yes'!", "God was speaking to me," "God told me to," "God's my best buddy," "God, the man upstairs." We make God commonplace, as if He were a chum or the genie in the lamp. Our use of God's name reveals that we do not fear Him. We think He serves us rather than being our Master and Lord. We indicate that we prefer a "personal revelation or guiding" over reading His Word. I believe the careless use of His name by His people has been a far worse witness to our children raised in the church than the blaspheming use of His name by unbelievers. It is wise to fear God and to revere anything associated with Him, particularly His name.

James knows that if we are not careful about how we approach our Lord. then we will not hesitate to defame one another. James confronts our ugliness with one another as aligning with Satan rather than submitting to His Spirit. James calls God's followers to return to God in humility and trust that He will deliver us from our sin.

Week 49, Day 3

Read It All: 1 Peter 1-2
Read a Bit: 1 Peter 1-2

The Revelation in Summary

1 Peter 1:10-11 — *As to this salvation, the prophets who prophesied of the grace that would come to you made careful searches and inquiries, seeking to know what person or time the Spirit of Christ within them was indicating as He predicted the sufferings of Christ and the glories to follow.*

Peter is determined to comfort the persecuted believers and knows that to do so he must encourage them in their faith that Jesus is the One the Old Testament anticipated and that their suffering is temporary but has eternal value as a witness to Christ's glory. Peter affirms the believers as members of God's family, part of His chosen race and holy nation. As His family, they are aliens in this world, awaiting their real home in His future kingdom. As they wait, they are to honor their Bridegroom and hate what they have been delivered from in this world. Peter's writings exhort believers to endure by identifying with the sufferings of Christ. This world can be so hard.

My friend's son was hit by a car on Christmas Eve, just before his second birthday, and killed. He and his twin brother had received toy cars as gifts and had gone outside, in the middle of the night without anyone noticing, to drive their little cars. The driver who hit my friend's son was a pastor. One twin survived, one twin died. The pastor, a neighbor, was beyond devastated. Many were in shock.

It is hard not to say stupid things on any day, but I think that in times of suffering, we really tend to show our lack of understanding. Some people said, "Well, at least you had twins"; "It could be a blessing as we don't know the future and all"; "I understand how you feel, I lost a child"; "Time heals"; and "What a waste." Gayle was gracious as some kept talking.

I wanted my friend to hear and see how thankful I was for her son's life. How the situation made me feel like I was holding my breath way too long, just praying for her. Her suffering reminded many to reprioritize their lives. I wanted her to know that her son's birthday will stay on my calendar and be an annual reminder to me to value the moments. I have a new love for the youthful, a new respect for people's pain, and a new playfulness that comes from thankfulness for life's little pleasures. I want to assure my friend that her little boy will not be forgotten, that it isn't awkward for her to talk about him, that we can rejoice over his birth and all the little funny moments with him.

She told me that one night, the week after his death, that she tried believing that God did not exist. She said it was so much worse, so much darker, as she realized that meant believing that all was just a game of chance, randomness. She said she knew God loved her son. She knew God mourned with her, and she knew it was a blessing to have any days with her little one. She hopes in God's promise of resurrected life. She is comforted by knowing His Word and remembering His faithfulness to warn her about this world's troubles.

Week 49, Day 4

Read It All: 1 Peter 3-5
Read a Bit: 1 Peter 3-5

Integrity

1 Peter 3:18 — *For Christ suffered once for sins, the righteous for the unrighteous, that He might bring us to God, being put to death in the flesh but made alive in the spirit.*

I love springtime! New life sprouting up everywhere. It's crazy how my severely pruned crape myrtles burst forth green. Brown bulbs bear bright blooms in the backyard. Even pockets of grass push through in my weed-strewn lawn. Miraculous! I get out in the yard and think about the possibility of a hydrangea hedge.

Spring has also brought about some of my greatest challenges in life. Spring was a time when I realized as a child that my family was in trouble. Spring was scary as I needed a job. Spring was when the baby I carried had anencephaly. Spring was when I discovered cancer. Spring has been marked by many burials amidst budding trees in cemeteries. I've sat in many Easter services hurting for the sorrowing. Life is fragile this side of heaven. The Apostle John pointed out that we would have much tribulation in this world even as he walked with The Resurrection and the Life.

Peter said to not be anxious but to trust in God's care of us. The Lord Jesus will make us perfect, whole in Him. He will give His children a crown of glory. God has integrity and, therefore, will keep His Word. The Lord Jesus Christ is Life. In Christ we have life, eternal life, ultimately bodily resurrected life. God Himself set the seasons. Spring reminds us that life is a miracle—a colorful, exciting, beautiful miracle, and the believer is aligned with the faithful Creator of miracles.

And when the Chief Shepherd appears, you will receive the unfading crown of glory. 1 Peter 5:4

*After you have suffered for a little while, the God of all
grace, who called you to His eternal glory in Christ, will
Himself perfect, confirm, strengthen and establish you.*
1 Peter 5:10

Week 49, Day 5

Read It All: 2 Peter 1-3
Read a Bit: 2 Peter 1-3

Dignity

2 Peter 1:13-14 — *I consider it right, as long as I am in this earthly dwelling, to
stir you up by way of reminder, knowing that the laying aside of my earthly dwelling
is imminent, as also our Lord Jesus Christ has made clear to me.*

Peter believes he is about to die. So facing death, Peter writes the believers
to encourage their faithfulness to Christ by affirming to them all Christ
has done for them and by warning them of the false teachers in their
midst. Peter closes the letter by providing dramatic details of the Last
Days to reinforce the truth that Christ will return and that they should
be ready to see Him. They are to be on their guard against false teaching
and be steadfast in growing in their knowledge of Him.

The way we prepare for death and honor our dead reveals a lot about
the value we place on life. My family tries to spend a week each year at
a condo overlooking a little inlet on the Gulf of Mexico in Florida. On
one visit, our daughter Sarah was out in the ocean, and we could see
from the shore that there was a pod of dolphins swimming her way. We
watched her to see if she knew she was about to have company.

Sarah was aware of the dolphins. Later she told us she had a
NatGeoMo (a National Geographic Moment). As the dolphins came
closer, she noticed that one was struggling to carry something, causing
the pod to move very slowly through the area. They kept having to stop
as the dolphin readjusted her load or let what she was carrying loose for
a little bit. But the load was apparently precious, and they maintained
close proximity to the slower dolphin and its cargo. As the pod arrived
right by Sarah, she realized that the dolphin was carrying a dead calf.
Sarah watches The Discovery Channel and had learned that whales do
something similar. There are a number of animals observed to grieve

their dead, particularly their offspring. A dolphin may carry a dead baby for days. Animals appear to experience emotional pain.

As Peter mourns his imminent death, his heart concern is that these persecuted new believers, his spiritual offspring, remain steadfast in the faith so that they will live devoted lives worthy of the Lord and powerful in their Gospel witness. Our lives have eternal value; Peter acknowledges this value in his last words to God's children.

1, 2, & 3 JOHN, JUDE

I love the apostle John's writings. His purpose is to intentionally assure believers that they are secure in Christ Jesus. John uses specific names for Jesus (Christ, King of Israel, Son of God, Son of Man—from Daniel 7) to affirm that the reader is following the One worthy of our devotion. John explains who I am in Christ, knowing that I oftentimes don't feel like I'm His, so I tend to doubt that I've been adopted into God's family. John greatly comforts me.

In his epistles, John expresses concern that the children of God doubt their abiding relationship with the Father, as the church is being influenced by those teaching justification by works, not relationship with the Son. The presence of these deceivers develops into a greater threat from one letter to the next. In 3 John, the deceivers are actually in the church, and John identifies them by name and commands his family of believers to remove from the church those who deny the apostolic teaching. The true family of God includes those who love the Son, accepting that they must be born of His Seed to be born of God (1 John 3:9).

Jude, like 2 Peter, exhorts the believers to stay faithful to God's revelation of Himself as delivered by the apostle. Some false teachers are saying that there is no future judgment, and so people might as well do as they please and enjoy what they can in this world. Jude reminds the church of God's sovereignty and holy judgment throughout history as well as His faithfulness to do as He says. Believers are to act on the word of the saints and to value purity during the delay in God's return so that they will help others be ready for His judgment.

These letters reveal the heavy concerns the church leaders had for their flock and the great influence false teaching still has on the church. God desires that His people are steadfast in enjoying the new life He has given them. God continues to mercifully care for His children through the teachings of these dear shepherds.

Week 50, Day 1

Read It All: 1 John 1-2
Read a Bit: 1 John 1-2

The Revelation in Summary

1 John 1:1-4 — *What was from the beginning, what we have heard, what we have seen with our eyes, what we have looked at and touched with our hands, concerning the Word of Life—and the life was manifested, and we have seen and testify and proclaim to you the eternal life, which was with the Father and was manifested to us—what we have seen and heard we proclaim to you also, so that you too may have fellowship with us; and indeed our fellowship is with the Father, and with His Son Jesus Christ. These things we write, so that our joy may be made complete.*

John is "the disciple Jesus loved," an eyewitness of the Deity of Christ at the transfiguration. After his Gospel book, he continues his teachings on abiding in Christ in this first epistle to an unknown Christian community. He knows that Christ's followers will struggle with appropriating God's gift of eternal life, so he continues to affirm God's faithfulness to His children.

John the apostle had heard John the Baptist preaching "Repent (return) for the Kingdom of heaven is at hand." The apostle teaches us what to do when we sin so that we continue in sweet fellowship with our Savior. John reminds us to not deny our sin but to confess it to the Lord, knowing that He has continually promised to restore us when we cry out to Him! He makes a way for the sinner to come back to Him and to fully receive all that He has for us.

> *If we say that we have no sin, we are deceiving ourselves and the truth is not in us. If we confess our sins, He is faithful and righteous to forgive us our sins and to cleanse us from all unrighteousness.* 1 John 1:8-9

God also included this teaching on repentance in His Law (Deuteronomy 30). His mercy has always been within our reach! No other belief system contains this great promise. All other world-views say "You failed, so now let's see you balance your good and bad in order to have some blessing at the end of your life." If eternal life is based on me getting it right now, then I have no hope whatsoever in tomorrow! The God of the Bible provides hope.

John knows that if we grasp this concept of God's mercy, then we will attain great comfort and encouragement in the faith. God securely loves His children. Just as He made a way in the law for those who marry into a family to remain in that family, He makes a way for me to enjoy an identity with Him forever. John knows that teaching continually on what to avoid or how to behave without teaching what to do when you err results in defeated Christians. John doesn't want his flock to experience what many believers have experienced: making choices that distanced them from God and then believing they would never be good enough to be right with Him. I've watched as some withdrew from their faith, avoiding any discussion of God. The Bible truth is that we weren't adopted as God's children because we were ever "good enough," and we don't stay in His family based on our goodness. We were never and will never be "good enough" for God. That's why He imputes His Son's righteousness to us. It is the only way for us to be righteous.

We become children of God by faith in His righteousness and His provision of our righteousness through His Son the Lord Jesus Christ. That is why when we fail, we can readily find forgiveness from God by returning to Him, crying out for His character to help us again and again. This is simply confessing our sin and trusting in the incredible power of the cross to cover that sin. God waits for us to return, and then He loves to restore. The more we embrace this truth, the more we stand in awe of the love of God for us, which empowers us to serve Him all the more closely.

Week 50, Day 2

Read It All: 1 John 3-5
Read a Bit: 1 John 3-5

Integrity

1 John 3:2-3 — *Beloved, now we are children of God, and it has not appeared as yet what we will be. We know that when He appears, we will be like Him, because we will see Him just as He is. And everyone who has this hope fixed on Him purifies himself, just as He is pure.*

The provision in the Law of God forgiving those who return to Him is not a loophole for sin. God's Word also warns that we can get so caught up in disobedience and then crying out to God when we are suffering sin's consequences that we begin to harden our hearts to the nature of God. We lose the joy and our purpose of representing Him as we cycle repeatedly through disobedience and destruction. Like the people in the times of the Judges, living by what seems right in our own eyes is death.

Integrity is characterized by a faith walk that is steadfast, refusing to compromise our beliefs to the degree that deadens our sensitivity to sin. I wish I didn't have any stories of people hardening their hearts to God. The encouragements in Scripture to endure and persevere are there for a reason, but many don't heed them. I've watched as professing believers left their spouses and children for another person, saying that the other person was God's real ministry for them. These are hearts so hard to God's truth that they not only rationalize their sin but label it "ministry." In one case, a lady I taught Bible Study with left her family for someone in prison that she had been writing letters to as part of an outreach to those with a life sentence. Her daughter, who had connected her to the ministry, was devastated.

God knows that His children need to spiritually develop, and He is patient with us. He says we are not yet what we will be, and He will help us be purified. John stresses the importance of persevering in the faith while assuring the reader that God is the One Who saved you, and He is the One Who will hold you securely in His family. When God adopts a child into His home, that child is united to Him for eternity. He is not indecisive on the people He places in His family. Salvation is God's work, not ours. It is His work, secured permanently through Christ, and because it's His work, it is trustworthy. It is lasting. It is not to be torn down and destroyed. It is not undone. It is not overcome or overwhelmed by lesser things. It is established by Christ for Whom and through Whom all things were made. Even when I run, I should have great confidence that my God will overtake me. He is the perfect Shepherd of the flock regardless of the stupidity of the lambs. We are secure in Him.

Week 50, Day 3

Read It All: 2 John
Read a Bit: 2 John

Dignity

2 John 6 — *And this is love, that we walk according to His commandments. This is the commandment, just as you have heard from the beginning, that you should walk in it.*

This short letter reminds me of some of the communications I've had with ladies doing mission work in countries where it is illegal to talk about the Lord Jesus Christ. We switch up words in our writing so as not to be so overt about the mission. I believe the "lady" in 2 John 1:1 is a house church, and the "chosen sister" (1:13) is another house church. The "children" would be those birthed in the Gospel. The letter is short as there isn't much that can be communicated safely unless in person. The persecution of believers must have been intense at the time of this letter.

We do show our love for one another by imitating one another, walking in the way of those whom we respect most. God sums up His commandments in the one to love Him by loving His Son. When we understand the mercy God has demonstrated to us through the gift of His Son, we are moved to show mercy to others, to love our neighbors as we've been loved. This is walking according to His commandments, realizing that Christ fulfilled God's Law and we need Christ.

I remember after years of not seeing much of my dad, praying one year specifically and regularly that he would have someone remind him of the Gospel and encourage him to study God's Word. Later that year, my brother invited us to his home, which was a few hours away, when Dad would be visiting too. When we arrived, my dad rushed to see me and asked if I had ever heard of a Bible study by Beth Moore that he was involved in. I was encouraged in that moment to continue to be intentional about praying for my family and that all would abide in the teaching of Christ.

Week 50, Day 4

Read It All: 3 John
Read a Bit: 3 John

Unity

3 John 4 — *I have no greater joy than this, to hear of my children walking in the truth.*

Children are a blessing from God. There are a number of events in this life that should be celebrated in a really big, beautiful way, and having a child is such an event. Having a baby completely changes your life. You'll never have a thought purely regarding yourself again. Your being is united to the existence of another. You'll see glimpses of the love of God in ways you've never noticed as you learn to have a deeper capacity to love sacrificially. You'll know what it means to have someone in your likeness (as God bore man in His image); through your child, your family is represented to others. You'll have dreams for your child that over time you'll need to amend, as you learn about your child's strengths and weaknesses, likes and dislikes. And you will share the desire that God has for His children, to walk in truth, so that your family's testimony of the Lord will expand and bear fruit.

Whether we are thinking of children in our homes or our spiritual children (those with whom we have shared His truth), we can be overwhelmed with the importance of family support. The parent is blessed by godly people who sacrifice to help teach children the words and the works of the Lord Jesus Christ through Bible studies and mentoring. Good parents see the importance of godly friendships, as they grieve the evil in the world. Parents see the cross of Christ in a whole new light as they realize that God didn't give up just anyone for our salvation, but He gave His child for us. Thoughtful parents may even cry fresh tears over the cross as they cradle their child in their arms. Good parents appreciate God's support and provision of Life.

The thoughtful parent loves when children walk in truth, including the truth of how to be forgiven. As my family grew in number and in years, I had many opportunities to express the importance of forgiveness as I expressed love for my children. I learned that oftentimes, my fears for my children were caused by my own struggles. I was struggling with wanting perfection for my children partly because I did want God to be glorified through them, but also because I thought that would keep them safe, and I wanted to appear to be the perfect or at least "pretty good" parent to others. So every time one of my children stumbled, I was tempted to make it about me and whether or not I was doing enough as their parent. My children reminded me that sometimes their struggles weren't a reflection of my parenting but an indication of their hearts. We discovered together that perfection isn't a possibility in this world apart from Christ, and as a family we can hold His mercy and grace close at hand for one another. Yes, it's a joy when His children walk in truth, the truth of His forgiveness.

In Luke 15, Christ tells of a Father who runs to greet his returning prodigal child. God's people celebrate the prodigal's return. We all love to see all His children walk in truth. Observing the journey can be hard on the guide, but I have found that the joys of being a parent far outweigh the times of irrational fear. I continue to work on the fear, remembering that our children are worth it.

Week 50, Day 5

Read It All: Jude
Read a Bit: Jude

The Revelation in Summary

Jude 20-21 — *But you, beloved, building yourselves up on your most holy faith, praying in the Holy Spirit, keep yourselves in the love of God, waiting anxiously for the mercy of our Lord Jesus Christ to eternal life.*

Jude states that he is greatly concerned about the influence of the ungodly on this flock of believers. In this short letter, Jude presents a solid case for the believers contending for their faith amidst evil. Jude's Old Testament references clearly remind the reader of God's great mercy and His capacity to judge evil. The prophets and apostles had warned the people of mockers in the last days, and Jude points out that the mockers have crept within the believers' gatherings.

We don't use the term "mocker" very often today, but I have witnessed firsthand the impact another type of woman can have on the home and in the church. The influence of a crabby woman can be significant. The crabby woman is never satisfied. She is incredibly selfish and has a way of making you think that you are responsible for her happiness. You aren't, of course, but she just wants a codependent partner in her misery. Beware! Crabby women sap your strength. They are high-maintenance people because self-idolization requires getting another to work hard to maintain your sense of importance. This results in a twenty-four hour job for the fool willing to take on the task.

I have been such a fool, so I've learned a few things firsthand about the crabby woman. Initially, she is rather hard to identify and frankly kind of fun, because she is constantly looking for entertainment. When a crabby woman is bent on having a good time, she is the life of the party. She is especially dangerous to a guy, as she usually takes very good care of herself and consequently can look very attractive. Many are perfectionists about their looks, which readily ensnares a man. Crabby women typically don't have a wide range of friends, so they can be very appreciative of your friendship. If you allow it, they will make you feel like you are the best thing that has ever happened to them . . . for a time. But your purpose in life will become rescuing and reaffirming them. Beware of letting your pride blind you from the ungrateful crabby woman. Watch out for the melodrama. It gets old. They have "cup empty" issues; year after year, it just isn't a good year for them or their families. "Woe is me" is their theme song.

God directs His children to be thankful, rejoicing, and living content lives. The crabby woman is continually in direct defiance of God. She mocks the gift of life God has given mankind and identifies with Satan in demanding attention for herself.

For my brothers in Christ I add this: Usually this woman is exotic in some very physical way. Beware of paying attention to the sensual traits that dim with time and hide the inner venom. Men can be drawn readily to that which is visually appealing, and pride may blind you as you sense that you look good on this woman's arm. Flee! Fear God and trust His word as the source of life over the lips of the woman who promises eternal satisfaction through enslavement to a hopeless crab. God's Word directs you to pursue the woman characterized as hardworking, independent, thoughtful, fearless, and composed (Proverbs 31). Prioritize time with women who are beautiful in representing God, and separate from those who would consume you in their misery.

REST TIME

Week 51, Days 1-5

Hebrews 4:1 — *Therefore, let us fear if, while a promise remains of entering His rest, any one of you may seem to have come short of it.*

The general epistles in the New Testament highlight the worthiness of God and the believer's call to endure suffering. These writers, along with God's flock, are experiencing intense persecution as the church is expanding throughout the Roman world. Many are tempted to abandon their new faith and so messages of Christ's supremacy over all belief systems are crucial for the preservation of His Body and for His offer of Refuge to continue to save lives. These letters are relevant reminders today of the believer's need to identify false teaching and flee deceptive leaders. I'm challenged by the teachings in these letters to stand firm in my faith, glorifying the Savior and appreciating suffering in this realm for its identification with His cross.

Journal any thoughts you wish to record at this point in your reading.

For the
Lamb
In the
Center of
The Throne
Will be
Their
Shepherd,
And will
Guide them
To Springs
Of the Water
Of Life

Revelation 7:17

NEW TESTAMENT REVELATION

The Book of Revelation is an epistle that is composed mainly of apocalyptic-style[27] communication. The author, John, writes to seven specific churches to encourage them to persevere during hard times. His inspiration for the churches comes from the visions he has experienced which depict the End Times. John's prophecy is the culmination of the Old Testament prophecy, and he unites the prophetic words in the Bible with graphic detail. The reader gains a view of the heavenly throne room of God and the culmination of His Story on earth.

---

[27] Apocalyptic writing is prophetic literature describing the End Times. "The word "apocalyptic" comes from a Greek word, 'apokalypsis,' meaning revealing or unveiling (http://bibleresources.americanbible.org/resource/apocalyptic-writing).

Week 52, Day 1

Read It All: Revelation 1-3
Read a Bit: Revelation 1-3

The Revelation in Summary

Revelation 1:1-3 — *The Revelation of Jesus Christ, which God gave Him to show to His bond-servants, the things which must soon take place; and He sent and communicated it by His angel to His bond-servant John, who testified to the word of God and to the testimony of Jesus Christ, even to all that he saw. Blessed is he who reads and those who hear the words of the prophecy, and heed the things which are written in it; for the time is near.*

The message of Revelation is very straightforward: Jesus is the Psalm 2 Anointed One who will restore the earth to God's original, created design. Christ will ultimately rule the nations in peace. The New Covenant will be fully enacted. God will resurrect His kingdom to include those who believe in Him.

The message of Revelation is written to the 7 churches to encourage them to be faithful to Jesus, anticipating Him as a Bride awaiting her loving Bridegroom. The churches are challenged to overcome their suffering by realizing that He will return and restore the earth; they are reminded to realize that He is worthy unto death.

John, possibly the Apostle, identifies the antagonists to his teaching as any who deny Jesus, the Lamb of God, as the Christ. The antagonists are clearly delineated as aligned with Satan, and their philosophy is to enjoy what the current world has to offer, as that is all there is to "life." In this book, we are reminded that Satan has two primary means of attacking the believer: deception and destruction. Christ combats both with the power of His Word and the power of His resurrection.

Revelation depicts Jesus' return to earth in the same way that He was witnessed as He ascended in Acts, in the clouds. His return includes His followers and His glorious restoration of His creation. The church is not mentioned after chapter 3 until the chapters on His Kingdom near the end of the book, thus the visions focus on Israel and her return to the King. John's Revelation is full of Old Testament references. The scrolls that play a dominant part in John's visions are connected to Jeremiah's discussion on scrolls, the land deeds. The description of a tribulation period is detailed and echoes many of the descriptions by numerous major and minor prophets. The Genesis 3 beast has a prime role in John's visions, as he is overtly attempting to kill all of Israel because they are no longer deceived by his lies, just as described in Ezekiel 37. Israel's repentance for her sin of rejecting the Seed of the woman begins.

The battle between the Seed and the serpent heads right back to the garden and culminates with the Tree of Life situated as originally planted, bearing fruit for the nations. God has faithfully revealed and preserved His character through the ages so that those who would believe and take refuge in Him would find Life. He is worthy!

Week 52, Day 2

Read It All: Revelation 4-9
Read a Bit: Revelation 4-9

Integrity

Revelation 4:1 — *After these things I looked, and behold, a door standing open in heaven, and the first voice which I had heard, like the sound of a trumpet speaking with me, said, "Come up here, and I will show you what must take place after these things."*

God's faithfulness to reveal so much about His creation edifies my faith, as He has provided fulfilled prophecy and glimpses into His heavenly realm to encourage us in our tribulations. His integrity through the ages motivates me to represent Him as best as I possibly can.

When you get to this section of Revelation, God pours forth detailed descriptions of His throne room in heaven and of His people on earth. You realize afresh that He sees all. Read carefully as you go through the text, considering what realm the visions depict. You will see His grand play unfolding. The tension is still the same: allegiance to the King or to the enemy serpent. The characters are familiar: the blood-stained Lamb, the martyrs, apostate Israel, the beast, the tribes, and the elders. The poetical passages echo the past: the words of Zechariah, Ezekiel, Isaiah, Joel, Amos . . . . The scenes are glorious: His presence, His Son, His armies, His creation, and His realm.

God is good. He reveals just what our little finite minds can bear so that we can continue to walk by faith and have His peace, regardless of our circumstances. Persevere.

Week 52, Day 3

Read It All: Revelation 10-13
Read a Bit: Revelation 10-13

Dignity

Revelation 10:5-7 — *Then the angel whom I saw standing on the sea and on the land lifted up his right hand to heaven, and swore by Him who lives forever and ever, who created heaven and the things in it, and the earth and the things in it, and the sea and the things in it, that there will be delay no longer, but in the days of the voice of the seventh angel, when he is about to sound, then the mystery of God is finished, as He preached to His servants the prophets.*

Repeatedly in this devotional, I have referred to a delay and to believers as the Bride awaiting their amazing Bridegroom. The delay is the time period between Christ's ascension and His return, the time period during which the loving Bride cannot see her blessed Bridegroom. Revelation is the believer's assurance that the delay will end. The marriage supper will occur. Revelation is our assurance that God remembers all He spoke through the ages via His prophets.

As we anticipate the end of the delay in His kingdom on earth, we continue to walk by faith, not seeing the fulfillment of all His Words and not sure of what step to take next. As a ministry leader, I often get asked how His children can know His will as they await His return. I'm encouraged by believers who purpose to live according to His will, but I think that in many situations, we cannot specifically discern the mind of God. We really do walk by faith, not knowing exactly what He would have us do. That is the essence of faith. But I also have learned that the more we know about God, through prayer and Bible study, the more we do have a sense of what would delight Him. This helps guide our walk.

In making decisions, it is good to do at least three things: (1) pray about the situation, looking in Scripture for guidance; (2) consider whether the decision being made will bring about His peace and His glory for you and others; and (3) get your spouse's input if you are married; if not, rely on one another for wisdom. But there is no set formula for finding out the will of God, and my idea of His will always needs to be tempered with what the Bible reveals about His will. God says a lot about His will in Scripture. Notice that His Word reveals that His will is more about character than behavior.

It is His will that man bear His image, ruling over all creation as God's representatives. Genesis 1:26-28

It is His will that you receive Him and become His child; believers are born of the will of God. John 1:12

It is His desire that men be saved by coming to the knowledge of the truth. As His representative, the believer is in God's will when he humbly and lovingly tells others about Jesus Christ, the mediator between God and men. 1 Timothy 2:3-4

It is His will that you work for His pleasure. Philippians 2:13

It is His will that you are sanctified, set apart as clean. That you abstain from sexual immorality as that represents God's purity in love. That you love your brethren and study to be quiet, to attend to your own business, to work with your hands so that you will meet your needs and be equipped to show mercy to those who are in need. It is God's will that you help outsiders as He is faithful to provide refuge for the foreigner. 1 Thessalonians 4:3-12

The will of God is something you do. It requires active involvement with His word, walking according to His revelation. Mark 3:35

It is the will of God to care for widows and orphans in their distress and keep oneself apart from the world. James 1:27

The Scriptures reveal that God cares deeply about your character and wills that you are different from the world. He planned and purposed for His children to receive His mercy and then to give His mercy to others. The world teaches you to shun the needy or to make them a special project in order to bring glory to yourself. God desires that His children are disciplined in their lives so that they can quietly help others that are in need.

It is good to consider God's will as we plan our days, to walk in His dignity, especially in troubling times. I have a concern that lengthens this discussion on the will of God. I am concerned that many do not believe God is personal. For them, the greatest question isn't what is God's will, but why would the Creator of the heavens and the earth be interested in me, particularly since no one else seems to be? Many aren't asking about God's will because they cannot imagine that He cares. Many aren't asking because they are too busy modeling what their parents did, which was to simply take care of themselves. Author and speaker Lael Arrington, in a lecture titled "Thoroughly Postmodern Millie and Willie,"[28] said:

> In the Middle Ages and in the Modern Age, life was perceived as a story with a beginning, an end, a plot, and characters. People visualized themselves playing a part in a larger story. However, the postmodern person has no sense of being part of a grand story. They see no author and no story. Each person lives in his or her own small story, trying to make it as interesting and enjoyable as possible.

I am concerned that many believers are not waking up and thinking about God's presence today. Rather, they are tempted to schedule too much, numbed by activity and social media, unfocused on what matters most, and oriented toward entertainment. I think we are caught up in a world more concerned about pleasing friends and self than pleasing God. That is the norm even for believers. That is living in the physical realm, walking by human reasoning over the revelation of God. The end of His delay will catch these children by surprise.

God values our loyalty to Him, and He desires to help us achieve our God-given desires, those right good desires He placed in our hearts. What we don't realize is that it is absolute joy to enjoy God. If the Bible is true, it does not take many chapters of His Revelation to see that He is intimately involved with His creation, especially mankind. He has created man after

---

[28] Quoted in Carol Kent, *Becoming a Woman of Influence: Making a Lasting Impact on Others* (Colorado Springs, CO: NavPress, 2006), 90-91.

His own image: He established order, provisions, and nations for mankind. He continues to discipline His people. He heals and directs us still.

Week 52, Day 4

Read It All: Revelation 14-18
Read a Bit: Revelation 14-18

Unity

Revelation 14:1 — *Then I looked, and behold, the Lamb was standing on Mount Zion, and with Him one hundred and forty-four thousand, having His name and the name of His Father written on their foreheads.*

At the beginning of the story, God described His creation as good. At the end of His Story, I see Him firmly planted in His creation, standing on Mount Zion and enjoying this Promised Land. God is ready to restore it all. Babylon, the epitome of those against the Son, will fall. Revelation 14-18 conveys how the enemy is completely overcome, and His children are united as one nation in His victory.

I am writing the last portion of this devotional while sitting with my husband overlooking the Gulf of Mexico. It has been a week of reflecting on God's magnificent creation. Just in our little spot of land, we have seen intricate shells of all sizes filled with weirdly asymmetrical creatures, sea oats, flowers surviving in the hot sand, a bonnet head shark, a large, skinny, star-fish, humanity in all shapes and sizes, pods of dolphins, and a multitude of shore birds. I could list much more. His creation is diverse. His creation is glorious.

I know His creation has been corrupted. Some of the sea life I described was washed up dead on our shore. Red Tide is just south of us. A tropical storm that threatens to turn into a hurricane is headed to the Carolina coast north of us.[29] If I venture to turn on the TV in our little condo, I'll get firsthand stories of the corruption. I don't turn on the TV, though, because I like being secluded, away from it all for a bit.

---

[29]   It became Hurricane Florence after I wrote this.

Revelation reveals that God also enjoys His creation. He enjoys you and me. He enjoys the nations. He enjoys a view from the mountain. He is ready to resurrect it all.

> *But if the Spirit of Him who raised Jesus from the dead dwells in you, He who raised Christ Jesus from the dead will also give life to your mortal bodies through His Spirit who dwells in you. For I consider that the sufferings of this present time are not worthy to be compared with the glory that is to be revealed to us. For the anxious longing of the creation waits eagerly for the revealing of the sons of God. For the creation was subjected to futility, not willingly, but because of Him who subjected it, in hope that the creation itself also will be set free from its slavery to corruption into the freedom of the glory of the children of God. For we know that the whole creation groans and suffers the pains of childbirth together until now. And not only this, but also we ourselves, having the first fruits of the Spirit, even we ourselves groan within ourselves, waiting eagerly for our adoption as sons, the redemption of our body.* Romans 8:11, 18-23

Week 52, Day 5

Read It All: Revelation 19-22
Read a Bit: Revelation 19-22

Priority

Revelation 21:3 — *And I heard a loud voice from the throne, saying, "Behold, the tabernacle of God is among men, and He will dwell among them, and they shall be His people, and God Himself will be among them, and He will wipe away every tear from their eyes; and there will no longer be any death; there will no longer be any mourning, or crying, or pain; the first things have passed away."*

I know that many, many scholars teach a *non*literal interpretation of Revelation. But as I get to the end of His Story, having read the hundred thousandth word of His Word, knowing the literal fulfillment of so many of the previous prophecies, and reading His consistent use of terms and images from Genesis through Revelation . . . I believe. I see His suffering martyrs avenged. I realize that the enemy and those aligned with him will be finally crushed. I believe in a bodily resurrection, just as Christ was the firstborn of the dead. I've anticipated the LORD of LORDS and KING of KINGS, the true tabernacle of God, dwelling among us. I've longed for death to be eliminated just as He says it will be. I'm ready for the New Covenant to be completely ratified. I'm done thirsting.

I know that His people have been like a Bride awaiting her gorgeous, tender Bridegroom. I'm ready for the wedding. I believe in the literal, full restoration of Jerusalem. I know He will create a New Heaven and a New Earth. These things have been specifically promised by God through the ages. I know His twelve tribes and His twelve apostles will fulfill His command to rule. I know that in His Sovereign care God has measured out all of these details and is planning a grand eternal celebration. The words of the prophets echo in my ears, and I hear and believe in His strategic deliverance of the nations.

I know the Lamb lights the way, as He has done since the foundation of the world. I know that His essence is glorious and His Spirit is moving mankind. I've envisioned walking by His Light, my faith turned to sight, with the nations. I've dipped my toes in the River of Life. I'm anxious to sit under the Tree of Life and to experience the garden restored, to receive His rest as Eden's gates are open wide and His people are at peace, with no fear of the serpent returning. I know we will finally see His face. I heed the words of His prophecy. I have His hope. He has given me a new heart.

He who testifies to these things says, "Yes, I am coming quickly."
Amen. Come, Lord Jesus. Revelation 22:20

Selected Bibliography

Arrington, Lael. "Thoroughly Postmodern Millie and Willie." Lecture series. Quoted in Kent, 90-91.

Baylis, Dr. Charles. 2018. Thebiblicalstory.org. http://thebiblicalstory.org.

Baylis, Dr. Charles. 1998-2007. Expositional study outlines. Dallas Theological Seminary, Dallas, Texas.

The Bible Project: Visual Storytelling Meets The Bible. 2018. https://thebibleproject.com.

Briscoe, D. Stuart. 2001. "Recommendation." Quoted in Yancey, 114.

Chester, Tim, and Steve Timmis. 2008. *Total Church: A Radical Reshaping around Gospel and Community.* Carol Stream, IL: Crossway.

Chesterton, G. K. 2001. *The Scandal of Father Brown.* Cornwall, UK: The Stratus House.

Fitzpatrick, Elyse. 2013. *Comforts from Romans: Celebrating the Gospel One Day at a Time.* Wheaton, IL: Crossway.

Green, Jay Patrick, ed. *The Interlinear Bible: Hebrew-Greek-English.* 2005. Peabody, MA: Hendrickson Publishers.

Kaiser, Dr. Walter C. Jr. 2009. "Jesus in the Old Testament." Gordon Conwell Theological Seminary. http://www.gordonconwell.edu/resources/Jesus-in-the-Old-Testament.cfm.

Kent, Carol. 2006. *Becoming a Woman of Influence: Making a Lasting Impact on Others*. Colorado Springs, CO: NavPress.

Lewis, C. S. 1960. *The World's Last Night and Other Essays*. New York, NY: Harper Collins.

Lewis, Eleanor, Pat Harley, and Linda Sweeney. 2009. *Invincible Love, Invisible War.*, Alpharetta, GA: Big Dream Ministries.

Mack, Wayne A., and Wayne E. Johnston. 2005. *A Christian Growth and Discipleship Manual, Volume 3: A Homework Manual for Biblical Living*. Bemidji, MN: Focus Publishing.

Melick, Richard Jr. 2014. *Called to Be Holy, Growing in the Likeness of Jesus*. Nashville, TN: Lifeway Press.

Payne, J. Barton. 2018. Ministry Safe (website) Training Videos. https://www.ministrysafe.com.

Polk, Laura. "20 Women Who Shaped History." iBelieve.com. Accessed September 14, 2018. https://www.ibelieve.com/slideshows/20-christian-women-who-shaped-history.html.

Powlinson, David. 2003. *Seeing With New Eyes: Counseling and the Human Condition Through the Lens of Scripture*. Phillipsburg, NJ: P & R Publishing.

Quest Study Bible. 1994. Grand Rapids, MI: Zondervan.

Shirer, Priscilla. 2015 *Fervent: A Woman's Battle Plan to Serious, Specific and Strategic Prayer*. Nashville, TN: B&H Books.

Sizer, Stephen. 2016. "Jesus Christ Foretold In All the Scriptures." *Stephen Sizer* (blog). February 1, 2016. http://www.stephensizer.com.

Spurgeon, C. H. "Peter After His Restoration." No. 2035-34:409. A Sermon Delivered On Thursday Evening, July 26, 1888. Metropolitan Tabernacle, Newington, NH. accessed August 17, 2018, https://answersingenesis. org/education/spurgeon-sermons/2035-peter-after-his-restoration/.

Spurgeon, C. H. "The Threshing Floor of Ornan." No. 1808-30:601. A Sermon Delivered On Lord's Day Morning, November 9, 1884. Metropolitan Tabernacle, Newington, NH. Accessed October 20, 2015. https://answersingenesis.org/education/spurgeon-sermons/1808-threshing-floor-of-ornan/.

Strong, James. 2016. *Strong's Exhaustive Concordance of the Bible*. Nashville, TN: Thomas Nelson.

Yancey, Philip. 2001. *Church: Why Bother? My Personal Pilgrimage*. Grand Rapids, MI: Zondervan.

Yancey, Philip. 1999. *The Bible Jesus Read*. Grand Rapids, MI: Zondervan.

Endorsements

Jodie inspires me and her siblings to grow in our faith. So grateful for all she has taught me-know you will benefit from her encouragement, too.
Janet Burns Townsend, Jodie's Mom, Administrator, Lakeland Eye Clinic

You may or may not get this from reading her devotional, but Jodie is super intelligent (her undergraduate degree is in Chemical Engineering), a real beauty (with curly red hair), and has a passion for encouraging women in their walk with Christ . . . and is pretty well written too. And she likes chocolate.
Scott Montgomery, Jodie's Amazing Husband, Senior Bridge Engineer

This book is the fruition of decades of faithful study and an unwavering desire to know God. As a young child, I remember waking up to find Jodie on her knees praying with her Bible close by every day. As I got older, I remember watching her tenacity as she raised three teenagers while getting her Master's in Biblical Studies. I am so proud of her for taking on this new challenge while I know it's been years in the making. I know this book will be a tool to understand His Story and will bless you on your journey as my mom's knowledge has already blessed me in my pursuit to know God.
Sarah Kate Wilder, Licensed Family & Marriage Therapist

Jodie's devotionals that accompany her *Finding Refuge: A Year in His Story* are insightful, heartfelt, and encouraging. She writes with the voice of authority, as one who has deeply studied and taught this Word for many years, and with the heart of one who has lived it and continues to share it daily with those she loves, who obviously include her readers. Jodie's organization of weekly readings into the concepts of Revelation, Integrity, Unity, Dignity and Priority allow us to focus on these concepts in Scripture and in life. You will be inspired, moved—to tears and laughter, convicted, and blessed.

Linda Devore, Master of Arts in College Teaching in English from Auburn University, PhD Studies in Literary Criticism from USF, Freelance Copyeditor, Owner of grammarnow.com

This devotional will be a blessing to you. Jodie puts in words what women need in their heart. As my wife battled cancer Jodie would call her weekly and lift her spirits. Her walk with Jesus was a constant encouragement in those dark days. She uses her talents to encourage others to become more like Jesus through it. Enjoy this devotional as it will draw you closer to the Lord. What every woman should have as part of their walk with the Lord.

Jack Oliver, Children's Pastor, Judson Baptist, Brentwood, TN

CPSIA information can be obtained
at www.ICGtesting.com
Printed in the USA
BVHW041355211118
533502BV00072B/1268/P